THE ILLUSTRATED HISTORY OF SPEEDWAY

To Lin

THE ILLUSTRATED HISTORY OF SPEEDWAY

Martin Rogers

Studio Publications

Acknowledgements

It is impossible to give adequate thanks to all the sources used in the preparation of this book, but some must be properly acknowledged, among them being: Stenners Publications Ltd (Stenners Speedway Annuals), Five Star Publications (Five Star Speedway Annuals), Websters Publications (Speedway Star, various annuals), Gresham Magazines, Speedway Mail, Who's Who of World Speedway by Peter Oakes, and many others, including programmes and handbooks of various tracks.

I am also especially grateful to Mike Rumens, who prepared the track-by-track section with painstaking devotion, and to Dick Barrie, Johnnie Hoskins, H. H. Howard, Ian Macdonald, Peter Morrish, Peter Oakes, Paul Parish, Philip Rising, Peter White, Alan Clark and various others.

Acknowledgements are due to the following who have supplied photographs: Stephen Bacon, Dick Barrie, T. Edenden, Lars Edgren, Johnnie Hoskins, Stephan Jarlvik, Daily Mirror, A. M. Photos, Trevor Meeks, Bill Meyer, Michael Patrick, Ray Page, Planet News Ltd, R.A.C., Barry Richardson, C. F. Wallace, and, especially, Alf Weedon and Wright Wood, those veterans of the camera.

Finally, my thanks to all of those speedway riders for performing the great deeds which form the story of this book.

Published by STUDIO PUBLICATIONS (IPSWICH) LIMITED,
37 Lower Brook Street, Ipswich, Suffolk, England.

ISBN 0 904584 45 3

Phototypesetting by: Galleon Photosetting, Ipswich, England.
Printed by Wm. Clowes & Sons Ltd, Beccles, England
Bookbinding by Ipswich Bookbinding Company, Ipswich, England.

Contents

Foreword

When he was a speedway writer, I always reckoned Martin Rogers would make a good administrator.

Now he's a good administrator, and he still has the ability to weave with words, never a bad thing when you are sitting down to write a book (as he and I both know).

We worked together on my autobiography, which was all about one bloke and twenty-odd years.

Now Martin has done his own thing on a thousand racers and fifty years of speedway. Personally, I prefer to race motor cycles.

Given that no book can mention all of the great names, and will be bound to place a different emphasis upon a variety of memorable and not so memorable occasions, there are few people better equipped to tell the story of speedway.

Martin has achieved a perspective by following the game and being closely involved with it in a variety of ways over a number of years. He always made it his business to find out the rider's point of view, and most of the boys reckon he is a fair judge.

He usually wrote nice things about me, so I am bound to agree with that assessment!

There seems to be something for everybody in this book; and that, I reckon, is what the story of speedway is all about.

by Barry Briggs, MBE

Introduction

Old Leonardo Da Vinci and Johnnie Hoskins have a lot to answer for.

Da Vinci, for whom the phrase 'a man of many talents' was surely fashioned, is reckoned to be the inventor of the world's first bicycle around 1493.

Hoskins, another unique and inventive character, gets the credit – or should it be the blame – for staging the first organised motor cycle speedway at West Maitland Showground, Australia, in 1923.

The motorised cycle appeared before the dawn of the present century. By 1902 there were reports of pioneering bravado by American racers. Five years later – about the time the T.T. Races were being introduced on the Isle of Man – historians recorded an event on a dirt track at Pietermaritzburg, South Africa.

By the time the 1914–18 war was over and done, the spirit of adventure was abroad, and it was then that speedway racing, as future generations have come to know it, began to evolve.

American riders Maldwyn Jones and Eddie Brinck were regarded as the earliest expert exponents of the art of sliding a motor cycle in a controlled movement.

But the organisation and evolution of speedway really dates from the time Johnnie Hoskins came upon the scene. He was born in New Zealand in 1892, and spent his youth in pursuit of adventure and cultivation of quick-witted enterprise. This found him perfectly fitted for the role of sporting innovator.

The story began in earnest in New South Wales, spread to other parts of Australia, and the British (who usually reckon to be in on the beginning of almost everything) did not start to build their speedway traditions until 1928.

When High Beech staged its initial speedway meeting, that man Hoskins was on his way to the 'old country'. And for the next half century, no man did more to establish the sport.

There have been hundreds of would-be promoters in all corners of the world, and innumerable flamboyant racers, personalities of vastly differing style, attitude and accomplishment. Most of the successful ones admit to some Hoskins influence.

We will introduce you to many of them along the road.

If it had not been Leonardo, and some say that it wasn't him anyway, somebody else would have invented the bicycle.

Teutonic motor maestro Gottlieb Daimler manufactured the first motor cycle. It could so easily have been someone else, but he got the credit, and deserved it.

Thus with John S. Hoskins. He spent his first thirty years as a wanderer, telegraphist, boxer, nurse, naval officer, wrestler, sheep shearer, sometime journalist and anything else that happened along. Then he ignited the spark which turned into a bush fire of speedway activity.

The fact is that Hoskins, adorned with the seal of office and the title Grand Master of Speedway at the 1977 British League Riders Championship Final at Belle Vue, Manchester, epitomises the feel of speedway racing and imbued it with its spirit.

The game has known highs and lows, but its essential character and optimism has seen it through. Obviously the ingredients for survival are there as well as those for success.

The ingredients? A mish-mash of show-business razzmatazz; sawdust ring feats calculated to make thousands of hearts beat that much faster than normal; speed, skill, daring, and the dash of men (and a few women) for whom there could be no greater thrill than to ride, fight, control and direct a racing motor cycle no matter what the occasion, never mind the varying elements, nor the others in the race for that matter.

Robert Findlay, a Fleet Street sports editor kindly disposed towards the sport, once wrote:

'You don't have to be crazy to be a speedway rider. But it helps.'

And on the face of it, you have to be just a little bit crazy. Who in his right mind would sit astride a potent, streamlined 500c.c. motor cycle with no brakes, and fling it through a series of tight turns on a loose surface for three or four laps of an enclosed track?

What orthodox motor cyclist would point his front wheel to the right in order to turn left, and apply all the power the throttle will provide when every instinct insists that this is the time to knock off?

But then, speedway has never followed the orthodox or the obvious. Hoskins and his successors have recognised that it is a sport apart. A business, too; big business.

Yet those essential qualities of buccaneering adventure live on. In half a century, the show has grown up without forfeiting its youthful vitality or eagerness to please – a raucous, boisterous creature to be sure, but with little or no hint of malice.

Unlike many other popular spectator and participant sports, it allows the emphasis upon entertainment to equal that laid upon the final result. The winners are cheered and remembered, of course. Feats of merit and valour by the losers are also generously acknowledged.

Thus the pursuit of success, the spirit of competition, and the sporting ties, too often debased and prostituted by players and watchers alike in some other sports, remain in a position of perspective in British speedway.

It lacks cynicism or snobbishness, has steadfastly refused to have anything to do with betting, and appeals today as it did years ago . . . to mums and dads, kids and their grandparents. A visit to the speedway is, as ever, an outing and a treat.

The manner of presentation can do so much to set the stage and the right atmosphere. Ultimately, though, memorable moments of high drama on the track induce the flow of adrenalin and surge of excitement which provide the speedway addict with his 'fix'.

Once hooked upon the sight, sound and smell of speedway racing, it is harder to give up than smoking. Take it from one who tried both.

Of course, there are people who live on in almost complete ignorance of the very existence of speedway, and many more who have no more than a faint idea of what it is like (or, as often as not, what it used to be like).

Ignorance is not bliss, especially for the press or public relations man, trying to remain patient while fending off questions with an all too familiar ring.

No, speedway didn't die off after its post-war boom. There are no longer 50,000 or 60,000 crowds at League matches. Happily, though, nor are there tracks forced into situations of bankruptcy and closure because of a failure to do the sums properly.

No, nobody calls it dirt-track racing nowadays. The Australians have never called the sport anything but speedway; and the British acknowledged the error of their ways and officially adopted the title in 1930!

And no, they don't race on cinders. The dimly-remembered era of leg trailers belongs firmly to the past. Shale track surfaces and the safer (saner?) foot forward technique have belonged to speedway folk lore for generations.

Some time-honoured sporting pursuits have failed to adapt from a previous time scale, but speedway racing has progressed, and seems as vital, active and appropriate to the day as in its exciting infancy.

It comes as a surprise to many people to hear that this is the best supported summer sport in Great Britain, though lacking the type of following devoted to cricket or horse racing, much more socially accepted and, some suggest, acceptable pursuits.

National newspapers, in particular, devote hundreds of column inches to those traditional sports. Speedway, a babe in arms by comparison, has a much more difficult time achieving such coverage. Sports Editors point out with some justification that it does not help to have meetings which tend to finish around the time the newspaper is being put to bed.

Yet those hard-to-find results and summarised scores add up to a consuming interest. This year, an estimated five million will support speedway racing in the most tangible fashion – by handing over their money at the turnstiles at any one of 40 tracks from Exeter to Edinburgh, from King's Lynn to Barrow-in-Furness. Theirs will be a weekly ritual from March to October.

There have been times when the measure of support was even greater. Huge crowds flocked to the earliest meetings, and tracks sprang up everywhere. In 1929, there were 64 recognised by the Auto Cycle Union.

Highest peak of interest followed the end of the Second World War. In 1946, a staggering 6,623,587 attended 13 tracks. At Wembley's final meeting of the season, 85,000 watched and cheered while 20,000 who had been locked out sat on the stadium steps and listened to a match commentary being broadcast.

Two years later, when the number of circuits had grown to 29, crowds for the season totalled 10,694,361.

Social change, altering life styles, new entertainments, and, especially, the advent of television contributed to a decline in such figures. And in some ways, speedway celebrated its heady successess but neglected to protect itself against the inevitable rainy day.

When support began to wane, and tracks closed, not all of the remedies were practical or inspired. Nothing fanned the slump more than the imposition of Entertainment Tax. Speedway always argued that it was punitively taxed. Although many circuits continued to attract sizeable attendances, such a chunk of the takings was handed straight to the Government that sooner or later, more were forced out of business.

It was not until 1960 that the trend was arrested, and revival began which paved the way towards the current situation, in which more League tracks are in operation than ever before.

There was a time when the real success centres were in the big cities. London dominated for years, with Manchester and Birmingham the obvious challengers. Nowadays the net has widened considerably. As often as not, the provincial towns and cities command the most enduringly enthusiastic following. Local identification is the name of the game.

There is a thread of togetherness, though, which suggests that although speedway bosses bicker amongst themselves from time to time, they do appear to have learned from lessons of the past.

Originally, numerous promotions flew off in various directions. There were arguments over riders, venues, and competitions. For some time, north and south barely nodded to one another. Not until a reconciliation took place in 1932 was speedway steered in a generally agreed course.

In 1964, there was an even more divisive split. The administration of the sport was torn apart. The Speedway Control Board seemed to be losing touch. The National League was in decline. The chirpy young Provincial League had ideas of its own and was not averse to going its own way, outside officialdom.

A full-scale inquiry headed by Lord Shawcross examined the rights and wrongs of the dispute, and recommended a revision in the organisation of speedway racing. Both sides accepted the proposals, the British Speedway Promoters Association was formed, and the creation of the British League signalled its arrival.

These last few years have been the most stable period of development the sport has known. There are those who would suggest that this owes a lot to the administrative power wielded by the promoters. It is a situation which might not have appealed to the old stagers and traditionalists, but it works well enough for most of the time.

There is a widespread belief that speedway racing is making vast strides towards new levels of acceptance and acceptability. There is just about the right amount of television coverage (and the right sort of coverage). The national newspapers have stepped up their interest. Magazine and local media support has rarely been anything but enthusiastic.

Commercial concerns, international, national, and local, have become more and more disposed to provide sponsorship support, an important and invaluable vogue of the times.

Some pundits, nevertheless, complain that the major policy decisions belong too much with the men who have a vested interest. As such, it can only be difficult for them to make moves which could prove unpopular with the paying customers. The trick, after all, is to stay in business before one can start to think of improving business.

The promoters can point out the problems on the other side of the coin. After all, they say, why should our business interests be left to an independent body who, for all their impartiality, probably do not appreciate all of the angles? It is not their own money at stake.

Time has made the modern promoter very much more conscious of his responsibility to public, riders, and the sport in general than some of the old-time fly-by-night operators who hustled to get in on the ground floor as tracks mushroomed everywhere. Speedway promotion was erroneously reckoned to be a licence to print money. But only the hard workers and the committed have survived. Today's bosses, indeed, have become the new Establishment.

The comparative sophistication of the present day contrasts vividly with the first few years, when almost anything went. Machinery provides a case in point.

Pioneer riders used stripped-down road bikes, and then converted racing machines. The Douglas and the Rudge held sway, followed by the JAP which enjoyed a lengthy period of supremacy which extended far to either side of the 1939–45 war.

The Czechoslovakian Jawa dominated for a decade, doing much to haul speedway into the modern era. And in the last two or three years, with the advent of four-valve power, the British Weslake has become a name to conjure with.

In 1928 it was possible to buy a new speedway machine, ready to race, for £70. Today you would not get much change out of £1,200.

Rewards have fluctuated, too. The earliest superstars such as Frank Arthur and Sprouts Elder could expect to earn up to £15,000 a year. Pickings were good for riders who were part of the post-war boom, when there was not too much austerity to worry anybody who could score points in good company.

Current performers of the standing of Ivan Mauger, Ole Olsen or Peter Collins can pick up earnings of £50,000 a year from racing; weekend trips to the continent are especially lucrative. Sponsorship and endorsements of various kinds may well double that figure.

But the financial structure of the sport is such that the average First Division rider makes a living best described as comfortable, rather than luxurious. And the National League (i.e. Second Division) regulars usually rely upon an income other than that derived from racing.

Nevertheless, most speedway riders through the ages have enjoyed the sport, the cameraderie and the fun and games and considered the money angle to be secondary.

The incentives are there, all the same. British youngsters have enjoyed an increasing number of opportunities over the last decade, and it is no coincidence that in international terms, England rules, OK?

The history of speedway is several stories rolled into one. League racing, the staple diet of the faithful fans, virtually warrants a history of its own. The world individual and team championships, Test matches and other major events have all added lustre.

In the final analysis, though, the gladiators of the track have made it all happen. Hundreds have given the best years of their lives; some gave life itself to the sport of speedway racing.

And all so that we could have fun and enjoyment from their efforts.

GENESIS

December 15, 1923. High summer in Australia.

February 19, 1928. Cool winter in England.

One story links those dates on two continents. Speedway racing was introduced to the world at West Maitland, near Newcastle in the coalfields territory of northern New South Wales. And British spectators discovered its impact and appeal at the King's Oak track, High Beech, on the fringes of Epping Forest.

The reputation of this new sport was quick to spread round the world. Many of the riders and officials who pioneered speedway under the southern sun, travelled 12,000 miles to perform similar missionary works.

Whatever its earliest origins, speedway traces its history from the day Johnnie Hoskins provided the Hunter River Agricultural and Horticultural Society with the most spectacular feast of entertainment.

The conservative officials of the Society recognised in their 31-year-old secretary a born entrepreneurial ability and showmanship to match. But they were dubious, to say the least, when Hoskins suggested motor cycle racing as a new attraction to be staged at the showground.

Johnnie was an enthusiastic motor cyclist, and the music of roaring exhausts appealed to him. The local bigwigs, however, were reluctant to sanction the racing activities he sought to promote.

An impromptu practice session which shattered the peace of a sunlit Sunday morning drew so much attention locally that they relented, and allowed Roaring John to incorporate motor cycle events into their midsummer Electric Light Carnival.

There were bands, bike races, trotting events, dancing on the green – all the fun of the fair. But it was the appearance of the gladiators on two wheels which stole the show and started the story of speedway.

Enthusiasts had come from all over the state. Hoskins recalled the scene in his book *Speedway Walkabout:*

'The competitors stripped down their precious models. Off came mudguards and lamps and they were ready to go. One or two riders had helmets of a kind which would have sent today's referees into a fit. Most had none. Gloves were considered superfluous. They just took off their coats, rolled up their sleeves and wheeled their assorted racing jobs on to the track'.

The track measured 706 yards and its oval followed the contours of the show ring. Race after race produced thrills and excitement, pile-ups and hectic battles.

'At the end of the day,' said Hoskins, 'riders wheeled their mounts, if they were still

Below: *Johnnie Hoskins, who started it all.*

wheelable, to the shelter of the cattle pens and horse boxes, too exhausted to care'.

The carnage must have been unbelievable, but a new sport was born. And the reaction of riders and watchers alike demanded regular repeat performances. Refinements were to follow.

Footrests dug into the dirt and unsuspecting souls were flung from their machines. So the inside rests were removed, and the rules amended to allow riders to put their foot to the ground when cornering.

While restrictions and regulations have never appealed too much to the freer spirits, some basic guidelines had to be set down. Protective clothing, helmets, leathers and so forth became the norm rather than the exception.

It was not long before a rider plunged through the flimsy wire surrounds and into the crowd. That unwanted distinction went to Charlie Spinks. After that a stout fence of wooden boards was nailed round the ring.

Maitland continued to run regular meetings, and inevitably, the word spread. A. J. Hunting, later to become the managing director of International Speedways, described a meeting in Sydney where heavy rain had made the track so dangerous that competitors moved the scene of the action to an adjoining cinder path.

The loose surface provided an even more spectacular setting than the grass and dirt had ever done. Hunting got into the act very quickly, and built Maroubra Park, then a Speedway Royale in Brisbane.

Meanwhile Hoskins moved his scene of operations along the road to Newcastle, where he was to lay the first red shale track. Later he set up in Sydney and, subsequently, in Perth, on the far west of the continent.

It had taken only a year or two for folk heroes to develop. Charlie Datson, Paddy Dean and teenager Billy Lamont were among the home-bred stars of New South Wales.

The arrival of an American party in 1925 stimulated tremendous interest. Eddie Brinck, the master of the broadside, and the first man to use the knee hook, commanded big appearance fees. He was accompanied by Sprouts Elder and Cecil Brown. Naturally the improving capabilities of the locals, notably Datson and Tommy Benstead, who became Harley Davidson sales manager in Sydney, helped to keep the visitors on their toes.

Crowds were gathering in their thousands and invariably there was plenty of variety for them. Every programme included machines of differing specifications, classes and categories. Scratch races were followed by handicap events. Track announcements, initially made by megaphone from the infield, kept the fans informed.

New names were beginning to emerge, especially up in Queensland where Vic Huxley, Frank Arthur and Dickie Smythe captured the imagination of the public. The question was, for just how long could the Australians hope to keep all of this good news to themselves?

The unsuspecting English knew nothing of what was going on – but Lionel Wills, a Cambridge undergraduate, changed all that. Wills, a member of the famous tobacco family, and a keen motor cyclist, was able to witness this new phenomenon of speedway racing when he went to Australia on a holiday-cum-business trip.

On arrival, he was attracted by an advertisement for a speedway meeting at Sydney Royale, and his breath was taken away by what he saw. Wills promptly sought out the manager to enquire about the possibility of competing in a future meeting.

Opposite top: *West Maitland – where it all began.*

Below: *. . . and some of the crowds who attended.*

Johnnie Hoskins proved to be a welcoming host, and as well as participating, Lionel learned quickly enough of other ventures up and down the country which were worthy of his inspection. He could hardly keep his findings and his feelings to himself.

Wills wrote home in excited fashion to tell fellow motor cyclists what was afoot. His reports in the trade press attracted a great deal of attention, and not a little scepticism.

To the English purists, the idea of riders actually putting their foot down was a new conception. The use of a steel sliding shoe was unheard-of, and the thought of having a knee hook on the outside of the machine did not meet with universal favour, either.

But Wills painted such a vivid picture that enthusiasts of similar enterprise were bound to try things for themselves. Two go-ahead clubs were particularly eager to involve themselves in anything that approximated to this exciting new aspect of motor cycle competition.

At Camberley, Surrey, the local club, inspired by E. O. Spence, claimed credit for many new events, including scrambles and even football on motor cycles.

It was on May 7, 1927, that they staged an event subsequently described in *Motor Cycling* as 'the first British Dirt Track Meeting'. It was held on the heath overlooked by the famous Military College.

C. Harman dominated the afternoon, winning the 350c.c., 500c.c. and sidecar finals. There was no hint of discrimination against the fair sex, either, with Fay Taylour winning the unlimited final.

Dirt track racing of a sort it may have been, but contemporary observers and reports suggest that this was no more than a pale descendent of that most historic of pioneering events at West Maitland.

On June 25, 1927, the enterprising South Manchester Motor Club held a meeting on cinders at Dodds Farm, Droylesden. The event was organised by Harrison Gill, who, more than half a century later, was still the machine examiner at Belle Vue.

Ron Cave took the 350c.c. and 600c.c. titles and the sidecar final as well. Fred Fearnley and Charlie Pashley, both officials of the club, also featured prominently in the results list.

Below: *The front page from the Daily Mirror of February 20th, 1928.*

GREAT NEW SERIAL BEGINS TO-DAY ON PAGE 15

Daily Mirror

THE DAILY PICTURE NEWSPAPER WITH THE LARGEST NET SALE

£10,000

No. 7,572 MONDAY, FEBRUARY 20, 1928 One Penny

ENGLAND'S FIRST SIGHT OF AUSTRALIA'S BIG SPORT

NEW WORLD'S SPEED RECORD—206 M.P.H.

Right: *Sprouts Elder, pride of America's west coast.*

Far right: *Fay Taylour, first lady of motor cycle racing.*

The difference between this meeting and its predecessor at Camberley Heath, was that this time races were conducted in anti-clockwise fashion, as in Australia.

But was it really speedway racing? Billy Galloway and Keith MacKay, a couple of the big names Down Under, would not have thought so. They arrived in England towards the end of 1927 with the express purpose of introducing the sport to a completely new audience.

Both were destined to feature in the High Beech meeting which most historians accept as having been Britain's first genuine speedway staging.

That February 19, 1928 date serves conveniently and accurately enough, though there are claims for other venues and ventures. Suffice to say that the King's Oak meeting was the first to be staged after the new A.C.U. sub-committee responsible for licensing tracks had come into being.

Jack Hill-Bailey, secretary of the Ilford Motor Cycle Club, had planned an open permit event at High Beech for November 9, 1927. But the A.C.U. would not grant permission for racing on a Sunday, and a large list of entrants had to be disappointed.

So put out were they, indeed, that many competitors were eager to go ahead and stage a meeting in defiance of authority. Fortunately, wiser counsels prevailed.

Eventually Hill-Bailey, working in concert with the Colchester Motor Cycle Club, obtained a permit from the Eastern Centre. The application list was opened once more, and the response was immediate.

The build-up to the day was distinctly unpromising, with wintry weather, grey skies, even snow in the area. But February 19 dawned bright and clear, and Epping Forest waited to receive riders, officials and enthusiasts, all eager to see what this new sporting venture was all about.

Little did anybody realise that instead of the 3,000 spectators who had been expected, something like 30,000 were to turn up. Tickets were snapped up, programmes sold out an hour before the start. It did not take long to fill up the centre green where the spectators were to be accommodated. Emergency measures meant that thousands more took up positions round the circuit. Many selected as the most suitable vantage point the upper branches of the trees surrounding the arena.

The *Motor Cycle* captured the essence of the occasion thus:

'A day's sport such as has never before been seen in England was provided for the thousands who thronged the King's Oak Speedway, near Loughton, last Sunday. True there was no real broadsiding on the quarter-mile dirt-track, but there was thrill upon thrill right from 10.30 a.m. to 5 p.m.'

Despite the presence of Galloway and MacKay, the occasion demonstrated just how much talent there was, just waiting for the opportunity to put Britain on the speedway map.

A. Barker (Ariel) won the opening race, by a walk-over! The first final, the Ilford Novice event, went to Fred Ralph, riding a 344 Coventry Eagle, and Ivor Creek (490 Norton) who was runner-up, later won the three-lap novice final.

Alf Foulds beat Galloway into second place in the first solo event, clocking two minutes, two seconds for five laps. And Reg Pointer won the three-lap final. Alf Medcalf recorded the fastest lap time of 26.8 seconds from a standing start.

Hill-Bailey, understandably overwhelmed, later described the meeting as 'a nightmare'. As the milling crowds disappeared into the dusk, who could have envisaged the repercussions?

On Saturday, March 3, the enterprising South Manchester club got in on the act, and held a meeting at the half-mile Snipe trotting track at Audenshaw. As at High Beech, spectators came from far and wide to see Galloway and MacKay demonstrate their broadsiding talents, and left talking about the ability and promise of many home-grown riders. Ginger Lees, later of Wembley and England, was one of them.

Greenford (on April 7) and Blackpool (on April 21) followed suit by opening vast 880 yard circuits. High Beech, closed for track re-building presided over and paid for by W. J. Cearns, reported back for business and Jack Hill-Bailey, none the worse for his baptism of fire, helped to form a British Dirt Track Racing Association. The effervescent Lionel Wills was appointed as its first secretary.

It was Wills who took one look at the Crystal Palace, where Cecil Smith and Fred Mockford had staged road races over a miniature course in the grounds, and suggested that a speedway circuit round the football pitch would provide much more thrilling fare.

And he was instrumental in arranging for

Left: *Billy Galloway, who showed 'em how.*

Hoskins to pack his bags and prepare to leave Australia so that he could assist with the full-scale introduction of speedway in Britain. There was no shortage of tracks, especially with so many new stadium developments going up to coincide with the introduction of greyhound racing. It was a relatively simple and completely logical step for such places to house an additional sporting activity.

Finding riders was the problem. Despite the exciting local talents displayed both in the south and north, an infusion of overseas performers of proven ability and experience was necessary to help so many tracks get into action.

Dirt Track Speedways, under the auspices of Jimmy Baxter, had Galloway and MacKay on their books and promptly snapped up Sprouts Elder from America and Stewie St. George from New Zealand. These two showed up at Celtic Park, Glasgow, in April, and then took themselves down to Stamford Bridge, London, for their May 5 opener, the first British meeting to be staged under floodlights. There Roger Frogley and Gus Kuhn showed impressive form for the locals.

Hoskins, of course, was good for a few riders when he arrived at last. J.S.H. brought with him the inveterate Charlie Datson, tiny Claremont discovery Sig Schlam, and Scots-born Ron Johnson.

Hunting, meanwhile, paraded a troupe including Frank Arthur, Charlie Spinks, Vic Huxley, Dickie Smythe, Frank Pearce, Ben Unwin and Hilary Buchanan. Soon, Paddy Dean and Billy Lamont also allied themselves with his International Speedways banner.

Theodore Goddard, a director of the company, told a luncheon at London's Savoy Hotel that British riders would be given every encouragement. He also laid down some of the principles of operation, including no betting, no Sunday meetings, and announced that agreement had been reached with the Greyhound Racing Association for long-term leases at several of their major tracks, including White City, Harringay, Wimbledon and Hall Green (Birmingham).

The Crystal Palace meeting of May 19 provided the first indication that the home riders were no mugs, after all. The pupils showed the new arrivals a thing or two about racing on a rain-affected circuit.

Lionel Wills – yes the same Wills who had been so wide-eyed with wonderment at his first sight of speedway in Sydney a couple of years before – rode his 499 Rudge-Whitworth to victory over Ron Johnson in the first of three 'international' match races.

Then Roger Frogley (499 Rudge) beat Datson (494 Douglas), a remarkable result for the youngster whose first outing on a speedway had been at King's Oak little more than a month earlier.

It was not until the third race that the diminutive Schlam, like Johnson mounted on a 345 Harley, achieved a victory over Les Blakeborough (348 Cotton). But in the individual final, Frogley and Wills again grabbed the major honours.

The weather did not dampen spirits, but it must have made life difficult for riders on the day. Across the capital, White City opened on the same evening and Ben Unwin set a remarkable track record of 126.8 seconds for four laps of the flooded 352 yard circuit. Nobody was deterred, though. A 78,000 crowd turned up for their second meeting a week later.

Other London tracks were equally quickly into the swing of things, but the next significant entry in the diary was the May 26 debut at High Beech of Jack Parker, a young man scheduled to dominate British speedway for years to come.

In the north, the White City track at Old Trafford, Manchester, had a spectacular opening, with Sprouts Elder performing an exhibition run on his Douglas.

Then came Belle Vue, who opened up for speedway at their Hyde Road Greyhound Track in July. This was the first of the provincial tracks launched by International Speedways, reckoned to be much like Harringay (where Hunting already reigned supreme) and second only to London's White City as a circuit which permitted the most enterprising and exciting racing.

Those local club pioneers were much involved in this first Belle Vue enterprise, in which Frank Arthur starred, capturing the Manchester Handicap and Golden Helmet

Opposite top: *Stewie St. George (New Zealand).*
Opposite bottom: *"Cyclone" Billy Lamont.*

Left: *Frank Arthur, star of International Speedways.*

events. But the likes of Eric and Oliver Langton and Alec Jackson displayed their skills, too; Jackson actually beat Vic Huxley in the handicap heat.

The Australians were becoming tremendous drawcards, and International Speedways split their riders into two groups to race on alternate evenings at the various circuits which continued to spring up.

But for some riders, there just could not be too much activity. Lionel Wills was a classic example. He recalled with glee racing against the likes of Datson and Johnson at Brighton's June opener, where he crashed and injured his left ankle.

But Wills happily limped to his Rolls Royce, drove back to London and competed again at Crystal Palace the same evening. Once again he crashed and that offending ankle finished its day's labours swollen to twice the normal size. Lionel declared that this had been 'the finest day's sport of my life'.

The devil-may-care cavaliering attitude of the experts from Australia and the States was matched by the enthusiastic zeal of riders such as Wills. And there were plenty more who displayed not just enthusiasm but genuine accomplishment.

Nevertheless, the overseas contingent held sway in the eight major competitions which were in force – scratch events dominated the season with match races a particular attrac-

Ron Johnson, one of the 1928 pioneers.

tion. Up for competition were the Golden Helmet, the Golden Gauntlets, Silver Helmet, Silver Sash, Silver Wings, Silver Armlet, Silver Pennant and Silver Wheel!

Vic Huxley's many victories included the last four named. Only 21, he pushed the new T.T. Douglas machine to a series of records and was invariably safe, reliable and popular.

At West Ham's opening meeting, Elder – later to become a director of the promoting Dirt Track Speedways company – won the Golden Helmet. And he signalled the arrival of speedway at Southampton on October 6 by collecting the Golden Gauntlets.

At this stage, Elder could command £100 appearance money, and on one day, rode at three different northern tracks to collect £350 for his efforts.

Frank Arthur also had his hands on both the Silver and Golden Helmets, the Golden Gauntlets and the Silver Sash. The acknowledged stars were prepared to concede that the British learned fast, but that did not diminish their appetite for winning. Indeed, it seems to have sharpened it!

Nevertheless, the likes of Frogley, Ivor Creek, Kuhn, Jack Parker from Birmingham, and the northern aces such as the Langton brothers and Frank Varey were quick to build their own reputation. It was obvious that these were natural performers, stars in the making.

As their opportunities increased, there seemed to be no stopping the spread of tracks. Circuits opened here, there and, it seemed everywhere from Swindon to Salford, from Middlesbrough to Bristol, and in places such as Bradford, Burnley, Coventry, Edinburgh, Bolton, Rochdale, Leicester and Huddersfield. Cardiff actually opened on Boxing Day.

All were only too eager to bring to their local public a taste of the thrills being purveyed at the big city centres.

Above: *The English could ride, too. Frank Varey ready for action.*

Left: *Colin Watson – from High Beech to Wembley.*

League Racing

While there were many who gave speedway a great welcome when it arrived in Britain in 1928, it was far from being wholly accepted. Indeed, it suffered a great deal of adverse criticism from some quarters, the press reaction was often no more than lukewarm, and the motor cycle manufacturers were not immediately impressed.

What a difference a few months made. Tracks began to spring up in every corner of the land. Sprouts Elder was the best advertisement the Douglas manufacturers could wish for. Frank Arthur remained faithful to his Harley-Davidson, and England's smiling Jim Kempster sang the praises of the Rudge. At the Motor Cycle Show at Olympia in November, no fewer than 17 manufacturers displayed speedway machines.

The image of the sport at large was improving, too. Nobody worked harder to project speedway racing than Colonel, the Master of Sempill – later Lord Sempill, the first patron of the Veteran Dirt Track Riders Association. He introduced many notable personalities from the world of sport, entertainment and public affairs. There could have been no more prestigious seal of approval for the infant sport than the appearance, albeit incognito, of His Royal Highness Prince George, later King George VI, who visited a big meeting at White City, London. On the same night, Major Henry Segrave – the new holder of the world land speed record – and Captain Irving, designer of his 231 m.p.h. Golden Arrow car, were guests of honour and assisted with the presentation of the event's prizes.

Right: *Fred Mockford – Crystal Palace and New Cross owed so much to his influence. He was the man who invented the starting gate in 1933.*

What the sport needed most, however, was improved organisation, a more unified direction of policy, and, as events were to prove, League racing.

A Southern Promoters Association was formed and with the A.C.U. formulated a new set of rules to govern the types of competition to be permitted and schedules for prize money payments.

The action which really caused speedway to take off was the decision to organise league competition between teams. Early programmes had relied too much upon the same old diet of scratch races, handicap events, and a series of individual tournaments distinguished only by the variety of titles used.

Jimmy Baxter of West Ham recognised the public need for something completely different. After a trial run featuring teams from West Ham and Southampton, he decided to press his colleagues to organise a league and thus the Southern Inter-Track League was formed for 1929.

Teams were to consist of four riders, with matches decided over six heats, the points awarded being four for a win, two for second place, and one for third. After only a few matches, Perry Barr and Hall Green, together with Wimbledon and Harringay, announced their withdrawal, but a new League was formed immediately with all but Hall Green returning to the competition.

Left: *Belle Vue, the 'Cocks of the North', won the National League in four successive years. This was the 1933 team at the start of that sequence.*
Back row, left to right: Eric Langton, Max Grosskreutz, Bronco Dixon, Bob Harrison, Eric Gregory, Bill Kitchen and Joe Abbott. On machine: Frank Varey (captain).

This time, it was agreed that there should be six-man teams, nine heats, and the more familiar 3–2–1 scoring system employed. The *News of the World* were sponsors of the competition and agreed to supply trophies.

The one drawback was the decision to outlaw the star category riders, who continued to ply their wares in individual events. Incidentally, to avoid any jealousy over the allocation of a number one, the system of identifying the stars started with Art Pechar (2), Jack Parker (3), Sprouts Elder (4), Roger Frogley (6), Frank Arthur (8), and Vic Huxley (11).

Soon enough the public made their feelings on the matter quite clear. They wanted the League to be open to everybody. Huxley was smuggled into the Wimbledon team, and gradually the opposition was relaxed.

Stamford Bridge, whose track was so narrow that push starts had to be employed – rather than the rolling starts used elsewhere, took full advantage of this peculiarity and emerged as the first Southern League champions. Chunky Gus Kuhn was the top rider, with 188 points from 80 starts. Wal Phillips and Les Blakeborough were his most successful aides.

The northern tracks were also quick to adopt League racing. After much debate and discussion, came the formation of the English Dirt Track League, sponsored by the *Sunday Chronicle*. Despite the somewhat pretentious title, this was an exclusively northern enterprise and its machinations, truth to tell, were shambolic to say the least.

After an original idea to have six riders to a race, the format was settled along the lines envisaged, tried, and dropped by the Southern League.

White City, Manchester, won each of their 18 matches and then resigned following a dispute. This left Leeds as the first champions, with 35 points from 23 matches. George Greenwood, Eric and Oliver Langton were the star men.

Unlike their southern counterparts, the northerners failed dismally to complete the scheduled fixtures. Belle Vue and Burnley quit in mid-season; Warrington were expelled. Bolton rode just once before Hanley took over their fixtures for a four match spell and then they pulled out as well. Long Eaton entered, but never rode at all.

It was much the same story in the following year, when Belle Vue began their sequence of

Right: *Len Steward, who rode for West Ham and Wimbledon and was later mechanic to Bluey Wilkinson, was the only coloured rider in League speedway.*

success which was to earn them the tag 'Cocks of the North'. With Arthur Franklyn, Frank Varey, and reinforced by the Langton brothers, they finished well ahead of the White City team, including Arthur Jervis and Frank Charles, though once again the table was not completed.

At least the competition was more realistically named the Northern League, and it could have learned a lesson or two from the Southern League which put on an extended competition. Wembley, inspired by Johnnie Hoskins (who had been shopping shrewdly for fresh talent in the north) and led by Jack Ormston were the new champions. They beat Belle Vue in a home-and-away affair designed to establish the best team in the land.

Some tracks failed to last the pace, and even with a much more streamlined line-up of just half-a-dozen participants, the 1931 Northern League again failed to complete its programme. Nevertheless, Belle Vue maintained their reputation, and even managed to field a second team in the Southern League (won again by Wembley) after Harringay had withdrawn.

With northern circuits closing almost as fast as they had appeared, regional rivalries were scrapped, if not totally forgotten, and in 1932 the National League was formed.

With only ten teams, there were two separate competitions. The first, the National Speedway Association Trophy, was conducted on championship lines and won by Stamford Bridge, who were to close at the end of the season.

After breaking an arm and suffering a lacerated shoulder riding for Sheffield at Wimbledon, international rider Squib Burton was ruled out of the second half of the season. So Sheffield did not contest the National League championship. Six of the nine teams were from London, and Wembley made it three in a row by finishing on top of the pile.

Belle Vue began a run of four successive National League victories in 1933, a year which began with several leading riders out of the country, touring Australia and then America under the wing of Johnnie Hoskins.

Provincial interest and involvement fluctuated. Plymouth stayed the course for three seasons, and the likes of Birmingham, Nottingham, Sheffield and Coventry flitted in and out of the picture.

Most important development of the 1933 season was the introduction of the electric starting gate, invented by Fred Mockford of Crystal Palace. Gone at last were those frustratingly ragged and often patently unfair rolling starts.

Belle Vue, with the Langtons, Bill Kitchen, Max Grosskreutz and Joe Abbott in their ranks, continued from strength to strength. For two successive years they won the League, National Trophy (sponsored by the *Daily Mail* from 1931 onwards) and the A.C.U. Cup.

By 1936, sufficient progress had been made for the spawning of an offshoot, effectively a second division (rather than the reserve competition which preceded it by a couple of years) though titled at first the Provincial League. Southampton inched to the first title, beating Bristol on race points; but those roles were reversed in the following season.

Meanwhile, who could halt Belle Vue? Harringay threatened to do so, but the loss through injury of Jack Parker cost them their chance. Even unfancied Hackney Wick were making a bold bid for the top, but the track death of the popular Dusty Haigh understandably jolted their hopes.

In 1937, though, there was a new name on the championship scroll – that of West Ham. The previous year the Hammers had finished stone last, and Johnnie Hoskins, who had moved over from Wembley and revived the club's fortunes if not the results, issued his 40,000 Supporters Club members with a miniature wooden spoon apiece!

Yet with the same side, Hoskins' Hammers came storming back, inspired by the Australian, Bluey Wilkinson, and Canadian Eric Chitty.

Belle Vue were still fallen from grace when New Cross took the 1938 title. Jack Milne was their star, with George Newton and Ron Johnson, two great little characters, providing excellent support. And Hackney, in the Second Division now, won the championship of the lower section.

It took the outbreak of war to deny Belle Vue another title. The men from Hyde Road were looking as invincible as ever and sat proudly at the head of the First Division table when the big shut-down came.

Newcastle led the way in an emasculated Second Division, with Sheffield, managed by Wilkinson – world champion the previous year – looking dangerously poised, just behind them.

When League competition resumed after a six year absence, Wembley smartly established themselves as the outstanding team.

The Lions, shrewdly bossed by Alec Jackson, took just four riders from the 'pool' – Tommy Price, Bill Kitchen, George Wilks and Bill Gilbert – and setting about building for the future.

This they did with such devastating effect that they were to win seven of the first eight post-war championship titles, up to and including the Coronation season of 1953. The one exception was in 1948, when they were forced to spend half of the season away from their traditional home, which was the stage for the XIVth Olympic Games.

Owner Sir Arthur Elvin insisted that everything about Wembley had to be just so. Nobody presented speedway racing with greater pomp, ceremony or style. And with exciting new discoveries coming along to augment the team, whether out of the training scheme, like Freddie Williams, or purchased,

Above: *Vic Duggan, so dominant in 1947.*

Left: *Wembley, all-conquering with seven National League titles between 1946 and 1953. How about this for a talented line-up? Standing, left to right: Trevor Redmond, Eric Williams, Bob Oakley, Tommy Price, Duncan King (manager), George Wilks, Dennis Cosby, Jimmy Gooch, Freddie Williams, J. Barrett (trainer). On machine: Bill Kitchen (captain).*

Right: *Olle Nygren, the first Swedish rider in National League racing.*

Below: *Wimbledon took over the winning mantle and helped themselves to seven National League championships between 1954 and 1961. On parade here, back row, left to right: Geoff Mardon, Barry Briggs, Cyril Brine, Ronnie Moore, Peter Moore. Front: Reg Trott, Dom Perry, Cyril Maidment.*

as was Brian Crutcher, the stream of talent kept producing the results.

Plenty tried to keep pace. Harringay concentrated their efforts on Australia, and their 1947 side contained four signings from Down Under, including the incredibly consistent Vic Duggan. But they still finished at the bottom of the League.

Wimbledon, shrewdly guided by Ronnie Greene, one-time European charleston champion, latterly decorated for his efforts as a wartime fire chief in London's Blitz, forked out the first £2,000 transfer fee for Alec Statham. Then Harringay paid Wembley £3,000 for Split Waterman and West Ham found a new record £3,750 to bring Australia's newest world champion Jack Young from Second Division Edinburgh.

But still the Wembley steamroller refused to slow down. And the sport itself, like Topsy, 'just growed'. In 1946 the National League was as usual the glamour competition, but a six-team Northern League re-established the grass roots. By the following year, there were three divisions, and youngsters fresh out of their services uniform, clamoured for opportunities. The overnight opening of several tracks gave them all the chances they needed.

Public interest and attendances swelled, and with no shortage of would-be riders or promotions, numbers climbed up to 37, still in three divisions, by 1951. It could not last. The punishingly high level of Entertainment Tax, the advent of television, and various other factors caused a few to totter, then a few more. Several promotions simply could not stand the financial strain of it all. After the bonanza of the immediate post-war years, budgets were set high, too high, and those who couldn't come to terms with the necessary adjustments went to the wall.

Thus, by 1954 it was back to just two divisions, and four teams pulled out of the Second Division during the course of the year. Within a couple of years even the apparently impregnable Wembley had followed the likes of Harringay and West Ham and opted out of the League.

Speedway, it seemed, was on the slippery slope to self-destruction. An amalgamation of those who remained left the National League with just eleven teams in 1957, with little Swindon the champions. And numbers continued to fall. The Dismal Jimmies were having a field day.

One centre seemingly unaffected by all of this was Wimbledon, where Ronnie Greene saw to it that his Dons took over the mantle of success previously enjoyed by Wembley. Apart from that audacious interjection in 1957, the south Londoners collected an incredible seven National League championship titles in eight seasons.

The sound basis provided by some experienced campaigners provided a platform from which the youthful Ronnie Moore, Geoff Mardon and Barry Briggs began to express their talents in exciting fashion. At one stage Wimbledon paraded a side which included seven World Finalists and internationals.

The first signs of a crack came when Norwich, brilliantly served by Ove Fundin, whipped the team of all the talents in the National Trophy. And in 1962, with Briggs and Björn Knutsson in devastating form, Southampton were champions, followed a year later by Peter Craven's Belle Vue and in 1964 by unfashionable Oxford.

But all of the National League outfits were playing to a contracting audience. Significantly, though, there were those who refused to let the sport curl up and die. There were promoters who believed that a new competition, sensibly structured and capable of paying its way, was ripe for introduction.

Some pilot – the traditionalists called them 'piratc' – meetings were held and did well enough to encourage visionaries such as Mike Parker, Reg Fearman and even the indestructible Johnnie Hoskins to get the Provincial League off the ground in 1960.

While the National League continued to meander along in its own way, keeping alive some of the legendary track names, albeit a diminishing number, the new League developed, and quickly. While standards were not especially high, interest was. The lively infant grew up in a hurry, so much so indeed that within four years the Provincial League bosses were quite prepared to challenge the order of things.

The Speedway Control Board, anxious to prop up the National League, made several overtures towards the new competition, but met with lukewarm response. And when the Board directed Wolverhampton, as 1963 champions, to move into the National League ranks for the following year, there was a refusal followed by open rebellion.

Above: *Ove Fundin, consistency itself for Norwich with 1,826 points in 148 National League matches between 1955 and 1964.*

The threat of suspension did not deter the Provincial League, and they blithely carried on with their own operation in the following year, although the A.C.U. licensing authorities declared the lot of them to be 'black'. Far from collapsing, they proved that they were eminently capable of running their own affairs.

This could not go on, and the R.A.C. ordered a commission of enquiry, headed by Lord Shawcross, to investigate the whole complex business of speedway and its administration in Great Britain. The upshot of it all was a marriage between the decaying National League and a jubilant, vindicated Provincial League – the new British League coming into being in time for the 1965 season.

With more power and responsibility vested in them, the promoters were determined to profit from the lessons of past experiences. They set about basing their business on a set of sound principles. While certainly not without flaws or exempt from criticisms, they did manage to lay the foundations of the most stable period the sport in Britain has known.

In such an atmosphere, teams could begin to plan and build with optimism. One of the great names, West Ham, lorded it over the rest in the first season of the competition, with an international heat leader trio of developing force in Ken McKinlay, Sverre Harrfeldt and Norman Hunter.

The honours were shared around at regular intervals until Dent Oliver, a former international turned manager, created a new Belle Vue set-up of traditional power. His signing of Ivan Mauger and the dash of Sören Sjösten was complemented by the steady stream of talent from the Hyde Road training ranks. With Chris Pusey, then Peter Collins coming along, the Aces picked up three successive championships and in 1972 dropped only five points in 34 matches.

The Manchester model of developing youthful stars gave Ipswich just the example they needed and in creating a championship-winning team in 1975 and 1976, they relied almost exclusively upon local riders. John Louis was the inspiration, Billy Sanders of Australia the only team member who was not a genuine son of Suffolk . . . and even he had been at Foxhall Heath since he was 16.

Much of the strength of the sport today goes back to the formation of a new Second Division in 1968. This has grown in strength and stature and provided an ideal training ground for new riders. Now it has adopted the title of National League, though it is still widely recognised as the junior competition.

Economics, as ever, determines that the British League is in effect the 'super league' with many of its teams operating out of the traditional plush big city stadia. Yet it is significant that many of the recent success tracks, some completely new but many revived after a lengthy absence, are situated in the provinces.

League competition has been the catalyst in a number of centres where once upon a time, no self-respecting promoter would have taken so much as a second look. That local identification theme again.

The modern supporters have so much more mobility than those of bygone days. Thus even towns of relatively small proportions can still attract a solid hardcore of support from the population in surrounding districts.

Right: *The first meeting of the British Speedway Promoters Association, the body formed after the R.A.C. enquiry headed by Lord Shawcross in 1964. These were the men who formed the British League. Back row, left to right: Ian Hoskins, Reg Fearman, Allan Martin, Norman Parker, Harold Jackson, Wally Mawdsley, Les Clarke, Charles Knott, Charles Foot, Bill Bridgett, Eddie Glennon, Peter Lansdale, Len Silver. Seated: Trevor Redmond, Charles Ochiltree, Johnnie Hoskins, Frank Varey, Mike Parker, Ronnie Greene.*

Above: *West Ham, winners of the inaugural British League championship of 1965. At the back are Tony Clarke, Sverre Harrfeldt, Malcolm Simmons, Ken McKinlay. Front: Norman Hunter, Brian Leonard, Reg Trott, Tommy Price (manager).*

Below: *Belle Vue, first team to win three successive British League First Division championships between 1970 and 1972. Back row, left to right: Ken Eyre, Chris Pusey, Eric Broadbelt, Peter Collins, Ivan Mauger. Front: Sören Sjösten, Alan Wilkinson.*

London, where once there were nine circuits, now has four – three of them in the British League, which has been sponsored by Gulf Oil since 1975.

If there is one area which appears to have a surfeit of tracks it is in the midlands, where a fistful of circuits in both divisions apparently operate quite happily side by side.

Nevertheless, a random glance at the map shows that League speedway encompasses most corners of Britain, with the majority of tracks sufficiently soundly based – even in these inflationary times – to give rise to optimism. The public want it, and there is no good reason why the diet of League racing cannot be sustained.

With the phasing out of a system of rider control, which had monitored the strength of all tracks and sought to guard against anybody achieving an undesirable or unfair level of power, managements are again being put to the test. Really, that is how it should be.

Those who swear by the value of their own efforts will have no complaints. But transfers, as ever, will continue to make the headlines. Not that big money guarantees success. Leicester, bottom of the Gulf League, paid Cradley Heath a new record of £12,000 to buy back Australian captain John Boulger in 1977 . . . and finished bottom again.

Hull, who equalled that figure when they signed Ivan Mauger from Exeter a year later, hope for better luck. Mauger, after all, did transform Belle Vue and later galvanised Exeter from also-rans to champions.

The quality of competition has never been higher or more stimulating. But if there is one move which could inject tremendous interest, it is promotion and relegation. Speedway has always skirted round this thorny topic. Teams have moved up and down, but no hard and fast rules have ever provided for anything which was automatic.

Maybe it is time for that. With 40 tracks, and the prospect of a few more to come, there are more teams than when the National League successfully operated three divisions after the war.

Conservatism has its merits but the sport cannot flourish if fear is the operative factor. League racing can continue to flourish without promotion and relegation, no doubt. The question to ponder is whether it might not boom even more if the promoters voted to take such a step.

Right: *Ipswich who won the First Division in 1975 and 1976. Standing, left to right: Billy Sanders, Ted Howgego, Ron Bagley (team manager), Tony Davey, Trevor Jones, Dave Gooderham, Mike Lanham. On machine: John Louis (captain).*

TEST MATCH STORY

After the welcome given by the public to team racing, it was only a matter of time before international matches were introduced. In 1930, football staged the World Cup for the first time. Test cricket was preparing for considerable expansion. Speedway was quick to join in.

Vivian Van Damm, the general manager of International Speedways – and later renowned for his involvement in such diverse entertainments as the Windmill Theatre and Grand Prix motor racing – tossed around the idea of speedway Test matches with Dickie Maybrook and *Speedway News* journalists N. Pritchard and R. M. Samuel.

The idea was first mooted in public by Lord Sempill, speaking at a luncheon arranged by the Association of Motor Cycle Track Racing Promoters in London just before the 1930 season opened.

Most promoters were taken with the idea, but for weeks nobody seemed capable of arriving at a final decision as to the format of a series. And everybody was too busily disputing claims as to whom should have the first match!

While others argued, Wimbledon stole a march on the rest. Most of the Australian stars were contracted to one or other of the International Speedways circuits. Bookings went out to them and to several of the star Englishmen such as Frank Varey and Jack Parker for what was ostensibly going to be an individual tournament.

With the top names all booked and confirmed, Wimbledon broke the news that they were to stage the first Test match between England and Australia.

There was uproar. The pioneer promoters thought no more of this ruse than would any of the contemporary collection, who have been known to react unfavourably when anybody tries to steal a march on them; but Wimbledon had a *fait accompli*.

The Australian authorities sanctioned the match, and thus on July 30, 1930 . . . the same day as Don Bradman and his cricketing colleagues were engaged against England in a Test match at Lord's . . . the first official speedway international was set to go.

An enormous publicity campaign was mounted. There were sandwich board men at cricket matches, banners and kites proclaiming the news flown at Ascot. The interest generated was huge.

An estimated 30,000 turned up at Plough Lane, and inevitably many of them did not manage to get inside the ground. Those who did saw Australia amble to a 35–17 victory over nine heats.

Above: *England, 1930. Left to right: Bob Harrison, Frank Charles, Jim Kempster, Squib Burton, Frank Varey, Wally Hull, Jack Parker, Eric Langton.*

Vic Huxley (Harringay) captained Australia. Not only did he win all of his races, but he broke the track record, too. Details:
England 17: Roger Frogley (Crystal Palace) 6, Jim Kempster (Wimbledon, captain) 5, Wal Phillips (Stamford Bridge) 4, Jack Parker (Coventry) 1, Jack Ormston (Wembley) 1, Frank Varey (Belle Vue) 0. Reserve was Gus Kuhn (Stamford Bridge).
Australia 35: Vic Huxley (Harringay, captain) 9, Frank Arthur (Stamford Bridge) 6, Max Grosskreutz (Belle Vue) 6, Billy Lamont (Wimbledon) 6, Ron Johnson (Crystal Palace) 5, Dickie Case (Wimbledon) 3. Reserve was Arnie Hansen (Southampton).

Despite the one-sided nature of this inaugural match, it was promptly decided to extend the series. Four more matches were raced, over 16 heats.

Right: *Australian mainstays Billy Lamont and Frank Arthur.*

England proved to have greater strength in depth over the longer formula, and won the next four matches, all enthusiastically supported. In the second, at Belle Vue, local hero Grosskreutz became the first to score a 12 point maximum, a feat emulated by Phillips at Stamford Bridge in the third, and by Huxley, comfortably the most successful rider in the series, in each of the last two matches.

England again won 4–1 in the 1931 series, their one reverse being by the odd point in a long-winded and often controversial second Test at Leicester Super. It was in this match that Squib Burton and Wal Phillips crashed and both suffered injuries which sidelined them for months.

Biggest problem in this match, though, was the number of false starts. Rolling starts were still the order of the day and a seemingly endless succession of heats had to be called back and started again.

The five match series was now established as an annual affair, and England usually contrived to win, with Jack Parker and Eric Langton their most consistent performers, ably supported by an increasing number of exciting newcomers.

It was a measure of the public appeal of the Tests that 84,000 watched the 1932 match at Wembley – the biggest crowd at any meeting up to that time.

The 1933 series was crammed with curios. The scoring system awarded four points to a race winner, with the result that individual and collective scores reached new heights. In the second Test at Belle Vue, for example, Ginger Lees claimed an incredible 22 points.

Missing from that match, and indeed, all but the first of the summer, was Eric Langton. At Wembley, he had won four races out of four, but was disqualified from his next for crossing the white line and going on to the grass. Eric disagreed, refused to take his last ride – and found himself left out of the team for the remainder of the series.

West Ham staged the final match, and an incredible 82,400 saw England win 74–52 to clinch the rubber.

In 1934, Australia won the Ashes for the first time, even though Langton was back to lead the England charts in each of the four matches in which he rode, and Lees was a model of consistency with double figures (and conventional 3–2–1 scoring) in each of the five Tests.

For once Huxley, hit by a rare injury, was not the dominant force for Australia. Instead, Grosskreutz, Ron Johnson and the fast-improving Bluey Wilkinson played the major role and the men from Down Under won 3–2.

England were back to their winning ways in the following year, and continued to call the tune until the outbreak of war. Yet the quality and appeal of these matches continued to thrill thousands.

In 1936 Frank Charles bettered the scoring record of his Wembley colleague Lees, and set a new series record for England, 69 points from five matches. Three years later Bill Kitchen bettered that by a solitary point.

As some of the elder statesmen faded, Wilkinson became the key man for Australia. So much so, indeed, that when he was injured after the first Test in 1937, the remainder of the series was scrapped and an England v Overseas series substituted.

But the following year, during which he won the world title, Wilkinson emphasised his prowess by rustling together 80 points, including an 18 point maximum at both New Cross and Wimbledon. Also chipping in with 18 at New Cross was Lionel Van Praag.

But if England ruled at home, they did not have things their own way when the series spread to Australia. Official Test matches there did not get under way until 1934–35, though an unofficial series preceded this by two years.

Frank Arthur and Johnnie Hoskins were prime movers in bringing the international stage to Australia. And riders such as Huxley, Grosskreutz, Van Praag, Phillips, Parker, Varey and the rest paid little heed to the threat of disciplinary action if the title 'Test matches' were used.

Officially, though, there were just five series in Australia before the war and the host country won the lot. The tourists soon discovered that there were plenty of accomplished riders quite happy to show them the way round the big, fast circuits.

Apart from 1935–36, when matches were of 12 heats, nine races were the order of the day. Initially Grosskreutz was the Australian mainstay. In the second series, he scored a 12 point maximum in each of the first four meetings. But Wilkinson proved to be no less consistent in the 1937–38 series, when he rode unbeaten, the first to do so in every match.

It was in Australia that the series revived in 1947–48, with 18 heats the formula used. Now the strength in depth of the host country was really emphasised. Admittedly England failed to send teams of ultimate ability, but in 27 matches spread over five series up to and including 1952–53, they won only twice.

Bill Rogers and Bill Longley were ever-presents as Australia chalked up a 5–0 win in the comeback series. The closest England came was within six points in the second Test at Sydney, where the Parker brothers, Jack

Left: *H. R. (Ginger) Lees, prolific scorer for England in 1933 and 1934.*

and Norman, and Bill Pitcher all got into double figures.

The Aussies responded by including Vic Duggan and Max Grosskreutz in the last three matches of the series, Aub Lawson in the last two, to remove any possibility of embarrassment.

In 1949–50, Lawson produced the most consistent scoring ever recorded in the series which Australia won 6–1. Lawson contributed a massive 117 points. England did contrive to win the sixth match at Melbourne, where Jack Parker and Ron Clarke claimed 14 apiece.

One year later, when Australia made a clean sweep of all seven matches, Lawson again collected double figures each time, totalling 105, with Buck Ryan a consistent support man.

Contrasting performances from the veteran and the baby of this England team.

Evergreen Jack Parker was massively consistent with 111 points. Teenager Reg Fearman scored 11 in seven matches.

A Parker 18 point maximum was the feature of England's 59–49 win in the second Test at Sydney in 1951–52. But this apart, the Aussies carried on in irresistible fashion. The following year, Parker's eighth consecutive tour, found him as usual at the head of the England score charts but complaining about the weakness of the side labelled England.

That was to be the last Lions tour for a further seven years, and in 1953 the matches in England also came to an end for a while. This was sad news, as the domestic series, revived in 1947, had contained many names and performances in keeping with the pre-war traditions.

In 1949 Australia had achieved a 3–2 success, with two 18 point maximum scores from Vic Duggan putting them on the way to victory. Duggan had concluded the previous series with a six-ride full score, a feat matched by Graham Warren at Wembley the next spring.

Parker, at West Ham in 1947, and debut maker Dent Oliver, at Belle Vue in 1948, demonstrated that such scoring was not an exclusively Australian prerogative. The Parker brothers provided England with a formidable first pairing in the latter series. Jack (58) and Norman (49) collected 107 of a possible 150 points. And in 1949, Oliver again scored 18, this time at Bradford.

Right: *An Australian team of superb talents, 1935. Left to right: Dickie Case, Mick Murphy, Jack Sharp, Max Grosskreutz, Vic Huxley, Lionel Van Praag, Bluey Wilkinson, Ron Johnson.*

For reliability, however, Tommy Price took the palm with double figures in every match in 1950, and Cyril Brine, who had failed to score in three previous appearances as a reserve in the preceding two years, bounced into the international reckoning with 11 at New Cross, 13 at Wimbledon and 16 at Wembley.

Jack Young proved still more effective for Australia, yet even his performances were overshadowed by those of young Ronnie Moore, whose 1952 record of 80 points from five matches included three 18 point scores. Not surprisingly, Australia won the series, 4–1. England had the consolation of taking the last match, 55–53 at Harringay, thanks largely to 16 points from reserve Dick Bradley, who was making his full international bow.

But within a year the series had come to a halt. There were those who felt that these battles between the two oldest rivals had lost something of their impact. No less significantly at this time, the New Zealanders were begging to make their presence felt.

Trevor Redmond was a pioneering prime mover in the Kiwi cause. A 1951 series against England 'C' was followed by the first of several visits to South Africa when Ronnie Moore and to an even greater extent Barry Briggs sharpened and honed their exciting talents.

Moore, born in Tasmania but essentially a Christchurch product, opted to represent New Zealand rather than Australia – and was the star turn when New Zealand were granted full Test status in 1953. He was spared the embarrassment of making a further decision on international pedigree the following year, when the England v Australasia (Australia and New Zealand combined) series was instituted.

This amalgam of the two Down Under countries was to maintain the impetus of international competition in England through some of the sport's darkest years. Half a dozen series of between three and six matches were staged and it was perhaps surprising that not until 1960, in the last such rubber, that the combined colonial stock came out on top, winning five matches and drawing the other.

Moore was masterly with 92 points from those six matches; and only fractionally less impressive was Peter Craven, whose record 83 for England included the top score in all but the New Cross international.

Above: *Australia, 1953. Back row, left to right: Arthur Payne, Keith Gurtner, Arthur Simcock (manager), Jack Young, Aub Lawson. Front: Johnnie Chamberlain, Ronnie Moore, Peter Moore, Jackie Biggs.*

If these two were the outstanding performers on either side during the Australasian matches – Moore collected 260 points in 21 appearances, Craven 219 in 18 – there were other major contributors. Young scored 228 in 19 matches, Briggs 215 in 20, while for the host nation, Ken McKinlay took 21 matches to amass 202 points, Brian Crutcher only 14 to total 176.

Others were also knocking on the international door. Some merely flattered to deceive. The United States had been good enough to defeat England in a solitary 1937 Test match at Wimbledon, against an England side of no mean accomplishment: Bill Kitchen, Joe Abbott, Jack Parker, Ginger Lees, Frank Charles, Tommy Croombs, Geoff Pymar and Claude Rye.

Jack Milne (18), Wilbur Lamoreaux (15), and Cordy Milne (11) were their mainstays on that occasion, as befitted the first three in the world championship of that year.

A revival was hinted when the U.S.A. sent a tour party to England in 1951. They won a couple of their five matches against an England 'C' team. But two decades were to elapse before the Americans again featured in international competition.

South Africa seemed to be a coming force, and in the first few post-war years their domestic scene flourished. The Springboks happily entertained visiting England, New Zealand and Overseas teams without ever suggesting that they could develop into a potent force outside their own country.

Nevertheless Henry Long, their first World Final qualifier, and scorer of 222 points in 20 matches against England tour teams, looked an accomplished performer, as did Buddy Fuller and Doug Davies, whose 66 in five matches in 1956–57 remains the best series return in the record books.

Of all the countries who entered the international arena after the war, none proved more impressive than the Swedes. They quickly established themselves as a force far ahead of that boasted by any other European country.

Olle Nygren, arguably the first of their great riders, soon attracted the attention of English clubs. Almost single-handed, he carried the first Swedish team to visit this country in 1951. They rode against England 'C' and were far from disgraced, losing at Exeter and Poole, with a 63–44 win at Wolverhampton sandwiched in between. Nygren scored an 18 point maximum in each of the first two matches.

Another five years elapsed before Sweden were rated strong enough to take on the full England side in a three-match series, but the improvement of Nygren, Dan Forsberg, Rune Sörmander and Ove Fundin had not gone unrecognised.

It was Fundin who set the Swedes on their way with an 18 point maximum in the 59–49 win at Wembley. Both he and Nygren were double figure scorers in each of the three Test matches, none of which had a more dramatic finale than the second at Wimbledon. The visitors won the match with a last race 3–0.

This was the start of an on-going series between the countries, which also embraced reciprocal visits to Sweden. And within five years, Great Britain – including the leading colonials – rather than England, provided the opposition.

Home advantage proved all-important, with the hosts winning 5–0 in series held in this country and in Sweden. Fundin registered an incredible 88 points from his home series, including four 18 point maximum scores. His 64 in England, one less than Björn Knutsson, included a score-less night at Belle Vue.

Craven, traditionally a top scorer for England and Great Britain, led the way both at home and abroad. Ronnie Moore and Barry Briggs also contributed freely.

Sweden, meanwhile, were busily expanding the international frontiers. A particularly hectic year was 1958, when they rode against England at home and away, Poland home and away, Australasia, Austria and even Holland.

Called upon for the more demanding matches, Fundin raced to an incredible 242 points from 16 internationals. Sörmander had 217, Nygren 216 from the same number of matches.

The Poles, another emerging nation, went meekly enough to defeat that year when Sweden and England came visiting. And in their first series in this country, the slaughter was terrible. England won all three matches by a huge margin.

But a couple of seasons later, and in spite of the most monumental exploits by Craven, the English discovered to their cost that Poland had improved out of all recognition. Twice little Peter was credited with a 21 point seven-ride maximum, and in the third match, at Leszno, when Poland tasted victory for the first time, he had to settle for 17 from six starts.

That gave him 111 points from a possible 114 in two visits. Small wonder that the Poles still talk of Peter Craven with reverence.

The developing talents of Florian Kapala, Marian Kaiser and Henryk Zyto encouraged Poland to believe that a bright future awaited them in the international arena. It was in this atmosphere of optimism and increasing interest that they were instrumental in getting the World Cup started, of which more anon.

The hoped-for international progress did not materialise, though, and, indeed, the British involvement diminished a great deal for a few years. And the next country to hit the international map was not Poland, but the U.S.S.R.

It had to be just a matter of time before Soviet Russia, so accomplished in so many sporting areas, decided to devote some attention to speedway racing. After some early individual successes, they turned their attention to team competition, initially in Poland in 1961.

Though beaten 5–0, the Soviets produced the outstanding rider of that initial series in Igor Plechanov, who scored 68 points and never failed to reach double figures. It was the start of the most astonishingly consistent international record.

Russia embarked upon competition with Sweden next, were due to visit England in 1963 only to pull out at the last minute, and eventually arrived for a three-match series the following year.

The drama of the first match, staged at Wembley before 26,000, was unforgettable. It was an occasion probably unrivalled in post-war British speedway history. The fact that the home side won 73–35 seemed to be almost incidental.

Vitaly Shilo suffered serious injury when he ripped into the safety fence. Yet nothing could quench the optimism and eagerness to learn of these smiling tourists, who promptly went to Coventry four days later and Great Britain were pushed to win a thriller 56–52.

Briggs in his prime – 83 points – led Britain to a clean sweep of success in five Test matches in 1965, and it was not until the next year, when England were considered to be more suitable opposition, that the Russians achieved a victory at Newcastle.

Whether against the best the commonwealth could offer or against a side stripped of the colonial supporting cast, Plechanov continued to grind out his incredible sequence of double figure scores. His 69 points in this series was his best and Boris Samorodov and Viktor Trofimov claimed double figures three times apiece.

Good individuals have continued to appear from time to time, yet as a collective unit the U.S.S.R. have not progressed too much since that point. They have made a number of sorties outside their own country, but there has been precious little in the opposite direction.

The Poles, by contrast, came bouncing back in the middle 1960's after some considerable reorganisation on the home front. A rude shock awaited Great Britain when they sent out a team in 1966 and never looked remotely like getting a result.

Pawel Waloszek hurried together an 18 point maximum in the first match at Bydgoszcz and Antoni Woryna, Andzej Wyglenda and Andrzej Pogorzelski also proved to be free scorers. The biggest upset, though, came the following year.

Great Britain found themselves on the wrong end of a 69–39 thrashing at West Ham, where only Colin Pratt could head Woryna, who rode with the aid of pain-killing injections and scored a brilliant 17. Partner Pogorzelski chipped in with a bonus point in each of his six rides.

With Nigel Boocock well to the fore, Britain came back to take the series, but they lost 3–2 to Sweden in the first meeting between the two sides for six years. However, British speedway reputation was climbing back, and the revival of the old tradition of a winter tour to Australia sparked added interest.

Changing faces in the England team

(a) Top: *Back row, left to right: Arthur Forrest, Wally Green, Ronnie Greene (manager), Split Waterman, Freddie Williams. Front: Peter Craven, Brian Crutcher, Eric Williams, Eddie Rigg.*

(b) Bottom: *Eric Williams, Tommy Price, Brian Crutcher, Ken McKinlay, Freddie Williams, Front: Eddie Rigg, Phil Clarke, Ron Mountford.*

Bottom: *The new technology. Tommy Price, former world champion, was appointed Great Britain team manager for the inaugural series against the U.S.S.R. in 1964. Here he checks to see how Yuri Chekranov is getting on with his Jawa/Eso machine.*

Below: *Colonials combined. Australasia, back row, left to right: Charlie New, Ron Johnston, George Allan (manager), Maury Dunn, Geoff Mardon. Front: Peter Clarke, Trevor Redmond, Ronnie Moore, Barry Briggs.*

Attempts to renew Down Under activity led to a couple of tours on a restricted basis, but the 1967–68 series was a full-blown affair and the England team was just about as strong as any to make such a trip.

The entente was not so cordiale when Terry Betts, one of the stars of a first Test win at Sydney, was hit on the head by a bottle thrown by a disgruntled spectator as Ken McKinlay's team rode on its victory parade. But tempers cooled, diplomacy prevailed, and the England boys went on to win the series by the odd match in five; Eric Boocock claimed 71 points including an 18 point show in the third Test at Sydney and the decider at Adelaide.

Australia turned the tables in the next tour, but England were back on top again the following year even though the splendidly consistent Jim Airey weighed in with tall scores in every match, for the second successive series. In 1969–70 he scored 79 in five matches.

With the series extended to seven, Australia again captured the initiative – without Airey, but boosted by the diligence and durability of John Langfield and Laurie Hodgson, whose bright promise was extinguished by a crippling accident. Nigel Boocock, having taken over from McKinlay as the elder statesman at the head of the tour party, hustled to 88 points in the series.

Reg Wilson, with 86 on his maiden tour in 1973–74, displayed a consistency of high standard. Two years later Peter Collins, with 97 in seven matches, did even better, despite collecting only a couple of points in England's only defeat – a controversial affair in Sydney in which skipper Chris Pusey was stretchered off.

Recent years have coincided with a decline in the Australian team strength. Yet they have still been capable of producing individual performances of great merit. John Boulger clocked up 109 points from seven matches in 1972–73. And Phil Crump later matched Lawson's record of topping the century mark in successive series.

Other colonial engagements have included the visit of Lions tourists to New Zealand at the end of several Australian trips; and, in 1969, England took on both Australia and New Zealand once more.

The Kiwis, with Ivan Mauger arrived as a world force, enjoyed a measure of success, with Briggs and Ronnie Moore playing their part. But the resources were all too thinly stretched after that.

Nevertheless, the commonwealth influence continued to be a significant feature of Great Britain team involvement. Sweden were punished for their 1967 audacity and went down 4–1, 5–0 and 5–1 in each of the next three series.

In the 1970 series Mauger twice collected the maximum 18, and 17 in two other matches. Briggs had one 18 and twice scored

17. Even in Sweden, where Britain won 2–1, Ivan scored yet another 18 at Gothenburg.

It was much the same story when Poland came back to face Great Britain in 1971. Andrezej Wyglenda was the only visitor to make any real impression, Poland lost 5–1, and twice found themselves on the wrong end of Mauger's flawless form.

But the English boys were beginning to flex their muscles. Martin Ashby totalled 158 points in 14 internationals during 1968, equalling the domestic record set by Ken McKinlay a decade earlier. Nigel Boocock was solidarity itself, while younger brother Eric (twice), Ray Wilson (twice), and Terry Betts all joined the relatively exclusive band of riders to have scored a six ride full maximum at international level.

England's reputation was further enhanced by Wilson and Betts who won the World Best Pairs in Boras, Sweden, in 1972; in the same year the English won an Inter-Nations Tournament which served as a prelude to an even more extensive competition sponsored by the *Daily Mirror* in the next season.

After a league series, spread over three weeks, a qualifying table read like this:

	P	W	D	L	Abd	F	A	Pts
England	6	5	0	0	1	233	155	11
Sweden	6	4	0	2	–	265	202	8
New Zealand	6	3	0	2	1	218	169	7
Australia	6	3	0	2	1	201	188	7
Norway and Denmark	6	3	0	2	1	193	196	7
Poland	6	1	0	5	–	182	284	2
U.S.S.R.	6	0	0	6	–	184	282	0

Semi-finals followed the form book, which left England to face Sweden at Wembley in the final. True to tradition, it was a memorable match, staged over 13 heats, at the end of which the scores were level at 39-all.

This meant a dramatic two-man run-off to decide the tournament. England paraded a side of proven experience. King's Lynn men Terry Betts and Malcolm Simmons had scored ten points each. Skipper Ray Wilson, 1971 World Team Cup maximum man, and in 1973 the first Englishman to become British champion since Jack Parker in 1947, had shown the right temperament for the big occasion.

But England manager Len Silver gambled on the 19-year-old Peter Collins, in his first year as an international racer, to confront Sweden's Anders Michanek, the successor to Fundin as the most reliable big time performer.

Collins gated, and led. Michanek was relentless in his pursuit. Finally he shaped to drive inside Collins coming into the pits turn. The teenager fell, Michanek was disqualified by senior A.C.U. referee Arthur Humphrey and amidst scenes of controversy and high drama rarely witnessed in international speedway, England had won.

That night was a watershed for both England and Sweden.

Below: *Great Britain team v U.S.S.R., Wembley, 1964. Back row, left to right: Dick Fisher, Brian Brett, Ron How, Ron Mountford, Tommy Price, Mike Broadbanks, Nigel Boocock, Ken McKinlay. On machine: Barry Briggs (captain).*

Bottom: *Captains Barry Briggs (Great Britain) and Igor Plechanov (U.S.S.R.) before the first race.*

The Swedes, with riders of the style and quality of Göte Nordin, Sören Sjösten, Bengt Jansson, then Bernie Persson and Anders Michanek, had seemed capable of sustaining their reputation at the highest level. Suddenly, too many of them were losing their bite.

In 1974, when commuting foreign riders were outlawed by the British League, the Swedes came back for a five match Test tour. England outclassed them from first to last. It was virtually the same story a year later when John Louis – 84 points in the series – included two 18 pointers and two of 17 in his haul.

England even went to Sweden and won as they pleased, with Ashby (18 at Stockholm) a revelation. Admittedly Michanek missed the first four matches because of illness, and came back with 18 at Mariestad. But the richly promising Tommy Jansson apart, the Swedes still disappointed.

Poland and Russia experienced similar difficulties. Even with the promise of Zenon Plech and developing maturity of Edward Jancarz, they were poor travellers. The Poles were drummed to defeat in seven successive internationals in 1974 and the Russians who followed them were probably saved from similar humiliation by the weather, which wrecked one match and prevented another from starting at all. One consolation for the Soviets was the excellent work of Grigori Chlynovski, who didn't taste failure on the entire tour.

Nobody, it seemed, could halt the England steamroller. Such has been the increasing dominance exercised by the English that series against other countries have been conspicuous by their absence from the fixture lists in the last two or three years.

In 1977 the Rest of the World provided the opposition, and even the assembled talents of leading riders from New Zealand, Australia, Sweden, Norway, Denmark, Poland and West Germany only managed to beat England 3–2.

Ole Olsen, whose Danish counterparts may well develop as the next significant international team, dominated proceedings with 67 points from five matches. Three home riders grabbed double figures on three occasions: Collins, Dave Jessup and the startlingly precocious 18-year-old Michael Lee.

It must be a source of disappointment that the Poles and Swedes have not sustained their promise of a decade ago, while the Russians appear to have gone back even further.

Even England's overseas activities appear to have lapsed apart from the on-going Australian tours.

It could be argued that the only balanced international tournament these days would be one which excluded England, which is as good a reason as any why the richly successful 1973 series has not been repeated, although there was a scaled-down version a couple of summers after that.

Tours, exchanges and series at club or lower league level continue to play their part. What British speedway must not do, however, is to fall into the trap of turning its back on continued international activity . . . for all its current position of eminence.

The road to even greater international recognition of speedway racing must still be via increased contact between the different countries.

Opposite top: *The new force. Poland, 1966. Back row, left to right: Pawel Waloszek, Antoni Woryna, Stanislaw Tkocz, T. Trawinski (manager), Marian Kaiser, Edmund Migos, Konstantyn Pociejkowicz, Andrzej Wyglenda. On machine: Andrzej Pogorzelski (captain).*

Opposite bottom: *England v Sweden in the final of the 1973 Daily Mirror International Tournament. This is the run-off between Peter Collins and Anders Michanek.*

Left: *The British Lions, 6–1 winners in Australia in 1973–74. Back row, left to right: Doug Wyer, George Hunter, Reg Fearman (manager), Eric Broadbelt, Nigel Boocock. Front: Reg Wilson, Jimmy McMillan, Peter Collins.*

Below: *Arguably no better England team has taken to the track, certainly in recent times. Back row, left to right: Terry Betts, John Louis, Martin Ashby, Peter Collins. Front: Malcolm Simmons, Ray Wilson, Dave Jessup.*

THE WORLD'S BEST

While League racing enabled the sport to establish an enduring appeal, the original concept of individual competition has never lost its attraction. World Championship Finals, instituted on an official basis in 1936, have consistently attracted huge crowds and provided the focal point for many a season.

Wembley will always be synonymous with the championship, though the spread of internationalism in recent years has decreed that the World Final also goes to Sweden and Poland these days.

Traditionally, though, the ultimate confrontation of the leading riders, chasing the world individual crown, has made for many electrifying and memorable occasions down the years.

It was back in 1926 that Johnnie Hoskins, never short of a new idea, first coined the phrase 'World Championship' and applied it to one of his meetings at Newcastle, New South Wales, which was won by one Roy Hindle.

A similar tag adorned other meetings in equally improbable outposts. Some historians claim that Vic Huxley won the first world title in Paris in 1931. Others put the year at 1933 and credit Claude Rye with that distinction.

But to all intents and purposes, the only truly authentic predecessor of the championships as we now know them was that held under the auspices of the London evening newspaper *The Star* from 1929 onwards.

At a time when individual trophy events abounded, executives of the newspaper suggested to the Southern Association of Track Racing Promoters a new competition, designed to establish just who was 'the best rider in the world.'

The Australian pioneers, American stars and top Englishmen were debarred from the newly-instituted League; and for the individual championships it was considered politic to stage one section for home riders and another for the overseas performers.

Thus the Star Riders Championship was born, and it operated on a match race basis, comparable with that employed today for the Golden Helmet. The first eliminator was at Southampton in June, 1929, between Billy Galloway and Sprouts Elder.

After a series of qualifying events, Frank Arthur and Vic Huxley met in the overseas final at Harringay in September. This one-off confrontation attracted a record crowd, and it was Arthur who took the title by two races to nil.

In the dash to the first turn in their second heat, Arthur fell. But a re-run was ordered, and next time he made no mistakes.

The English section was crammed with plenty of legendary names, Jim Kempster, Colin Watson, Gus Kuhn and Ivor Creek among them – but it was Roger Frogley who took the crown. He beat Jack Parker in the domestic decider at Wimbledon. Frogley had been a doubtful starter, having crashed his aeroplane a few days before the Star Final. But he was nerveless when it mattered.

By the following year, when overseas stars and home riders alike contested all of the major competitions, the emphasis had switched dramatically. The organisation was different, too, with the top dozen scorers from the first 15 Southern League matches going to a grand final at Wembley, with three riders in each of the eliminating heats.

The qualifiers showed several changes from

the previous season, though Roger Frogley, Watson and Kempster were among ten – yes, ten – Englishmen. Just two Australians made it to Wembley, and in the event they contested the prize. This time Huxley reversed the 1929 result, beating Arthur in the decider.

For the following year, each track staged its own qualifying round. There was much more of an Australian flavour about this final, but Englishman Jack Parker (Southampton) began as the hot favourite for the title.

However, Ray Tauser helped himself to a slice of history, by becoming the first rider from the United States of America to qualify for the final. Furthermore, he won it, beating Huxley, his skipper at Wimbledon, in convincing fashion.

After the formation of the National Speedway Association in 1932, the championships became truly representative, and the northern aces wasted no time in making their presence felt. Eric Langton (Belle Vue) won the event, with Huxley second once again, and his Australia and Wimbledon team mate Dickie Case third.

Tom Farndon (Crystal Palace) was a popular winner in 1933, when each of the eight teams in the National League provided two qualifiers. His colleague Ron Johnson collected second position and Bluey Wilkinson, the popular Aussie from West Ham, was third.

With Huxley absent, suffering from the only major injury of his career, the Englishmen had things very much their own way in 1934. For the first time, they provided the winner, runner-up and third place man.

Jack Parker, making his third final appearance in four years, and with his latest team of Harringay, stunned the crowd and the much fancied Eric Langton by taking the Belle Vue man from the back in the decisive race. Wembley's own Ginger Lees was third.

The 1935 championships adopted the format which has become so familiar in subsequent seasons. After each track had staged its own qualifying round, the final was held over 20 heats with the now traditional formula of 16 riders each meeting the others once.

Tom Farndon was the biggest pre-meeting favourite thus far; but a second half final crash at New Cross the night before put him and Ron Johnson out of the final. In fact Farndon never recovered consciousness, and within 48 hours he had died.

So it was that Frank Charles, wooed out of self-imposed retirement by Wembley, waltzed to the title with a 15 point maximum. The 14th heat, his fourth, was the crucial one. Here he was confronted by unfancied Jack Ormston and Australian hope Max Grosskreutz, both also unbeaten to this stage.

Charles remained cool while his two challengers missed an opportunity to earn themselves a place in the all-time hall of fame.

Such was the success of the Star Championships that sooner or later somebody was bound to come up with the idea of investing the competition with a World Championship status. Naturally, Johnnie Hoskins was one of the prime movers.

Wembley's Arthur Elvin was not so easy to convince. But eventually the other promoters persuaded him, and press and public alike received the idea with rapturous enthusiasm.

Controversially, each rider came to the first official final with a credit total of bonus points, accumulated from earlier qualifying rounds. Eric Langton led the way, with Lionel Van Praag (Wembley and Australia), Frank Charles, George Newton and Jack Parker all just one point behind.

Almost inevitably, this meant bad news for any other rider who happened to strike outstanding form on the big night, but lacked the necessary bonus points.

And so it proved. Wiry Bluey Wilkinson was untouchable on the night, scoring a maximum. But with only ten points to carry forward, he could manage a grand total of only 25.

Van Praag beat Langton in heat 20 to force a run-off. Then, after a false start, he repeated the treatment and thus became the first official World champion. In addition to his starts and point money, Van Praag earned £500 and a handsome trophy.

The unfortunate Wilkinson had £100 and a silver medal to console him . . . he had to wait for two more years before it was his turn.

The competition was immediately accepted, and has since accumulated the greatest legend

Abbreviations:

A	— *Australia*
EG	— *East Germany*
SA	— *South Africa*
USSR	— *Soviet Russia*
Cz	— *Czechoslovakia*
N	— *Norway*
S	— *Sweden*
W	— *Wales*
D	— *Denmark*
NZ	— *New Zealand*
Sc	— *Scotland*
WG	— *West Germany*
E	— *England*
P	— *Poland*
USA	— *United States*

and most enduring popularity, leading to this day to the high peak of almost any speedway year.

The records contain details of the doughty deeds of 16 men who have been crowned as champion of the world, and many more who strove for similar immortality and fell short.

Wartime and its aftermath robbed others of their chance. Adolf Hitler saw to it that the 1939 final, scheduled for September 7, did not take place, much to the chagrin of the leading qualifiers and especially the top four due at Wembley: Cordy Milne, Bill Kitchen, Wilbur Lamoreaux and Eric Langton. Any one of them must have been in with a strong chance of joining the all-time greats.

After hostilities ended, the *Sunday Dispatch* sponsored a British Riders Championship for three years, before the world championships were revived.

Tommy Price took the first post-war crown, a performance he repeated when the championship proper was re-introduced in 1949.

For Jack Parker, victory in the 1947 British Riders Championship was the closest he came to collecting a world title, which would surely have been an appropriate recognition of his lengthy domination of the sport.

Parker's victory over Vic Duggan was the turning point of this meeting. Duggan had been in unbelievable form all year – he was as dominant in every competition as Huxley had been in 1930 – but it all went sour for him this time.

Right: *Lionel Van Praag (Australia), 1936.*

However, the following year belonged to the laconic Australian from Harringay. He dropped a point in his opening ride, then rattled off four impressive victories to take top spot. Just a point behind were the indestructible Ron Johnson, and Alec Statham, lone conqueror of Duggan.

Then it was back to the competition proper, with the modern day catalogue unfolding.

Of the 32 finals staged to date, Ove Fundin, Ivan Mauger and Barry Briggs claim 14 titles between them. We will have a look at their exploits in greater detail elsewhere.

For the meantime, the following summary of what happened in the finals staged thus far should provide the historians with all the facts.

1936

THIS is where it all began. Wembley, September 10. Other tournaments had preceded it, but this was the first official World Final, with the top qualifiers coming from an original list of 63 entries, including 11 nationalities. The crowd was 75,000.

All the riders started with a credit of bonus points gained from previous rounds. Eric Langton led; Lionel Van Praag was one of four riders just one point behind. Yet on the night neither could tame Bluey Wilkinson who scored five wins in as many rides.

With bonus points added, however, a run-off between Van Praag and Langton was required and the 27-year-old Australian won by inches to collect the £500 prize and the trophy. So it was that he went into the record books; Wilkinson's turn came later.

Scorers: Lionel Van Praag (A) 26 (14 at Wembley), Eric Langton (E) 26 (13), Bluey Wilkinson (A) 25 (15), Frank Charles (E) 20 (8), Cordy Milne (U.S.A.) 20 (11), Vic Huxley (A) 18 (8), Dickie Case (A) 16 (7), Jack Ormston (E) 16 (7), George Newton (E) 16 (4), Jack Milne (U.S.A.) 15 (6), Morian Hansen (D) 15 (5), Bob Harrison (E) 15 (5), Wal Phillips (E) 12 (5), Ginger Lees (E) 11 (4), Arthur Atkinson (E) 10 (4), Bill Pitcher (E) 8 (2), Norman Parker (E) (res) 7 (1).

Left: *Jack Milne (United States of America), 1937.*

Right: *Bluey Wilkinson (Australia), 1938.*

1937

ALTHOUGH the bonus points system continued, nominations for the second championship were limited to 48. This time, Jack Milne of the United States led the qualifiers and made sure with a 15 point maximum in front of Wembley's 85,000.

In fact it was a clean sweep for the Americans, with Wilbur Lamoreaux and Jack's brother Cordy Milne claiming the next two places. This trio seemed far better equipped than the rest to deal with a very deep, heavy circuit.

Unluckiest men in the championship this year were erstwhile favourite Bluey Wilkinson, who broke his wrist and missed qualification, and Eric Langton, the strongly tipped Englishman. A broken toe proved too much of a handicap for him in the Final.

Scorers: Jack Milne (U.S.A.) 28 (15 at Wembley), Wilbur Lamoreaux (U.S.A.) 25 (13), Cordy Milne (U.S.A.) 23 (10), Jack Parker (E) 21 (10), Ginger Lees (E) 19 (9), Lionel Van Praag (A) 17 (6), Frank Charles (E) 17 (7), Eric Langton (E) 16 (4), George Newton (E) 16 (5), Bill Kitchen (E) 16 (9), Morian Hansen (D) 15 (8), Eric Chitty (C) 15 (4), Joe Abbott (E) 14 (6), Arthur Atkinson (E) 14 (6), Frank Varey (E) 11 (3), Tommy Croombs (E) 8 (2), Alec Statham (E) (res) 0 (0).

1938

BLUEY (ARTHUR) WILKINSON, the wiry Australian who had been undefeated on the first World Final night but missed the title, made amends this time. Under a new bonus points system, he went to Wembley a point ahead of a fistful of close rivals.

Wilkinson had suffered concussion and damaged a shoulder in a crash at New Cross the previous evening; and he was known to be suffering from cartilage trouble, too. But he had vowed to take the title and 14 points on the night ensured his success.

Once again there was a strong American challenge, with Jack Milne scoring 14 on the night, Wilbur Lamoreaux 13, but the best this earned them was second and third placing overall. No complaints from them or the 93,000 crowd, though.

Scorers: Bluey Wilkinson (A) 22 (14 at Wembley), Jack Milne (U.S.A.) 21 (14), Wilbur Lamoreaux (U.S.A.) 20 (13), Lionel Van Praag (A) 18 (11), Cordy Milne (U.S.A.) 15 (8), Bill Kitchen (E) 15 (9), Alec Statham (E) 13 (8), Eric Langton (E) 13 (8), Benny Kaufman (U.S.A.) 12 (7), Jack Parker (E) 10 (6), Arthur Atkinson (E) 10 (9), Tommy Price (E) 8 (4), Tommy Croombs (E) 8 (4), Geoff Pymar (E) 7 (2), George Newton (E) 7 (2), Frank Varey (E) 4 (0), Jack Ormston (E) (res) 0 (5).

1949

THE first World Final to be held after the war – replacing the British Riders' Finals staged in 1946 (won by Tommy Price), 1947 (Jack Parker), and 1948 (Vic Duggan) – attracted a capacity crowd to Wembley and provided a home winner in Tommy Price, 38.

Injury ruled out Vic Duggan, and Jack Parker – beaten only by Price – was arguably the unluckiest rider on the night. On such occasions though the trick is to keep winning and Price did that to perfection.

It was a memorable end to a season's long pursuit of the prize, for which 224 riders from a dozen countries had entered. Most important departure from past tradition was that no bonus points were carried forward; the result on the night was all-important.

Scorers: Tommy Price (E) 15, Jack Parker (E) 14, Louis Lawson (E) 13, Norman Parker (E) 10, Bill Kitchen (E) 9, Wilbur Lamoreaux (U.S.A.) 9, Aub Lawson (A) 8, Ron Clarke (E) 8, Bill Longley (A) 8, Cyril Roger (E) 7, Bill Gilbert (E) 6, Graham Warren (A) 5, Ken Le Breton (A) 4, Lloyd Goffe (E) 2, Cliff Watson (A) 1, Oliver Hart (E) (res) 1, Dent Oliver (E) 0.

Right: *Tommy Price (England), 1949.*

Top right: *Freddie Williams (Wales), 1950 and 1953.*

Opposite page: *Jack Young (Australia), 1951 and 1952.*

1950

FREDDIE WILLIAMS, a 24-year-old from the Welsh steel town of Port Talbot, was the surprise winner of the fifth world championship final – and the third Wembley rider to take the title.

Cheered by a 93,000 crowd including a coach-load of relatives who had made the journey from Wales, he broke the track record in the first race, and never looked back.

This was the year in which two future world champions made their debut in the final. One was Australia's Jack Young, who topped the qualifying round scores. The other? Ronnie Moore, at 17 the youngest finalist there has been. And he was excluded from his first race for unfair riding!

Scorers: Freddie Williams (W) 14, Wally Green (E) 13, Graham Warren (A) 12, Aub Lawson (A) 10, Jack Parker (E) 8, Tommy Price (E) 8, Split Waterman (E) 8, Cyril Brine (E) 7, Ronnie Moore (NZ) 7, Jack Young (A) 7, Dent Oliver (E) 6, Danny Dunton (E) 5, Cyril Roger (E) (res) 5, Vic Duggan (A) 4, Jackie Biggs (A) 3, Ron Clarke (E) 3, Arthur Payne (A) 0, Mike Erskine (E) (res) 0.

1951

FOR THE first time, a three-man run-off was needed to determine the world championship.

Wiry Australian Jackie Biggs looked a certainty after winning his first four rides, but, incredibly, he finished last in his fifth, then had to settle for third place in the decider.

Jack Young, also of Australia, took the title by beating Split Waterman and Biggs after all three had totalled 12 points. For Young, the brilliantly consistent skipper of Second Division Edinburgh, it was the night of nights.

Defending champion Freddie Williams flattered to deceive, winning his first race, but it was a memorable occasion for the family nonetheless, with brother Eric making his bow. Once again, Wembley pulled in 93,000.

Scorers: Jack Young (A) 12, Split Waterman (E) 12, Jackie Biggs (A) 12, Ronnie Moore (NZ) 11, Jack Parker (E) 10, Louis Lawson (E) 10, Eddie Rigg (E) 8, Aub Lawson (A) 7, Bob Leverenz (A) 7, Freddie Williams (W) 7, Jeff Lloyd (E) 6, Eric Williams (W) 6, Cyril Brine (E) 3, Norman Parker (E) 3, Ernie Roccio (U.S.A.) 2, Alan Hunt (E) 2, Dick Bradley (E) (res) 2.

1952

JACK YOUNG collected his second successive title, this time as a West Ham rider. He had been transferred from Edinburgh for a record £3,750 fee. This was a more convincing performance than that of the previous year, full of mature confidence.

Freddie Williams was a consistent scorer but a surprise defeat at the hands of Swedish teenager Dan Forsberg – the first continental qualifier since Morian Hansen in 1937 – dented his chances.

For the first time, a European round was staged and thus the entry was more representative than before. Forsberg wasn't the only teenage newcomer, though, as Poole's Brian Crutcher, also 18, made his first appearance in a World Final.

Scorers: Jack Young (A) 14, Freddie Williams (W) 13, Bob Oakley (E) 12, Ronnie Moore (NZ) 10, Dick Bradley (E) 9, Dan Forsberg (S) 9, Arthur Payne (A) 9, Arthur Forrest (E) 7, Jeff Lloyd (E) 7, Henry Long (SA) 7, Brian Crutcher (E) 6, Split Waterman (E) 6, Graham Warren (A) 5, Derek Close (E) 4, Cyril Roger (E) 2, Ron How (E) 0.

1953

THERE WAS an even more marked international flavour in Coronation Year, with seven continental rounds being staged, but the glory belonged to a former winner – Freddie Williams, who rode consistently on a track which was tricky following rain.

Split Waterman, such a flamboyant and popular performer, looked to be the favourite as he won his first four rides. But in his critical fifth outing, Williams won and Swedish champion Olle Nygren kept Waterman pegged back in third spot.

In a run-off for third place, Geoff Mardon struck a first for New Zealand when he held off the challenge of Nygren, who fell on the notoriously treacherous pits bend. In spite of bad weather, 90,000 turned up to watch the Final.

Scorers: Freddie Williams (W) 14, Split Waterman (E) 13, Geoff Mardon (NZ) 12, Olle Nygren (S) 12, Jack Young (A) 10, Ronnie Moore (NZ) 9, Jeff Lloyd (E) 8, Arthur Forrest (E) 7, Aub Lawson (A) 7, Brian Crutcher (E) 6, Rune Sörmander (S) 5, Graham Warren (A) 5, Eric Williams (W) 4, Alan Hunt (E) 3, Jackie Biggs (A) 2, Dick Bradley (E) 2, Dent Oliver (E) (res) 1.

1954

RONNIE MOORE, 21, signalled the fact that the times were changing. His five-ride maximum established him as the clear winner of a Final in which youth was very much to the fore. And he did so with an injured leg cased in a special protective plaster.

Brian Crutcher, a year younger, settled for the runner-up spot and Olle Nygren was relegated to third after a run-off. Nevertheless, this was the first time a Swedish rider had made the rostrum.

Especially interesting in the light of future events, three young riders made their first appearance in the Final and subsequently each of them won the title. They were Barry Briggs, Peter Craven and Ove Fundin.

Scorers: Ronnie Moore (NZ) 15, Brian Crutcher (E) 13, Olle Nygren (S) 13, Jack Young (A) 11, Split Waterman (E) 9, Barry Briggs (NZ) 9, Eddie Rigg (E) 7, Fred Brand (E) 7, Jackie Biggs (A) 7, Arthur Forrest (E) 5, Geoff Mardon (NZ) 5, Tommy Price (E) 5, Trevor Redmond (NZ) 5, Aub Lawson (A) 4, Peter Craven (E) 3, Ove Fundin (S) 2.

Top left: *Freddie Williams (Wales), 1950 and 1953.*

Right: *Ronnie Moore (New Zealand), 1954 and 1959.*

Left: *Peter Craven (England), 1955 and 1962.*

Right: *Ove Fundin (Sweden), 1956, 1960, 1961, 1963 and 1967.*

1955

PETER CRAVEN was the darling of the fans as he collected the title for the first time. The diminutive thrill-maker from Belle Vue underlined his growing reputation with a display of typical character and panache.

It was ironic that Brian Crutcher, widely tipped as the next English world champion, should be dogged by misfortune. He came down at the first turn in heat 13 and was excluded. But he still reached a double figure total.

Ahead of him, New Zealand pals Ronnie Moore and Barry Briggs lined up with Eric Williams for a run-off to determine second, third and fourth. The more experienced Moore sauntered to victory and the other two came off while disputing the final place.

Scorers: Peter Craven (E) 13, Ronnie Moore (NZ) 12, Barry Briggs (NZ) 12, Eric Williams (W) 12, Brian Crutcher (E) 10, Ove Fundin (S) 10, Jack Young (A) 10, Olle Nygren (S) 9, Arthur Forrest (E) 7, Arthur Wright (E) 6, Ron Johnston (NZ) 6, Billy Bales (E) 6, Kjell Carlsson (S) 3, Phil Clarke (E) 2, Henry Andersen (N) 2, Cyril Roger (E) 0.

1956

THE first televised final coincided with another most significant 'first' as Ove Fundin of Sweden collected the championship. The 22-year-old from Tranas, in his second season with Norwich, kept cool while others faltered.

Not for the first time, Crutcher tossed away a title chance by crashing. Craven, the defending champion, won his first race in brilliant fashion but dropped a valve while leading in his second.

This was a significant year with riders from Eastern Europe involved in the qualifying rounds for the first time. But even without Olle Nygren – he elected to miss the final and rode in the Swedish T.T. instead – the Swedes remained the dominant force.

Scorers: Ove Fundin (S) 13, Ronnie Moore (NZ) 12, Arthur Forrest (E) 11, Peter Craven (E) 11, PeO Söderman (S) 10, Barry Briggs (NZ) 10, Ken McKinlay (Sc) 10, Brian Crutcher (E) 9, Peter Moore (A) 8, Eric Boothroyd (E) 7, Alan Hunt (E) 6, Dick Fisher (E) 5, Doug Davies (A) 4, Ulf Ericsson (S) 2, Olle Andersson (S) 2, Gerry Hussey (E) 0.

Right: *Barry Briggs (New Zealand), 1957, 1958, 1964 and 1966.*

1957

ANOTHER first – with Barry Briggs topping the pile. But the husky Kiwi needed a run-off against holder Fundin to win, and controversially the Swede crashed in that deciding race when being put under the most severe pressure.

Because of the withdrawal of Wembley from League racing, the track was for the first time a wholly neutral venue. Unfortunately little more than 50,000 watched the event, indicative of the sport's falling support at the time.

Nevertheless it was an interesting and closely-contested Final, and no fewer than eight countries were represented, a new record. Missing for the first time in seven years was Ronnie Moore, who had gone off to pursue a short-lived car racing flirtation.

Scorers: Barry Briggs (NZ) 14, Ove Fundin (S) 14, Peter Craven (E) 11, Aub Lawson (A) 11, Rune Sörmander (S) 11, Ron Johnston (NZ) 9, Ken McKinlay (Sc) 8, Bob Roger (E) 8, Ron How (E) 7, PeO Söderman (S) 7, George White (E) 4, Aage Hansen (N) 4, Ian Williams (W) 3, Dan Forsberg (S) 2, Josef Hofmeister (WG) 0.

1958

THE problems of preparing the Wembley circuit for its one meeting of the year were highlighted this year, with track conditions leaving something to be desired. One man who didn't mind the bumps was Barry Briggs, who successfully defended his title.

Briggo won even more convincingly than in 1957. This time he rattled together a fine maximum, and his heat 12 win over Ove Fundin, was the most important. Slow from the start, he battled his way round the outside to overhaul two opponents.

Despite the track problems, there was plenty of interest and incident for a 61,000 crowd to enthuse over. These included a plane-load of Swedish supporters who saw Fundin pushed into the runner-up position for the second year in succession.

Scorers: Barry Briggs (NZ) 15, Ove Fundin (S) 13, Aub Lawson (A) 11, Peter Craven (E) 11, Ken McKinlay (Sc) 11, Olle Nygren (S) 9, Ronnie Moore (NZ) 9, Ron Johnston (NZ) 8, Gerry Hussey (E) 7, Ron How (E) 7, Peter Moore (A) 5, Mike Broadbanks (E) 5, Rune Sörmander (S) 4, Jack Geran (A) 3, Josef Hofmeister (WG) 2, Joel Jansson (S) 0.

1959

SO KEEN were the organisers to see if Barry Briggs could become the third first man to win the crown three times in succession that they flew him back from New Zealand to compete. Originally Barry had intended to remain Down Under.

Instead, it was Ronnie Moore, his great friend and mentor, who collected his second championship, winning with a faultless maximum as he had done in 1954. Superb starting technique and masterly control put Moore a cut above the rest.

Once again Fundin had to settle for second. The major news aspect about the 1959 Final was that for the first time an Eastern European rider qualified. He was Mieczyslaw (Mike) Polukard of Poland.

Scorers: Ronnie Moore (NZ) 15, Ove Fundin (S) 13, Barry Briggs (NZ) 11, Aub Lawson (A) 11, Olle Nygren (S) 11, Brian Crutcher (E) 10, Arne Carlsson (S) 8, Peter Craven (E) 7, George White (E) 7, Geoff Mardon (NZ) 6, Rune Sörmander (S) 6, Mieczyslaw Polukard (P) 5, Josef Hofmeister (WG) 4, Ron How (E) 3, Peter Moore (A) 3, Cyril Roger (E) 0.

1960

NEVER before had three riders tied for first place, but that's how it happened at Wembley in this year. Ove Fundin beat Ronnie Moore and Peter Craven in the run-off after all had totalled 14 points; and it was a win which was to have repercussions.

The Swedish star maintained his remarkable record of consistency and this success almost certainly clinched the staging of the following year's final for his country. Moore, only man to beat him, came closest to doing so again in the run-off.

Peter Moore was the shock merchant, and his fellow Australian, the remarkable Aub Lawson, was making his last appearance at the age of 45. Polukard, first of the Poles, was only reserve but three more Polish riders qualified for the Final.

Scorers: Ove Fundin (S) 14, Ronnie Moore (NZ) 14, Peter Craven (E) 14, Peter Moore (A) 12, Ron Johnston (NZ) 10, Barry Briggs (NZ) 9, Stefan Kwoczala (P) 8, Ken McKinlay (Sc) 6, Josef Hofmeister (WG) 6, Jack Young (A) 6, Rune Sörmander (S) 5, Chum Taylor (A) 5, Aub Lawson (A) 4, Henryk Zyto (P) 4, Bob Andrews (E) (res) 2, Marian Kaiser (P) 1, Brian Elliott (E) 0.

1961

FOR the first time, the World Final was staged away from Wembley – at Malmö, Sweden, on a cool, grey September evening. The occasion turned out to be a Swedish celebration, with Ove Fundin winning his third title, and fellow countrymen taking the next two places.

Björn Knutsson was in brilliant form but a fall in heat 16 when he met Fundin spoiled his chances of taking the title at the first attempt. Fundin was allowed the luxury of handing a point to Göte Nordin which enabled him to qualify for the run-off.

Though only 22,000 saw the Final, the atmosphere was electric and history in the making. Not the least interest centred upon Igor Plechanov, the first Russian to qualify for the championship finale, riding on the then revolutionary new ESO (Jawa) machine.

Scorers: Ove Fundin (S) 14, Björn Knutsson (S) 12, Göte Nordin (S) 12, Barry Briggs (NZ) 12, Ronnie Moore (NZ) 10, Bob Andrews (E) 10, Florian Kapala (P) 8, Ron How (E) 7, Rune Sörmander (S) 7, Peter Craven (E) 6, Ken McKinlay (Sc) 5, Cyril Maidment (E) 4, Igor Plechanov (USSR) 4, Stanislaw Tkocz (P) 3, Ray Cresp (A) 3, Mike Broadbanks (E) 2.

1962

BACK to Wembley came the Final and the enduringly popular Peter Craven brought the title to England once again. When Craven was at his best, there was nobody to compare with him for entertainment value; and this was such a night.

Barry Briggs, the only man to defeat Craven, must have ruefully reflected upon his inability to start as he carried on. He had a disappointing third placing in his first race, and was unbeatable after that.

The British fans – there were 62,000 of them – also had the opportunity to see Plechanov for the first time. His energetic style stamped him as the most exciting of the overseas contingent.

Scorers: Peter Craven (E) 14, Barry Briggs (NZ) 13, Ove Fundin (S) 10, Björn Knutsson (S) 10, Göte Nordin (S) 9, Ronnie Moore (NZ) 9, Ken McKinlay (Sc) 9, Bob Andrews (E) 9, Sören Sjösten (S) 8, Igor Plechanov (USSR) 7, Rune Sörmander (S) 7, Ron How (E) 6, Arne Carlsson (S) 3, Pawel Waloszek (P) 2, Ron Mountford (E) 2, Mike Broadbanks (E) 2.

1963

RIDERS have defied all sorts of odds to appear in a World Final and indeed Ronnie Moore had won the 1959 title when recovering from a broken leg. Ove Fundin emulated that achievement by taking his fourth title with a broken ankle in plaster.

The third heat started the fireworks. New Russian sensation Boris Samorodov was excluded after a clash with Ron How; and in the re-run Fundin equalled the ten year-old Split Waterman track record of 68.4 seconds.

After that, there was no holding Fundin; or Samorodov for that matter. He bludgeoned his way to 11 points from four rides in a most sensational debut. But Björn Knutsson and Barry Briggs nudged him out of a rostrum placing.

Scorers: Ove Fundin (S) 14, Björn Knutsson (S) 13, Barry Briggs (NZ) 12, Boris Samorodov (USSR) 11, Göte Nordin (S) 10, Sverre Harrfeldt (N) 10, Nigel Boocock (E) 8, Ron How (E) 7, Leo McAuliffe (W) 7, Peter Craven (E) 6, Peter Moore (A) 6, PeO Söderman (S) 5, Dick Fisher (E) 5, Jim Lightfoot (E) 4, Per Tage Svensson (S) 1, Arne Carlsson (S) 1.

1964

WHO CAN forget the rain-soaked Ullevi Stadium, Gothenburg, and the heroics both from officials and riders who saw to it that this Final went on against all the odds? Barry Briggs won't. He won with 15 points.

The New Zealander, the form man of the season, made light of the conditions and saw to it that there would be no repeat of the 1961 Swedish beanfeast. And Igor Plechanov achieved the best Soviet placing to date.

He brilliantly rode round Fundin on the last turn of their second and third place run-off. It was the last breath-taking thrill of a night on which 25,700 bedraggled fans could only wonder how proceedings went on at all.

Scorers: Barry Briggs (NZ) 15, Igor Plechanov (USSR) 13, Ove Fundin (S) 13, Boris Samorodov (USSR) 11, Björn Knutsson (S) 10, Ron How (E) 10, Cyril Maidment (E) 8, Gennady Kurilenko (USSR) 7, Nigel Boocock (E) 6, Mike Broadbanks (E) 6, Ken McKinlay (Sc) 6, Andrzej Wyglenda (P) 4, Bob Andrews (E) 4, Zbigniew Podlecki (P) 3, Jaroslav Wolf (Cz) 3, Dick Fisher (E) 1.

1965

BJÖRN KNUTSSON had been threatening to win the world crown for several years. At Wembley, saluted by 70,000 he achieved the feat at last to hoist himself into a position of eminence which his record in other competitions warranted.

Yet, surprisingly, Knutsson had been missing from British speedway for a year, after the formation of the new British League which in its inaugural season excluded commuting Swedes. Bengt Jansson in heat 3 was the only man to beat him.

Of the growing Eastern European contingent, Plechanov again stole the honours. And he flew from the start to defeat Fundin in a run-off for third place. Gating was all-important on a track which had been affected by afternoon rain.

Right: *Bjorn Knutsson (Sweden), 1965.*

Scorers: Björn Knutsson (S) 14, Igor Plechanov (USSR) 13, Ove Fundin (S) 13, Barry Briggs (NZ) 10, Bengt Jansson (S) 10, Brian Brett (E) 9, Sören Sjösten (S) 9, Nigel Boocock (E) 8, Andrzej Pogorzelski (P) 7, Antoni Woryna (P) 6, Leif Larsson (S) 5, Reg Luckhurst (E) 5, Ken McKinlay (Sc) 4, Jimmy Gooch (E) 3, Lubos Tomicek (Cz) 2, Andrzej Wyglenda (P) 2.

1966

GOTHENBURG again . . . and Briggs again. Mounted on the ESO machine which he had pioneered in British League racing the previous year, Barry repeated his 1964 Ullevi performance of five starts, five wins.

The title and placings were effectively decided in one race, the ninth. Briggs beat Sverre Harrfeldt and Antoni Woryna who were undefeated apart from this one reverse. Thus the first four had 13 heat wins between them.

For both of the other men on the rostrum, there was ample consolation. It was the first time that a Norwegian had been thus placed, and Woryna's third was the best achieved by a Polish competitor up to this stage.

Scorers: Barry Briggs (NZ) 15, Sverre Harrfeldt (N) 14, Antoni Woryna (P) 13, Ivan Mauger (NZ) 11, Torbjörn Harrysson (S) 10, Göte Nordin (S) 9, Leif Enecrona (S) 8, Igor Plechanov (USSR) 8, Stanislaw Tkocz (P) 7, Björn Knutsson (S) 5, Marian Kaiser (P) 5, Andrzej Pogorzelski (P) 5, Mike Broadbanks (E) 4, Leif Larsson (S) 3, Nigel Boocock (E) 2, PeO Söderman (S) 1.

1967

THE old master beat his heir apparent when Ove Fundin collected his fifth world title in front of 75,000 at Wembley. Fundin nonchalantly wheeled out an untried JAP/ESO hybrid and won with 14 points, defeating Bengt Jansson in a run-off.

Experience and temperament counted for everything. Fundin had done it all, seen it all before. And yet the technically brilliant Jansson, ten years younger, had already beaten Ove in their earlier meeting.

Ivan Mauger, the man who was ultimately to equal Fundin's all-time record of five wins, achieved a solid third placing in only his second World Final appearance. Anders Michanek made his debut.

Scorers: Ove Fundin (S) 14, Bengt Jansson (S) 14, Ivan Mauger (NZ) 13, Igor Plechanov (USSR) 12, Barry Briggs (NZ) 11, Eric Boocock (E) 9, Anders Michanek (S) 9, Ray Wilson (E) 7, Bernt Persson (S) 6, Andrzej Pogorzelski (P) 6, Antoni Woryna (P) 5, Rick France (E) 5, Colin Pratt (E) 4, Jerzy Trzeszkowkski (P) 3, Andrzej Wyglenda (P) 2, Jochen Dinse (EG) 0.

1968

AS IN two previous Finals in Gothenburg, a New Zealander won with 15 points. Not Barry Briggs this time, however, but Ivan Mauger, with a display which emphasised the improvement and style he had shown for a couple of years.

Mauger won with a most polished and professional display, and runner-up Briggs (later found to be suffering from septicaemia) was well beaten, with the rest nowhere at all.

Sweden, hoping for something for their fans to cheer, produced the most exciting rider of the night in Torbjörn Harrysson. But it was Poland's Edward Jancarz who was the most

Left: *Ivan Mauger (New Zealand), 1968, 1969, 1970, 1972 and 1977.*

successful newcomer, winning a run-off for third.

Scorers: Ivan Mauger (NZ) 15, Barry Briggs (NZ) 12, Edward Jancarz (P) 11, Gennady Kurilenko (USSR) 11, Torbjörn Harrysson (S) 10, Pawel Waloszek (P) 10, Anders Michanek (S) 9, Hasse Holmqvist (S) 9, Ove Fundin (S) 7, Gunnar Malmqvist (S) 7, Antoni Woryna (P) 5, Martin Ashby (E) 5, Reidar Eide (N) 3, Jerzy Trzeszkowksi (P) 3, Bernt Persson (S) 1, Nigel Boocock (E) 1.

1969

IN A display no less conclusive than the one with which he picked up his first title a year earlier, Ivan Mauger conquered Wembley and the rest of the world, although the 75,000 fans were not totally enraptured.

Many English followers were disappointed when Mauger sat in behind Belle Vue colleague Sören Sjösten to produce a heat 20 form-buster. This denied England's Nigel Boocock the possibility of a third-place run-off.

In the event it was left to Barry Briggs to claim second spot by beating Sjösten, but nobody could get within yards of Mauger on this night. For the first four of his races, at least, he looked untouchable.

Scorers: Ivan Mauger (NZ) 14, Barry Briggs (NZ) 11, Sören Sjösten (S) 11, Nigel Boocock (E) 10, Hasse Holmqvist (S) 10, Edward Jancarz (P) 9, Ove Fundin (S) 9, Ken McKinlay (Sc) 7, Andrzej Pogorzelski (P) 7, Jan Mucha (P) 7, Ronnie Moore (NZ) 6, Henryk Glucklich (P) 5, Valeri Klementiev (USSR) 4, Torbjörn Harrysson (S) 4, Zbigniew Podlecki (P) (res) 3, Andrzej Wyglenda (P) 2, Howard Cole (E) 1.

1970

NO MAN had achieved three successive title wins . . . until Ivan Mauger, ambassador of the increasingly international-flavoured speedway of the seventies, followed his triumphs in Sweden and England with this super show in Wroclaw, Poland.

A 65,000 crowd expected home riders to dominate and indeed the host nation provided the second and third placed men. Neither Pawel Waloszek nor Antoni Woryna had looked quite convincing enough, even before Mauger beat them in his fourth and fifth rides.

Indeed, Mauger described this win as his best so far, one which demonstrated that if you have the talent and the temperament, it's possible to win anywhere. Disappointingly down-field were former winner Barry Briggs and future champion Ole Olsen, making his debut.

Scorers: Ivan Mauger (NZ) 15, Pawel Waloszek (P) 14, Antoni Woryna (P) 13, Sören Sjösten (S) 9, Henryk Glucklich (P) 9, Valeri Klementiev (USSR) 8, Barry Briggs (NZ) 7, Andrzej Wyglenda (P) 7, Anders Michanek (S) 7, Ole Olsen (D) 6, Jan Mucha (P) 6, Hans Jurgen Fritz (EG) 5, Vladimir Gordeev (USSR) 5, Edmund Migos (P) (res) 4, Gennady Kurilenko (USSR) 3, Zygfryd Friedek (P) 2, Trevor Hedge (E) 0.

Right: *Ole Olsen (Denmark), 1971 and 1975.*

1971

IN ONE of the most exceptional performances in the world championship's history, Ole Olsen, 24, became the first Danish rider to take the crown . . . and a 15 point maximum in Gothenburg, together with a winning margin of three points, didn't overstate his superiority.

Normally it is taken for granted that the prerequisite of any would-be champion is the ability to make five consistent starts. Olsen gated like a novice at times, yet swept past all opposition – including Ivan Mauger – in carefree fashion.

Vladimir Gordeev of the Soviet Union was one of the star turns of the night, but his 11 point total and fifth placing was subsequently declared null and void. An F.I.M. investigation and fuel analysis found that he had used a banned nitro additive.

Scorers: Ole Olsen (D) 15, Ivan Mauger (NZ) 12, Bengt Jansson (S) 12, Ray Wilson (E) 11, Vladimir Gordeev (USSR) 11, Anders Michanek (S) 11, Bernt Persson (S) 9, Jim Airey (A) 8, Sören Sjösten (S) 8, Nigel Boocock (E) 6, Ronnie Moore (NZ) 5, Eric Boocock (E) 4, Leif Enecrona (S) 4, Jiri Stancl (Cz) 3, Tommy Jansson (S) 1, Jerzy Szczakiel (P) 0.

1972

FOR the second year in a row, Ole Olsen looked the best rider on show – but he didn't win this time. A disastrous first race fall put him out of the Wembley reckoning, although, just as Björn Knutsson had done in 1961, he won four races in dashing style.

Ivan Mauger was back to claim the title which he had relinquished to Olsen the previous September. Even so, he required a run-off against surprise merchant Bernie Persson before collecting his fourth title, thus equalling the record of Barry Briggs.

And what of Briggs? In what was to be his last big effort to win a fifth title, he began with a fine victory, then crashed in his next outing. He was taken to hospital with a hand injury, and he never did get to another World Final.

Scorers: Ivan Mauger (NZ) 13, Bernt Persson (S) 13, Ole Olsen (D) 12, John Louis (E) 11, Christer Löfqvist (S) 11, Aleksander Pavlov (USSR) 8, Anders Michanek (S) 8, Pawel Waloszek (P) 6, Viktor Trofimov (USSR) 6, Nigel Boocock (E) 6, Viktor Kalmykov (USSR) 6, Anatoly Kuzmin (USSR) 4, Grigori Chlynovski (USSR) 3, Barry Briggs (NZ) 3, Eric Boocock (E) 2, Valeri Gordeev (USSR) 2, Jan Simensen (S) (res) 2, Jimmy McMillan (Sc) (res) 2.

Left: *Jerzy Szczakiel (Poland), 1973.*

1973

JERZY SZCZAKIEL of Poland provided the biggest sensation in the history of the world championships, winning the title after Ivan Mauger had fallen in a run-off. Even the Polish authorities seemed totally stunned by the shock result.

Sure, the Poles had hoped to provide the winner, just as they had planned at Wroclaw three years earlier. This time, in front of a record 130,000 crowd at Katowice (Chorzow) their best chance appeared to lie with new wonder boy Zenon Plech, but he had to settle for third.

Following some splendid performances in Britain and elsewhere, Sweden's Anders Michanek was perhaps the hottest premeeting favourite. His challenge crumbled into insignificance – but his time was coming.

Scorers: Jerzy Szczakiel (P) 13, Ivan Mauger (NZ) 13, Zenon Plech (P) 12, Ole Olsen (D) 11, Grigori Chlynovski (USSR) 10, Vladimir Paznikov (USSR) 8, Pawel Waloszek (P) 8, Valeri Gordeev (USSR) 7, Jan Mucha (P) 7, Anders Michanek (S) 6, Edward Jancarz (P) 6, Peter Collins (E) 6, John Boulger (A) 6, Ray Wilson (E) 5, Vladimir Zaplechny (USSR) 2, Bernt Persson (S) 0, Andrzej Wyglenda (P) (res) 0, Tommy Jansson (S) (res) 0.

Right: *Anders Michanek (Sweden), 1974.*

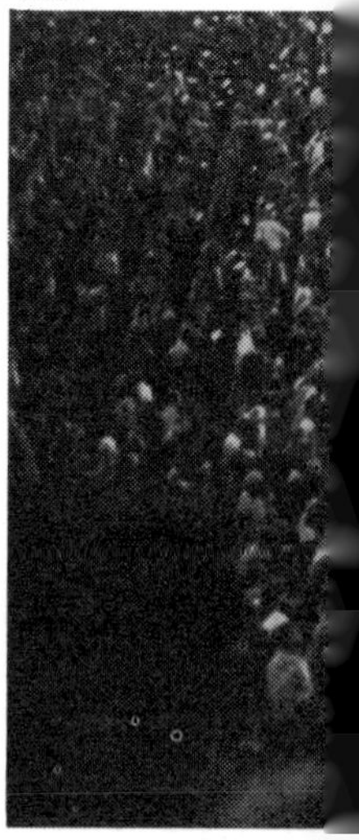

1974

THERE have been convincing world title winners but never before had a rider won with four points to spare, as Anders Michanek did at Ullevi . . . where as usual, it rained, and, also as usual, the winner collected maximum points.

Nobody had expressed any particularly strong fancy for Michanek, who didn't ride in British League this year and had so often flattered to deceive in previous World Final appearances. Yet on this occasion he was different class.

Main talking-point was the first public view of the ERM four-valve machines. Most of the Swedes used them at some stage of the meeting. And despite the difficult track conditions, they produced the results . . . especially Michanek.

Scorers: Anders Michanek (S) 15, Ivan Mauger (NZ) 11, Sören Sjösten (S) 11, John Louis (E) 9, Bengt Jansson (S) 9, Peter Collins (E) 9, Tommy Johansson (S) 8, Zenon Plech (P) 8, Christcr Löfqvist (S) 8, Grigori Chlynovski (USSR) 6, Terry Betts (E) 6, Dave Jessup (E) 5, Mikhail Krasnov (USSR) 3, Tommy Jansson (S) (res) 3, Ole Olsen (D) 2, Edward Jancarz (P) (res) 1. Vladimir Gordeev (USSR) 0.

Top left: *Ove Fundin receives the congratulations of Peter Craven and Ronnie Moore after their three-man run-off at Wembley, 1960.*

Bottom left: *Ullevi Stadium, Gothenburg, 1964. The rain, and how to deal with it!*

Top right: *Wembley, 1965. Left to right: Nigel Boocock, Ken McKinlay, Andrzej Pogorzelski, Jimmy Gooch.*

Centre top: *Arne Bergström, father of Swedish speedway, beams paternally after Ove Fundin has beaten Bengt Jansson in the 1967 World Final decider.*

Centre bottom: *Ullevi again – and it isn't raining for once!*

Centre: *Peter Collins powers to victory at Katowice, Poland, 1976.*

Bottom right: *And the band played on . . .*

Right: *Peter Collins (England), 1976.*

1975

AFTER crashing out of the '74 Final in his second ride, Ole Olsen stormed back into the big time rankings with a thoroughly accomplished Wembley win watched by 85,000, biggest crowd there for more than two decades.

Biggest controversy surrounding the track preparation and the lack of specialist attention it received during the evening. Some unscheduled watering unsettled England's great hope Peter Collins, strongly fancied on a track usually lucky for him.

But dust, water, opposition – nothing could interrupt Olsen's victory march. He was resolute from first to last. But for England there was the rare pleasure of providing a rider on the rostrum in John Louis, who beat Ivan Mauger in a run-off.

Scorers: Ole Olsen (D) 15, Anders Michanek (S) 13, John Louis (E) 12, Ivan Mauger (NZ) 12, Peter Collins (E) 10, Phil Crump (A) 10, Malcolm Simmons (E) 10, Viktor Trofimov (USSR) 8, Tommy Jansson (S) 7, Bernt Persson (S) 5, Ray Wilson (E) 5, Edward Jancarz (P) 4, Valeri Gordeev (USSR) 4, Zenon Plech (P) 4, Marek Cieslak (P) 1, Henryk Glucklich (P) 0, Vladimir Gordeev (USSR) (res) 0.

1976

FOR 14 years England had waited for a world champion. Peter Collins, 22, succeeded where so many others had failed and his victory in Katowice put the seal upon a build-up which had promised such a reward for two or three years.

As if this wasn't enough, England also provided the runner-up in Malcolm Simmons and Phil Crump produced Australia's best placing since the palmy days of Jack Young. The Poles were badly out-gunned, and not just by the new technology of Weslake and Street machinery.

Ivan Mauger, for the second year in a row, just missed the top three. A carburation fault cost him victory in his second ride, though later on he did beat Collins. But on this grey Silesian day, nothing could take away Peter's moment of joy.

Scorers: Peter Collins (E) 14, Malcolm Simmons (E) 13, Phil Crump (A) 12, Ivan Mauger (NZ) 11, Zenon Plech (P) 11, John Louis (E) 9, Doug Wyer (E) 8, Egon Müller (WG) 8, Scott Autrey (USA) 7, Jiri Stancl (Cz) 6, Chris Morton (E) 6, Edward Jancarz (P) 5, Marek Cieslak (P) 4, Jerzy Rembas (P) 3, Anders Michanek (S) (res) 2, Valeri Gordeev (USSR) 1, Vladimir Gordeev (USSR) 0.

1977

A FEW weeks short of his 38th birthday, Ivan Mauger defied his critics and carved another slice out of the record books by collecting his fifth title. For once, the Gothenburg meeting didn't produce a maximum. But of course, it rained.

Peter Collins defied all medical advice and rode despite having suffered a nasty leg injury only six days before the event. His efforts were filled with bravery, but not enough to retain his title.

Ole Olsen looked the likely winner right up to the 18th race, which had to be re-run. But ice-cool Mauger made no mistake. Then Olsen won a third-place run-off against 18-year-old British champion Michael Lee, whose debut display almost stole the show.

Scorers: Ivan Mauger (NZ) 14, Peter Collins (E) 13, Ole Olsen (D) 12, Michael Lee (E) 12, Finn Thomsen (D) 10, Bengt Jansson (S) 9, Egon Müller (WG) 8, Anders Michanek (S) 8, Tommy Nilsson (S) 6, Billy Sanders (A) 6, Bernt Persson (S) 6, John Boulger (A) 5, Edward Jancarz (P) 4, Jiri Stancl (Cz) 3, Jan Verner (Cz) 1, Jan Mucha (P) 1.

WORLD TEAM CUP

The booming interest in Test match competition bore new fruit in 1960, when the World Team Cup was inaugurated. The Polish motor sports magazine *Motor* of Warsaw initiated the tournament, designed to crown the leading speedway country.

Classified by the F.I.M. as being second only to the world individual championship, the Team Cup has grown in stature over the last decade or so, providing a ready barometer of international rankings.

Apart from its 16 heat formula, the event has several features which enable it to stand apart from just about every other international competition – not the least being the comparative regularity with which countries not involved in the final stage have been allocated the responsibility of staging such a major occasion.

Geography has seen to it that a number of the minor speedway countries have competed in the qualifying stages. Yet apart from Great Britain and/or England, Sweden, Poland, Czechoslovakia and the U.S.S.R., only one other nation has been represented in the Final.

And Australia, who would probably have won such an event had it been introduced 50 years earlier, made their first appearance in 1976 a memorable affair – they won the title!

In its first two years, in fact, Australia and New Zealand competed against England in the British qualifying competition. Subsequently, colonial riders were included under the Great Britain banner, a situation which continued for more than ten years.

Latterly, the Aussies and New Zealanders have been granted separate affiliation to the F.I.M., after coming under the jurisdiction of the British Control Board more or less since the year dot.

The English had decided to go their own way, discontinuing the reliance upon commonwealth talent, and that decision coincided with the start of a sequence of flamboyantly successful results.

In the first few years of the event, though, the British contingent tended to take the World Team Cup rather less seriously than some of their opponents. An analysis of the results year by year will bear that out.

1960 (GOTHENBURG)

The Ullevi Stadium celebrated a Swedish success, with those supreme performers Ove Fundin and Olle Nygren scoring maximum points. Sweden had been awarded the first World Team Cup in recognition of their world championship achievements and as a consolation for missing allocation of the World Final; so theirs was a fitting victory.

England had them in their sights for a while, but a measure of the home team's superiority was the fact that only twice did they fail to provide the heat winner. Ron How headed Rune Sörmander in heat 6, and Ken McKinlay won the next race after Björn Knutsson had retired because of engine failure.

The Czechs picked up a few crumbs; but Poland were outclassed, with Florian Kapala, their most experienced international, and Stefan Kwoczala and Henryk Zyto, their

Above: *With teams like this, no wonder the Swedes dominated in the 1960's. Left to right: Göte Nordin, Björn Knutsson, Ove Fundin, Arne Bergström (manager), Per Olaf Söderman, Rune Sormander, 1963.*

British-based World Final qualifiers, all notable absentees.

Sweden 44 (O. Fundin 12, O. Nygren 12, R. Sörmander 11, B. Knutsson 9).
England 30 (P. Craven 8, K. McKinlay 8, R. How 7, G. White (res) 6, N. Boocock 1).
Czechoslovakia 15 (A. Kasper 5, L. Tomicek 4, F. Richter 3, J. Mahac 3).
Poland 7 (K. Pociejkowicz 3, M. Kaiser 2, M. Polukard 2, J. Malinowski 1).

1961 (WROCLAW)

The Poles made up for their disappointment of the previous year, and were roared to a thrilling victory by an appreciative home crowd. Their one-point winning margin remains the closest World Team Cup Final result so far.

This time the Poles paraded a much stronger team, with old hand Mike Polukard a trump card at reserve. But Marian Kaiser was their individual star. Sweden gave them a run for their money, though, and surrendered the title with reluctance.

Fundin gave another confident display and Sörmander was also good value. England hardly did themselves justice and the Czechs were even less of a force than on their previous appearance.

Poland 32 (M. Kaiser 10, H. Zyto 7, F. Kapala 6, M. Polukard (res) 5, S. Tkocz 4).
Sweden 31 (O. Fundin 11, R. Sörmander 10, B. Knutsson 7, P.-T. Svensson 3).
England 21 (P. Craven 8, B. Andrews 6, K. McKinlay 4, R. How 3).
Czechoslovakia 12 (L. Tomicek 7, A. Kasper 4, B. Bartonek 1, M. Svoboda 0).

1962 (SLANY)

Shocks were indicated when host nation Czechoslovakia showed early, and favourites Sweden failed to score in the first two races. Even Fundin did not trouble the scorers in his opening heat. But the Swedes swiftly made amends.

They settled down to win the important races, with Sören Sjösten providing the thrills to complement the talents of Knutsson and Fundin. The fact that Göte Nordin suffered with bike troubles did not interrupt their rhythm.

For the first time, British representation included a commonwealth flavour. Ronnie Moore was particularly impressive without being able to stimulate a genuine challenge to the Swedes. Poland's Kaiser was best of the rest.

Sweden 36 (B. Knutsson 10, S. Sjösten 10, O. Fundin 9, G. Nordin 4, R. Sörmander (res) 3).
Great Britain 24 (R. Moore 10, B. Briggs 8, P. Craven 6, R. How 0, C. Maidment (res) 0).
Poland 20 (M. Kaiser 9, F. Kapala 5, J. Maj 4, P. Waloszek 2, M. Polukard (res) 0).
Czechoslovakia 16 (L. Tomicek 7, B. Slany 4, J. Wolf 3, J. Prusa 2).

1963 (VIENNA)

On a bumpy and often difficult track, the Swedes again displayed the sort of team work which wins championships. Old hand PeO Söderman, in what turned out to be his only World Team Cup Final appearance, collected a highly creditable double figure score.

There were other splendid individual performances. Barry Briggs rode to a maximum using his grass track engine; because of flight delays the British arrived late and there was no time to install another motor.

Beaten only by his Southampton team mate, Knutsson was the pick of the Swedes. Antonin Kasper inspired the Czechs who were suitably delighted with second place. But the Poles disappointed, and never got to grips with the conditions.

Sweden 37 (B. Knutsson 11, P. Söderman 10, O. Fundin 7, G. Nordin 6, R Sörmander (res) 3).
Czechoslovakia 27 (A. Kasper 10, S. Kubicek 7, L. Tomicek 5, M. Smid 5).
Great Britain 25 (B. Briggs 12, P. Craven 8, D. Fisher 4, P. Moore 1).
Poland 7 (H. Zyto 4, S. Tkocz 1, J. Maj 1, M. Kaiser 1, A. Pogorzelski (res) 0).

1964 (ABENSBERG)

The same story as far as the Swedes were concerned; another splendidly organised display of talent and temperament. They were always the class team on a deep, difficult cinder surface which provided many riders with a few problems.

The energetic Russians didn't mind too much, though. They enthusiastically set about their first Final appearance and were good value for the runners-up position. Young Gennady Kurilenko, only rider to beat Knutsson, took the eye.

The British contingent, apart from a couple of early wins by Briggs, seemed ill at ease. Greatest encouragement for a new-look Polish squad was the promising debut of Andrzej Wyglenda.

Sweden 34 (B. Knutsson 11, G. Nordin 10, R. Sörmander 7, O. Fundin 6, S. Sjösten (res) 0).
U.S.S.R. 25 (I. Plechanov 8, G. Kurilenko 8, Y. Chekranov 6, B. Samorodov 3).
Great Britain 21 (B. Briggs 9, K. McKinlay 7, N. Boocock 3, R. How 2, B. Brett (res) 0).
Poland 16 (A. Wyglenda 8, Z. Podlecki 3, A. Pogorzelski 3, M. Rose (res) 2, M. Kaiser 0).

1965 (KEMPTEN)

With a display of buoyant confidence, Poland swept to a win which was all the more breathtaking because of the lack of impact they had made on the international scene in the preceding three or four years. But the new brigade was something else.

The Swedes were never too far in arrears, but the Poles pulled out something extra when it was required. Wyglenda maintained the good impression created the previous year; he alone beat Knutsson but Fundin spoiled his maximum chance with a last heat win. Pogorzelski was equally accomplished but Knutsson put an end to his winning sequence.

Ken McKinlay was the only British race winner, and their chances were wrecked when Briggs crashed in his first ride. Neither he, nor his bike, were up to it after that.

Above: *The Russians make their first appearance. Left to right: Farid Szajnurov, Gabdrakhman Kadirov (manager), Viktor Trofimov, Boris Samorodov. On machine: Igor Plechanov.*

Poland 38 (A. Wyglenda 11, A. Pogorzelski 11, A. Woryna 9, Z. Podlecki 7).
Sweden 33 (B. Knutsson 11, B. Jansson 8, O. Fundin 8, G. Nordin 6).
Great Britain 18 (K. McKinlay 7, N. Boocock 6, J. Gooch (res) 3, C. Monk 1, B. Briggs 1).
U.S.S.R. 7 (V. Sokolov 2, Y. Chekranov 2, G. Kurilenko 2, I. Plechanov 1, V. Trofimov (res) 0).

1966 (WROCLAW)

Before 65,000 delighted fellow countrymen, Poland emphasised their dominance with another power-packed display. Everything was geared to their success, and not one of the other teams involved could do anything to halt their victory march.

Wyglenda again came so close to a maximum and it was fitting that Knutsson, a brilliant but lone flag waver for Sweden, should be the man to deny him. Woryna – previously headed by the outstanding Boris Samorodov – claimed the heat 14 win over Knutsson.

For the British, it was an education. At the half-way stage they had only two points, one of them a gift. They had neither the pace nor the power and crashed to just about their most comprehensive defeat in post-war international competition.

Opposite top: *The Swedes, jubilant again after a famous 1970 win at Wembley. Left to right: Anders Michanek, Bernie Persson, Bengt Jansson, Sören Sjösten, Ove Fundin, with Arne Bergstrom never far behind.*

Opposite bottom: *The first all-English winners, left to right: Terry Betts, Peter Collins, Ray Wilson, Malcolm Simmons, Dave Jessup.*

Poland 40 (A. Wyglenda 11, A. Woryna 11, M. Rose 10, A. Pogorzelski 8).
U.S.S.R. 26 (B. Samorodov 10, I. Plechanov 6, V. Trofimov 6, F. Szajnurov 4).
Sweden 22 (B. Knutsson 11, L. Enecrona 4, G. Nordin 3, O. Fundin 2, L. Larsson (res) 2).
Great Britain 8 (N. Boocock 4, I. Mauger 3, B. Briggs 1, T. Betts 0, C. Pratt (res) 0).

1967 (MALMO)

Göte Nordin set the stage with a smart first race win and the Swedes, back on home territory, were on the way to their fifth World Team Cup title. Though their winning total equalled the lowest thus far, they always looked to be in control.

Holders Poland made a patchy start and although Woryna – who matched Nordin for style and confidence – and Wyglenda showed up well, it was not enough to ruffle their hosts. Bengt Jansson made a valuable contribution on his first appearance.

Igor Plechanov had his best return in this competition and registered three impressive victories, including one in heat 15 which spoiled Nordin's maximum. Briggs was the only heat winner for the British.

Sweden 32 (G. Nordin 11, B. Jansson 9, O. Fundin 6, T. Harrysson 6).
Poland 26 (A. Woryna 10, A. Wyglenda 9, J. Trzeszkowski 5, A. Pogorzelski 1, Z. Podlecki (res) 1).
U.S.S.R. 19 (I. Plechanov 9, V. Trofimov 4, B. Samorodov 3, G. Kadirov (res) 2, F. Szajnurov 1).
Great Britain 19 (B. Briggs 8, E. Boocock 5, R. Wilson 4, I. Mauger 2, C. Pratt (res) 0).

1968 (WEMBLEY)

At last a British success. Approaching the competition with real determination, and conscious of the need to be at their best in front of a home crowd for the first time, Great Britain did all that was asked of them, and more.

Skipper Barry Briggs got up from his sick bed to inspire the rest. Newly crowned world champion Ivan Mauger joined the select band of maximum scorers. Above all, though, it was a genuine team effort to which everybody contributed.

Fundin showed his traditional liking for Wembley, but Sweden were never a serious threat. Chunky Edmund Migos collected a couple of gutsy wins for Poland. The Czechs, surprise qualifiers, were game but out of their depth.

Great Britain 40 (I. Mauger 12, N. Boocock 10, M. Ashby 8, B. Briggs 7, N. Hunter (res) 3).
Sweden 30 (O. Fundin 11, A. Michanek 7, B. Jansson 7, O. Nygren (res) 3, T. Harrysson 2).
Poland 19 (E. Migos 8, E. Jancarz 6, H. Glucklich (res) 2, A. Wyglenda 2, P. Waloszek 1).
Czechoslovakia 7 (A. Kasper 3, L. Tomicek 2, J. Holub 1, J. Wolf 1).

1969 (RYBNIK)

Britain had broken the spell at last – but could they win in Poland? The answer, this time, was no. But they gave a much more encouraging display and were only a single point adrift with two races to go.

However, big guns Edward Jancarz and Andrzej Wyglenda made sure of a Polish win and Britain, who didn't have the best of fortune, had to settle for a highly creditable second spot.

The Russians re-appeared with a new-look team with the emphasis very much on youth. They shaped impressively, too, which is more than could be said for the Swedish contingent. Anders Michanek was their only race winner.

Poland 31 (E. Jancarz 11, A. Wyglenda 11, S. Tkocz 4, H. Glucklich 3, A. Pogorzelski (res) 2).
Great Britain 27 (I. Mauger 9, B. Briggs 8, N. Boocock 5, M. Ashby 5).
U.S.S.R. 23 (V. Smirnov 9, G. Kurilenko 8, V. Klementiev 5, Y. Dubinin 1, V. Trofimov (res) 0).
Sweden 12 (A. Michanek 7, O. Fundin 2, S. Sjösten 2, B. Jansson 1).

1970 (WEMBLEY)

The Swedes upset the international form book and raced to a comprehensive win which made a nonsense of their disappointments in individual and team competition in the previous year. And old maestro Fundin was the inspiration.

Ove, who had spent an earlier part of the season riding for Wembley before making a controversially premature departure, had to admit second best when Briggs broke the track record in heat 2. After that, he was unbeatable.

This was the most comprehensive team performance since 1960, with every member contributing double figures. And it was also

the first time since 1963 that the host nation had failed to win the title.
Sweden 42 (O. Fundin 11, B. Jansson 11, A. Michanek 10, S. Sjösten 10).
Great Britain 31 (B. Briggs 11, I. Mauger 9, E. Boocock 5, Ray Wilson (res) 4, N. Boocock 2).
Poland 20 (J. Mucha 6, A. Woryna 5, E. Migos (res) 4, H. Glucklich 3, P. Waloszek 2).
Czechoslovakia 3 (V. Verner 3, M. Verner 0, J. Stancl 0, Z. Majstr 0, J. Holub (res) 0).

1971 (WROCLAW)

Ray Wilson wrote his name in the record books as the first Englishman to score a World Team Cup Final maximum. And he and his colonial colleagues finally laid the Polish bogy, racing to a victory of almost stunning proportions.

The home favourites, watched by a capacity crowd which was at first silent, then derisive, did not even manage a single heat win, and only just managed to edge Sweden out of third place.

The Russians, including three debut makers in the event, gave an encouraging display but were never remotely in contention. The victory margin might have been greater had not Briggs pulled out of one race when in the lead.
Great Britain 37 (Ray Wilson 12, I. Mauger 10, J. Airey 9, B. Briggs 6).
U.S.S.R. 22 (G. Chlynovski 8, V. Smirnov 7, Vladimir Gordeev 4, A. Kuzmin 3).
Poland 19 (H. Glucklich 6, P. Waloszek 5, A. Woryna 4, E. Jancarz 4).
Sweden 18 (A. Michanek 9, S. Sjösten 3, B. Jansson 3, L. Enecrona (res) 3, B. Persson 0).

1972 (OLCHING)

Another clear-cut British success in the first Final to be held on neutral ground since 1965. The venue made no difference, and this win wrapped up a year in which the individual, pairs and long track titles had also come to Britain.

It was Ivan Mauger, consistency personified, who led the way, and he only missed a maximum when he was slow from the start in heat 16 and couldn't catch Henryk Glucklich. His example was inspiration enough for the rest.

The other nations were left to battle it out for the minor placings. Sweden began brightly

enough but unaccountably lost their way, and in a run-off series between the Eastern bloc representatives, Russia clinched overall second spot.

Great Britain 36 (I. Mauger 11, J. Louis 9, T. Betts 8, Ray Wilson 8).

U.S.S.R. 21 (A. Kuzmin 6, G. Chlynovski 5, V. Kalmykov 5, V. Trofimov 5).

Poland 21 (Z. Plech 7, H. Glucklich 6, P. Waloszek 5, Z. Dobrucki (res) 3, M. Cieslak 0).

Sweden 18 (C. Löfqvist 6, A. Michanek 4, T. Jansson 4, J. Simensen 3, G. Nordin (res) 1).

Below: *Terry Betts and Ray Wilson give Peter Collins the traditional salute after the Belle Vue teenager had scored a maximum on his World Team Cup Final debut, 1973.*

1973 (WEMBLEY)

This was the year in which England, rather than Great Britain, embarked upon a modern-day sequence of international domination. The British team, by design, excluded Mauger and relied exclusively upon home-produced talent.

Not only did this prove successful as a matter of policy but it also coincided with the start of a record-breaking run by Peter Collins. In this, his first Final and only his second Wembley appearance, he smashed the track record and grabbed a maximum.

Michanek was not so far behind in the individual stakes, and Sweden provided a spirited but not quite successful challenge. Biggest let-down was the nerve-racked and ineffective display from Jerzy Szczakiel, a fortnight after his world title win.

Great Britain 37 (P. Collins 12, T. Betts 9, M. Simmons 8, Ray Wilson 8).

Sweden 31 (A. Michanek 11, B. Persson 9, B. Jansson 6, T. Jansson 5).

U.S.S.R. 20 (Vladimir Gordeev 7, V. Paznikov 5, G. Chlynovski 4, A. Pavlov 2, V. Trofimov (res) 2).

Poland 8 (Z. Plech 5, E. Jancarz 2, P. Waloszek 1, J. Szczakiel 0).

1974 (KATOWICE)

If the Poles had suffered embarrassment enough at Wembley the previous September, this was even more inglorious and the 80,000 crowd whistled their disapproval. In the midst of such disappointment the locals managed a generous tribute to England.

And how well such applause was earned. John Louis helped himself to a maximum and Collins collected his second successive full score, though he was a trifle fortunate. Michanek led him until his bike failed yards from the line in the last heat.

Sjösten signalled his return to favour with a fine performance, but the Russians, like their hosts, simply did not look to be up to the requirements of the occasion.

England 42 (J. Louis 12, P. Collins 12, D. Jessup 10, M. Simmons 8).

Sweden 31 (S. Sjösten 10, A. Michanek 9, T. Jansson 7, C. Löfqvist 5).

Poland 13 (Z. Plech 4, J. Mucha 4, A. Jurcynski 3, A. Tkocz (res) 2, J. Szczakiel 0).

U.S.S.R. 10 (M. Krasnov 5, Valeri Gordeev 4, V. Kalmykov 1, A. Kuzmin 0).

1975 (NORDEN)

Another Collins full score, another England display of power, precision, confidence and style. The holders soon recovered from the shock of seeing Louis trail in last in the opening race and by the half way stage they were three ahead of Russia.

After the interval they stepped up the momentum, and pulled away to another superb victory. The Soviets gave their best account of themselves for some years, with Valeri Gordeev denying Malcolm Simmons the lot.

The elder Gordeev, Vladimir, was the only U.S.S.R. rider who failed to win a race. Michanek recorded the solitary Swedish win. The Poles? They were even more unhappy than in the previous year's debacle, despite track conditions which were perfect.

England 41 (P. Collins 12, M. Simmons 11, M. Ashby 10, J. Louis 8).
U.S.S.R. 29 (Valeri Gordeev 8, V. Trofimov 8, G. Chlynovski 8, Vladimir Gordeev 5).
Sweden 17 (A. Michanek 8, T. Jansson 4, B. Persson 2, S. Sjösten 2, S. Karlsson (res) 1).
Poland 9 (M. Cieslak 4, H. Glucklich 2, J. Rembas (res) 2, E. Jancarz 1, Z. Plech 0).

1976 (WHITE CITY)

The greatest upset occurred in the British qualifying round when Australia were shock conquerors of England's best. The Aussies proved that this was no fluke by lifting the title on their first World Team Cup Final appearance.

At least the absence of the holders left the way clear for three teams to involve themselves in the most keenly-contested championship to date. Poland gave a surprisingly lively account of themselves and the Swedes were always in the running.

Ultimately the Australians hauled themselves clear, inspired by Phil Crump whom only the brilliant Michanek could tame. Then victorious skipper John Boulger celebrated by halting a Michanek full score with his heat 16 win.

Australia 31 (P. Crump 11, P. Herne 7, B. Sanders 7, J. Boulger 6).
Poland 28 (E. Jancarz 9, M. Cieslak 7, Z. Plech 6, J. Rembas 5, B. Proch (res) 1).
Sweden 26 (A. Michanek 11, B. Persson 8, L-A. Andersson 5, B. Jansson 1, C. Löfqvist (res) 1).
U.S.S.R. 11 (Valeri Gordeev 5, G. Chlynovski 2, Vladimir Gordeev 2, V. Paznikov 2).

1977 (WROCLAW)

England made no costly qualifying round mistakes this time, and set themselves up for one more outstanding performance in Poland. And the host nation, recovering some composure, battled hard to keep them in their sights.

The Collins maximum sequence came to an end, as it had to some time, though in fairness neither he nor Simmons were at peak fitness. But the team pulled together splendidly, with teenager Michael Lee collecting the track record on his Final debut.

The introduction of reserve John Davis was another vital factor, for his two wins helped to ward off the challenge of Poland – well led by Jancarz – and the up-and-coming Czechs. The Swedes, though, were terribly disappointing.

England 37 (P. Collins 10, D. Jessup 9, M. Lee 9, J. Davis (res) 6, M. Simmons 3).
Poland 25 (E. Jancarz 10, B. Nowak 6, J. Rembas 6, M. Cieslak 2, R. Fabiszewski (res) 1).
Czechoslovakia 23 (J. Stancl 8, A. Dryml 5, J. Verner 5, V. Verner 5).
Sweden 11 (A. Michanek 5, B. Persson 4, B. Jansson 2, T. Nilsson 0, S. Karlsson (res) 0).

Below: *Australia, 1976 winners. Left to right: Phil Crump, Billy Sanders, John Boulger, Phil Herne, Garry Middleton, Peter Moore (manager).*

THE BEST OF THEIR TIME

Right: *Vic Huxley – magnificently consistent.*

Like the devotees of almost any and every other sport, speedway old-timers tend to grow misty-eyed as memories take them back to the early days. It was ever thus. Things are never as they used to be.

For all that, the glamour, the excitement and the personalities who coloured the first decade of speedway racing in Great Britain achieved a status which was larger than life.

Inevitably, a number of those heroes were visitors from across the sea. But as the seasons followed one another, home-bred riders got themselves into a position in which they could hold up their heads with pride.

Just how does one evaluate classifications at such a distance? It is virtually impossible. All one can do is to recall via the record books and the recollections of their contemporaries the impact made upon the scene by those who were indisputably the best of their time.

Eddie Brinck, who taught Americans and Australians alike the primitive arts of broad-siding, never did make it to England. He was due to have been included in a 1928 advance party; but a few weeks earlier was killed in an accident at a half mile track in the United States.

One American who did come was Lloyd (Sprouts) Elder. As far as British speedway is concerned, there has probably never been another to match his legendary status.

Elder, from Fresno in California, was apprenticed to a racing stable, but simply kept growing; hence the nickname of 'Sprouts'. Nature saw to it that he was to turn to horses of a different variety. Instead of becoming a jockey, he took to racing motor cycles on board tracks.

As memories of the First World War faded, he built a reputation as western states hill-climbing champion, and rode for some years on half-mile and mile tracks. When he went to Australia, his impact was immediate, first at Sydney, then Maroubra Park – and so, too, was the stir he caused in England when the sport took its first grip upon the public.

Elder was the first of the big money men. In the first three seasons in British speedway, he was reputed to have earned £50,000. He lost most of it, by all accounts.

Though he rode for Southampton in 1930, Elder was for the most part a free-lance, and a phenomenally successful one at that. But it was at the end of that season that the promoters decided that appearance monies would not be paid in future. Instead they offered a new schedule of start money and increased prizes. It may well have been no coincidence that in the following year, Sprouts rode only on the continent.

Always prepared to adventure, he had already headed a party (which included Frank Varey, the Langton brothers and Max Grosskreutz) to South America. But he was no stranger to Europe, either, having raced in France, Denmark and elsewhere.

A serious back injury in America more or less finished his career, though ironically, he was destined to suffer injuries as a Highway Patrol man back in Fresno, more serious than he had ever sustained on the track. When his wife died in 1957, Elder killed himself: an improbably melancholy end to a life story of one of the great characters.

Another tall, lean pioneer with the talent for making money was Frank Arthur, the 'wizard' of Brisbane whose Australian reputation preceded him.

When speedway came north to Queensland, he was a quick learner, and became the first man in the world to lap at 50 m.p.h. Not surprisingly, Arthur made an immediate impact on his arrival in England in 1928, and a stack of titles and track records came his way.

He was an obvious nomination for the new star class in 1929, which meant being automatically debarred from competing in the first League competition. But Arthur etched his name into the record books by becoming the

Above: *Dickie Case – the former dining car attendant who served up the goods for Australia.*

Left: *Eric Langton, architect of many Belle Vue and England successes.*

first winner of the Overseas Final of the Star Championships, when he beat Vic Huxley 2–0 at Harringay.

Subsequently Arthur became the driving force at Stamford Bridge, and was a key contributor to their 1932 success when they won the League Trophy in the first competition to embrace teams from both north and south.

The only rider to feature in each of the first four Star Finals, he never repeated his initial achievement. But he was an automatic choice

Right: *Jack Parker, a man of many tracks before the war.*

Far right: *Great Aussies, Bluey Wilkinson and Max Grosskreutz.*

for the early Test teams, and was instrumental in bringing international racing to Australia.

Arthur became an influential figure in the revival and development of the sport Down Under, which had waned after the exodus of so many top stars. But speedway there came to life again in the mid 1930's and drove forward in determined fashion after the Second World War, with Frank still involved as one of the most progressive and successful of promoters.

Vic Huxley was another of the early Aussies to make an instant impact. When League racing was introduced, it was decided that several of the trophies which had been contested the previous year should be discontinued. The Silver Wings, Silver Wheels, Silver Pennant and Silver Armlet were struck off the fixture list.

But Huxley helped himself to those that remained, winning the Golden Helmet, Golden Gauntlets, Silver Helmet and Silver Sash. And his inclusion as captain in the Wimbledon team helped to break through that early ruling which denied the public the chance to see star class riders in the League.

In 1930, not only did Huxley avenge his previous defeat at the hands of Arthur in the Star Championship – winning the first such Final to be held at Wembley – but he was in a class of his own.

The end of season dinner, given by the International Speedway and Motor Track Racing Association included a little ceremony in which he was presented with a gold cigarette case. The inscription – The Undisputed Speedway Champion of 1930 – said it all.

At one stage, Huxley held 52 different track records at 35 circuits where he had ridden. So dominant was he that even his rare failures made headlines.

In the Test series, which got under way in this year, he captained Australia throughout and was top scorer in four of the five matches. Huxley went on to score 367 points in 45 international appearances.

There was a soft centre to the man. A confirmed animal lover, he frequently brought a pet to meetings; sometimes a marmoset, and, for a long time, a sealyham terrier named 'Rags'.

Leadership was another of his talents. Other riders could always rely upon him for a friendly word of advice. For seven years, Huxley was captain of Wimbledon.

But in individual competition he was as tough as they come. Ruthless in the battle for first bend supremacy, he wasted no time in adjusting after the introduction of the starting gate.

Vic was three times British Individual Champion, and his record in the Star Championships spoke for itself. While 1930 was his only victory, he was runner-up on three other occasions.

For sheer durability, few riders can match the record of Ron Johnson, another who wore the Australian colours with distinction. His total of 59 'caps' against England, all but four of them in this country, remained a record for years.

Johnson was born at Duntocher in Scotland, but went to Australia with his parents when he was six years of age. It was Johnnie Hoskins who gave him his first start at Claremont, Perth, in 1926, and they travelled together to play their part in the introduction of speedway racing to England.

A diminutive thrill-maker, Johnson had a career that was dogged by many niggling injuries. He qualified for six of the seven Star Championships, actually rode in five of them and was runner-up to Tom Farndon, then his Crystal Palace team mate, in 1933.

In the following season, he began a lengthy association with New Cross, and was still in their colours in 1948 when he finished as runner-up to Vic Duggan in the British Riders Championship . . . at the age of 41.

Ironically, Johnson never rode in a World Final. He was a reserve in 1937 but did not get a ride. And he was one of the 1939 qualifiers. That Final did not take place because of the outbreak of war.

Max Grosskreutz, a protégé of Arthur and one of the originals from Brisbane, also appeared with distinction after the war, although his career was essentially at its zenith in the early years.

Son of a German father and Danish mother, he was named Maximillian Octavius Grosskreutz, and as a youngster worked as a cane-cutter in the far north of Queensland. When he started racing, he read his own obituary on no less than three occasions, wrongly identified by reporters who filed their story before checking the facts!

Sadly, several of his contemporaries and friends were killed on the track, among them Sig Schlam, Buzz Hibberd and Indian Allen. This sequence of tragedy prompted a new appraisal of the whole business by Grosskreutz, whose successes owed much to tactical safety and awareness as well as machinery which was always up to the job.

Though injury ruled him out of the historic first World Final, he lent his famed bike, nicknamed 'Pinto', to Bluey Wilkinson who

Left: *Great Englishmen, Tommy Farndon and Frank Charles, both of whom met with a tragic death.*

raced to a flawless maximum.

Max was third in the 1935 Star Final – he won four races, and fell off in the other – while his international record comprised 57 appearances against England, just two less than Johnson managed. He collected a record 374 points in 44 matches in this country, while his 1935–36 total in Australia showed maximum scores in each of the first four internationals, followed by three wins and a disqualification in the last.

Yet it was as a member of the all-conquering Belle Vue team that he made arguably his greatest impact. Harringay once offered to pay £7,000 for his transfer, but instead he turned to promotion and was the man who successfully introduced licensed speedway to Norwich in 1937.

More mercurial, but a rider who made no less of an impact upon early enthusiasts was Billy Lamont, who touchingly remained faithful to Johnnie Hoskins, the man who had given him his first opportunities back home, when Wembley were casting around for a team.

Tom Morgan, top speedway scribe of the day, described 'Cyclone' Billy Lamont as a rider whose apparently reckless riding gave him the title of 'the man with a month to live'. Bill scorned the niceties of track craft. He rode the outside of the track flat out and took a course so near the fence that he was called the 'programme snatcher'.

With an accolade like that, who needed a

place in the annals of record-breaking?

A chance meeting with Frank Arthur was the start of a colourful career for 'Demon' Dicky Case. He was serving as a steward on the Brisbane to Bundaberg train, and struck up a conversation with the great man whom, it transpired, lived in Toowoomba, his own home town.

Encouraged by Arthur, he quit the railroad and crossed the world, embarking upon a spell of prolific Test match scoring which extended to 39 appearances and 279 points against England.

Case qualified for four successive Star Championship Finals and for the first World Final, but never bettered the third place he achieved at Wembley in 1932, behind Eric Langton and Vic Huxley, his erstwhile Wimbledon team mate.

In later years, he made a significant contribution to the sport as a director and guiding light of the famed Rye House training school.

They didn't have training schools when Arthur Wilkinson started racing at his home town track of Bathurst, New South Wales, as a 16-year-old in 1927. But the kid was an astute observer and quick learner and within a few months had beaten Lionel Van Praag in the state championships.

Like every Australian then or now whose hair colouring inclined towards the golden hue of sunset, Arthur was nicknamed Bluey, and soon enough his name became known much further afield. He did a newspaper round to help raise the boat fare to London.

On his arrival, Bluey was taken under the wing of Buzz Hibberd, and signed for West Ham. He had an inauspicious first year, but in 1930 often gave even the brilliant Huxley something to think about in individual competition.

Chosen to ride for his country in the third Test of the inaugural series, he was an ever-present until his retirement in 1939, when he became promoter at Sheffield.

His 359 points in 38 matches in England and 181 in 23 appearances in Australia were both pre-war records.

In between times, Bluey became the darling of the dockland fans, and in 1936 was unbeaten in that first World Final, but accumulated bonus points determined that he had to be content with third place overall.

His 27th year was his most astonishingly successful. He started it by scoring a maximum in each of the five Test matches of the 1937–38 series against England. Wilkinson came back to this country as the reigning Australian champion, and promptly helped himself to a series of individual titles. And he topped the Australian score charts in each of the five internationals, amassing an unsurpassed 80 points.

Bad luck had denied him the world title two years earlier; injury ruled him out in 1937. But this, surely, would be his year. If the form book meant anything he looked certain to be crowned as champion of the world.

Well, he was – but not before undertaking a visit to a faith healer whose skills enabled him to overcome a troublesome cartilage injury, and a trip to Tottenham Hotspur Football Club on the morning of the Final for intensive treatment on a shoulder he had hurt in a second half crash at New Cross the night before.

This was just the sort of situation to bring the best of this gritty, gutsy rider. For technical accomplishment, perhaps, he was not the match of Huxley and others were more flashily brilliant; but Bluey Wilkinson simply refused to acknowledge that there was ever the possibility of defeat.

Off track, he kept himself much to himself. Manager Hoskins, rarely at a loss for a good story line, was left dumb-founded when Wilkinson slipped away one afternoon to get married in secret.

The headlines which mattered to Bluey were those that recorded the results which ultimately declared him as one of the sport's heroes.

Ironically, he met an untimely death . . . not on the track, nor as the consequence of war, but when returning home from the pictures on his motor cycle in July, 1940. A swerving lorry knocked him from his machine. When they picked him up, Wilkinson was dead.

Time has emphasised the quirks of the 1936 scoring system which denied Wilkinson the title of the first official world champion.

Instead that quite unique honour belonged to Lionel Van Praag, yet another Australian.

Riding on the track where he had led Wembley Lions to many distinguished achievements, the dashing 26-year-old from Sydney, in his tenth year as a speedway racer, carved his name with pride.

His previous record at the highest level had been good without suggesting qualities out of the ordinary. But Lionel reacted like a champion when the chips were down. He beat the hotly favoured Eric Langton in the 20th heat to force a run-off.

And after a false start (Langton broke the tapes but was given another chance) Van Praag repeated the performance to determine the destination of that first crown.

Dark-haired, debonair and renowned as a practical joker, the new champion was beloved by the Wembley faithful, not always so popular elsewhere. Yet this night of nights belonged to him, and subsequent performances confirmed that he was a man of rare mettle.

At both domestic and international level he was a redoubtable customer. In 56 Test matches he scored 382 points and even after the Second World War, could still mix it with the best on both sides of the globe.

It was wholly in keeping with the character of the man that on even more important battle fields he won the George Medal for exceptional bravery.

Later he was involved in the revival of solo racing Down Under, and half a lifetime later served Australia as team manager against the visiting British Lions.

For longevity of sustained performance, though, it is debatable whether any rider achieved more in the sport's first quarter of a century than Jack Parker, one of England's own.

A former B.S.A. works employee, this modest midlander had his first taste of speedway at High Beech in 1928, and was still capable of commanding the headlines when the sport was celebrating its Silver Jubilee in Coronation Year.

A man of many tracks, he captained Coventry, Southampton, Clapton and Harringay before hostilities interrupted proceedings, then embarked upon a complete new career as the elder statesman at Belle Vue.

Although Parker did not win a World Final, he was never found wanting at the highest level. Don Clarke of the *Sunday Mirror*, one of the most experienced of speedway journalists, rated him the finest rider of all time.

Jack appeared in the first official Test match in 1930 and was still going strong in 1951, when he became the first to make 50 home international appearances. Not surprisingly his points haul of 862 in 94 matches against Australia leaves behind all challengers on either side. Of those, 460 came in 52 matches on home soil, the rest spread over eight successive tours amongst which that of 1950–51 proved the most productive, with 111 points in seven meetings.

Parker had been runner-up to big Roger Frogley in the first English Final of the Star Championships, and five years later at Wembley he brilliantly took the most prized individual crown of the day.

Injury cost him a place in the first official World Final. Yet eleven years later, he was a popular and deserving winner of the British Riders Championship, again at Wembley. He beat Bill Kitchen in a run-off after both had scored 14 points.

Track-crafty Parker struck the biggest psychological blow in his second ride when he swept past Vic Duggan, who was the hot favourite. That night, perhaps, was the high point for Jack, but consistency and durability were features for which he will always be remembered.

This was never more vividly illustrated than by his near stranglehold on the British Match Race Championship in the years immediately after the war. So consistently did he defend that particular prize that the Golden Helmet event was dubbed 'Parker's Pension'.

The career of Roger Frogley, the 1929 conqueror of Jack Parker in that first year of the Star Championships, was much more meteoric and relatively short-lived. Nevertheless, he was probably the first home-bred rider to suffer nothing by comparison with the overseas stars.

Farmer's son Frogley took to racing with remarkable style, breaking speed records at

High Beech and Stamford Bridge. Later he became the popular skipper of Crystal Palace, while brother Buster, another first-season Star finalist, captained Wembley.

Subsequently the Frogley brothers used their skill and imagination in another high-speed direction, launching the Hertfordshire Aero and Flying Club at Broxbourne, which was followed by a profitable air ferry business.

London, very much the focal point of the competitive activity in the first two or three years, boasted several equally accomplished English discoveries. Rival sets of supporters sang the praises of smiling Jim Kempster, the Rudge-mounted Wimbledon favourite, Colin Watson – whom Wembley snapped up on the closure of White City – and plucky little white line expert Tommy Croombs who went on to become a West Ham favourite for a decade.

Watson, a one-time coach-builder from Plaistow, also found his way across to the Custom House and rode in their team in 1946 at the age of 55.

Stamford Bridge followers would hear no ill of Wal Phillips, sleek and stylish former J.A.P. apprentice whose first sight of the sport was when Elder was performing spectacular broadsides at an early Stamford Bridge meeting.

Phillips, who lapped at over 100 m.p.h. in road racing competition at Brooklands, and rode speedway at the Bridge later the same day, was 26 times an England international. A badly broken leg at Sydney in 1936–37 ended his track career. But with Wimbledon, for whom he had also ridden, and later Harringay, he became a shrewd administrator as well as maintaining his reputation as an innovator and machine development expert.

Great characters abounded, none more so than the inimitable Phil Bishop. He chirpily confessed to having broken just about every bone in his body in a series of hair-raising accidents which earned him the title of 'King of Crash'. An untimely end befell him, one of five victims of the 1970 Lokeren road disaster.

When it came to winning, and winning consistently, Tom Farndon commanded attention. He began at Coventry, his home town track, while still in his teens. Jack Parker and his younger brother Norman took the fair-haired youngster under their wing. But it was after his move to Crystal Palace that easy-going Farndon began to establish himself as one of the first of the really great English riders.

In no time at all he was an international regular. A total of 138 points in 20 Test matches barely does credit to his ability.

In 1933, at the age of 22, Farndon won the Star Championship Final in typically dashing style. He was a vividly physical rider, and master of tracks of all shapes and sizes.

This was emphasised when Crystal Palace closed and the team moved in 1934 to New Cross. The switch from the flat-out 440 yard circuit to a 262 yard 'frying pan' gave Tom no problems.

It was during this season that he established a new slice of history by adding to his Star title the British Match Race Championship and the London Riders title.

Farndon seemed destined to collect another title in 1935, when his record of successes showed tremendous consistency. At one stage, he held a track record at every circuit in the National League.

The night before Wembley's gala occasion, he crashed in the second half final at New Cross. His absence threw a pall of gloom over the Star Final, and 24 hours later, Tom Farndon was dead. It was a tragedy for British speedway which knew no parallel until Peter Craven was mortally injured in 1962.

Tragedy of a different kind befell Frank Charles, winner of the 1935 Star Final with a 15 point maximum. The big, strong northerner had been plucked from retirement by Wembley only weeks earlier. Less than four years on, he was to lose his life in an accident during the national gliding championships at Great Hucklow, Derbyshire.

Charles, who began as a beach racer back in 1924, and won his first race when Blackpool opened only to be disqualified for looking round (!) achieved something of a record when the League got under way.

It was probably a commentary upon the informality of the northern-based English Dirt Track League that Charles rode for Manchester White City, Preston, Burnley, Belle Vue and Leeds in its inaugural season.

It was with Belle Vue that he eventually settled down, and it cost Wembley £1,000 to buy him. In 1936 he scored what was an incredible 69 points in five Test matches against Australia, including 18 in the defeat at New Cross when Jack Parker, next best Englishman, scored eight. Charles needed 21 internationals to score 179 points.

For some time, the northern contingent were considered to be beyond the pale. Eventually regional difficulties were forgotten and with the birth of the National League in 1932, more opportunities presented themselves to the riders from the out of town tracks.

This provided Belle Vue with just the chance they welcomed, and as well as making their presence felt in team tournaments, they also got the opportunity to advance the claims of Eric Langton in the Star Championships. Fittingly, this home-grown star of Hyde Road won the premier individual title that year.

Four years later, he came within a whisker of lifting the first World Final. Eric led the qualifying scorers, and needed only to register his fourth win at Wembley in heat 20 to take the title.

But Lionel Van Praag decided otherwise, beating him in that race and again in a memorable run-off. Langton was never again so close to a place alongside the all-time greats.

Yet until Jack Parker finally overhauled him, this long-time trials enthusiast could point to an international record second to none.

In England alone, he totalled 345 points in 35 Test matches. This quiet, almost dour Yorkshireman also raced in New Zealand and Australia and eventually emigrated to Perth.

Eric and his brother Oliver were established motor cyclists when they rode in the open meetings at Blackpool and Belle Vue. In 1929 Eric was one of the first to employ the foot forward style, and it was a year of significance for Oliver, too. He suffered an injury which spoiled his career chances but in later years he was the mechanical genius and inspiration behind many of Eric's successes.

After switching from Leeds to Belle Vue, whom he captained for six years, Eric was a consistently dominant force in the Aces team which strode from one success to another.

He missed the best part of the 1933 Test series after a flare-up in the opening match; it was in the same year that he gave up the British Individual Championship because he disagreed with the method of running the competition.

For the greater part of his career, though, Langton was far removed from controversy. He was canny, clever and, above all, dependable.

If Eric was northern solidarity personified, his Belle Vue colleague Frank Varey excelled at the unpredictable. A former apprentice at the Scott motor cycle factory in Saltaire, he had ridden in trials, hill climbs and sand races, had even been a sidecar passenger, when speedway racing overtook the north.

Varey broke the track record at the first Hyde Road meeting, and soon began what was to become one of the most effective and renowned of partnerships with Langton. They provided an enduring base for a team of so many talents.

Frank, who favoured a colourful jersey, earned the nickname of 'Red Devil' from excited fans as a result of his exploits in Argentina as a member of Elder's South American touring team.

Purists may claim that Varey, 16 times an England rider, owed much to his huff and puff style, and did not rate among the all-time technical greats. Nevertheless, his rumbustious character left an indelible impression.

Some of his finest efforts were during the wartime, when he was British Individual Championship runner-up in 1942, winner two years later. Above all, he spared no effort to keep the flag flying and the interest alive in those dark years.

Later he was a successful promoter, and renewed his partnership with Langton at Sheffield, though it was not until the new Provincial League that he really cut a dash in the administrative field. And at 65, he came out of retirement to boss his beloved Belle Vue for a short but successful spell.

Vying for the title of the most spectacular rider in the 1930's was Harold (Tiger) Stevenson, who captained West Ham for more than ten years. The legendary Elder was an early mentor, and Stevenson learned well, for he went on to win the British Individual Championship, represented his country 27 times, and, in Australia in a 1933–34 season of free-lance activity, won 48 of the 53 races he started.

His West Ham colleague Arthur Atkinson, who qualified for each of the four World Finals up to the war, was equally consistent. When Johnnie Hoskins went north to scour for talent, Atkinson was one of his first discoveries, but his Wembley career was cut short by injury.

Unconscious for three weeks, he retired to farm in Yorkshire, and after an abortive comeback attempt at York in 1931, seemed to be lost to the sport. But when Hoskins switched to West Ham, it did not take too much talking to persuade Atkinson to return.

Not only did he enjoy rewarding times on track, but he also met, courted and married Eileen (Tippy) Thorpe, who was Hoskins' secretary. The newly-wed couple celebrated their honeymoon on the 1937–38 England tour to Australia.

A co-director of West Ham in later years (with Stan Greatrex) he made another comeback in 1951, when 39 years of age. Tippy took over his shares at the Custom House and at Rayleigh, and ran both shows with legendary efficiency.

Jack Ormston was another of those northern discoveries spotted and lured to Wembley by Hoskins, though he made an unfortunate start, crashing in his first meeting.

But the boy from County Durham soon became a man of some standing. In 1932 he captained the famous Lions to victory in the National League, National Trophy and London Cup. At Sydney Royale in the following Down Under summer, Ormston was virtually unbeatable.

The wanderlust took him off to Canada and the United States in the company of Frank Arthur, Ray Tauser, George Greenwood and Billy Lamont. On his return to England midway through the next season, Jack found himself placed in the 'pool' and promptly announced his retirement.

It was short-lived. Tom Bradbury-Pratt got him back for Hall Green, Birmingham, in 1934, and took him down to Harringay in the following year. It entailed a small matter of a 524 mile round trip for home meetings, but that did not appear to bother Ormston. He was second in the Star Final that year.

A great friend of the Frogley brothers, Jack became increasingly enthusiastic about flying, and once competed in the King's Cup. In more recent years, he earned a considerable reputation as a trainer of racehorses at Richmond, Yorkshire.

Ginger Lees, one more product of the north who made a name for himself at Wembley, was the first rider on either side to score double figures in each of five Test matches in an England v Australia series. That was in 1934, the year in which he also grabbed third place in the Star Final.

His exploits of the previous summer were no less remarkable, for in the first four internationals he scored 20, 22, 13 and 17 points! The scoring system was changed for that year, though, with four points awarded to a race winner.

The record books were not so kind to some contemporaries, whose impact lacked the supporting evidence of statistics. Exciting leg trailer George Newton, for instance, was so spectacular with New Cross. His efforts earned him a place amongst the World Final qualifiers each year up to the war. Despite coming to the first two with a dozen bonus points to his credit, Newton failed to produce his best when it counted.

Indeed, in the 1937 Final at Wembley, he had the unenviable distinction of falling three times after winning his opening race.

Oddly enough, it was on the same track that he had enjoyed his finest hour, scoring 16 points on his international debut the previous season.

Other names flitted across the scene. Cyril (Squib) Burton was one of the early provincial stars, first at Leicester, then Sheffield. Injuries limited him to just one Star Final appearance. In London again, Claude Rye was a notable name at Wimbledon in their formative days; later he built even more of a reputation for himself and became a multi-millionaire business tycoon.

While a fleeting acquaintance with the excitement of those pioneer days was enough for some, Joe Abbott from Burnley vowed to ride until he was 50. He began at Preston, and later moved to Belle Vue where he was paired with Frank Charles.

Another of those who appeared in the first Test match, Abbott reached the inaugural World Final, but injury postponed his Wembley appearance for a year.

After wartime work in a munitions factory, he had a spell as team manager at Sheffield before coming back to ride, first for Harringay, then Bradford. In 1949, racing for Odsal against Harringay, he was killed in a track accident.

Belle Vue simply could not fail to produce likely prospects, and a newspaper advertisement, in which Hyde Road boss E. O. Spence offered trials to novice riders, started Bill Kitchen on a distinguished career.

Kitchen had raced on sand, in the T.T. and in grass track events before trying speedway, and within no time at all he was hailed as an overnight sensation, heading many of the stars of the day. In a matter of weeks he earned the first of his 32 England caps.

Bill earned an England record which only Jack Parker and Eric Langton among his contemporaries managed to surpass. In this country alone he scored 254 points including 70 in the five 1939 matches, a record.

After being runner-up in 1941 and 1943, Kitchen was the 1945 British Champion, some consolation for the postponement of the 1939 Wembley Final for which he had been a leading qualifier.

No stranger to team successes as a result of his Belle Vue association, he subsequently captained Wembley in a sequence of matching triumphs; and in 1946 and 1947 he experienced the bitter-sweet taste of finishing as runner-up in the British Riders Championship.

In more recent times, he was the first track inspector appointed by the Speedway Control Board.

So many riders were unfortunate enough to lose potentially their best years because of the 1939–45 break. Imperturbable Alec Statham was one such. He began at Hall Green, switched to Southampton, then retired to concentrate on the management of a garage.

Above: *Bill Kitchen, a great competitor.*

Left: *Tiger Stevenson, stalwart of West Ham.*

But he came back and in the years up to and including 1939 displayed flashes of brilliance which suggested that one day he could beat the world. More was seen of him after hostilities ended. In 1948, having arrived at Wimbledon via Bradford – he was the first rider to be transferred for £2,000 – he was placed third in the British Riders Championship. Alec was the only man to defeat Vic Duggan that night.

Yet the 1930's Englishmen had to fight a battle for recognition and supremacy against a continuing challenge of overseas opposition. Their 1970's counterparts might argue that things have not changed!

Whereas the Aussies were by far the most prominent visitors, the United States came up with several to follow in the tyre-treads of Elder.

Ray Tauser, a former boxer and wrestler from Portland, Oregon, blazed a comparatively short but spectacular trail around the capital. Wembley gave him his first chance, and after that he was big news at Wimbledon.

In 1931, he beat Huxley in the Star

Championship Final, and cashed in upon his newly-acquired title by riding round the world. Despite many offers, he made 1932 his last season in England and quit the sport to become a pioneer of free-fall parachuting.

Four years elapsed before the brothers Jack and Cordy Milne arrived from Pasadena, California, and they soon made a major impact upon the British scene.

Jack wore the colours of New Cross, while Cordy gravitated between Hackney, Bristol and Southampton.

Cordy was fourth, third and then sixth in his first three World Final appearances. He led the bonus points scorers who qualified for the ill-fated 1939 championship.

Jack did not win a race in his World Final debut. He did not lose one a year later, when he added a 15 point maximum to the 13 bonus points he had taken with him to Wembley.

His was a wholly appropriate win, for his displays throughout the season had been of the highest quality. The large and vociferous contingent from the Old Kent Road received his success with rapture.

It might have been better still had the crowd burst into a refrain of the 'Star Spangled Banner' since the 1937 Final was a real United States show.

Wilbur Lamoreaux (Wimbledon) won four of his races and claimed the runner-up position with Cordy Milne making it an American 1–2–3. Although he was born in Illinois, it was on the west coast that he first saw speedway racing – Elder was racing at White Sox Park, Los Angeles, in 1932 – and Lamoreaux soon hitched up with the Milnes to make his own reputation.

Wimbledon made an unsuccessful application to be allowed to sign him in 1935, but got their man two years later. Shy and retiring, Lammy was a game little customer idolised by the fans, and he collected another 13 point haul in the 1938 World Final, once again with four wins.

He was the only one of the American superstars to reappear here after the war, and had spells with Birmingham and Wembley without quite recapturing his former brilliance.

Benny Kaufman, a doleful-looking fellow countryman and team mate at Wimbledon, was another rising force in the years up to the Hitler-enforced break. But one can only speculate as to whether he may have emulated the Milnes or Lamoreaux.

Thus Jack Milne, latterly a successful businessman and, with brother Cordy, involved in the revival of speedway activity in the west during the late 1960's (after the best part of two decades of little action or interest) remains to this day the only American to win the world crown.

Johnnie Hoskins called Jack 'a champion among champions'.

From neighbouring Canada came Eric Chitty and Jimmy Gibb, who learned the basics of the craft in California before coming over to join West Ham.

Both were good enough to qualify for a World Final place, and Chitty, indeed stayed around long enough to become a major force. He won each of the first three wartime British Riders Championships at Belle Vue.

During the war, Chitty took a touring team to Germany to entertain the troops, and another accomplishment for which he is fondly remembered was a fine singing voice. He accompanied many bands of reputation and even made a couple of recordings.

And in the first hint at the growth of internationalism which was later to become such a feature of British speedway, cosmopolitan Hackney included Danish flier Morian Hansen, the first continental to feature in the world championship story.

Hansen, who looked more Latin than Scandinavian, tried his luck at West Ham in the early 1930's, before establishing himself as the Wick idol in 1935. In the following year, when his brother Balzar also appeared briefly, he was fourth in the First Division score charts.

He became a wartime flier with the Royal Air Force, and received the George Medal and the D.F.C.

All of this was perhaps a far cry from the days of the European Economic Community; but even at that formative stage, British promotions and the public were not slow to adopt the rule of thumb – if they are good enough, let them all come!

PICKING UP THE PIECES

The long, tedious, destructive business of war robbed British speedway of half a dozen seasons. It was not considered safe to permit the assembly of large crowd gatherings; and most of the riders were kept busy elsewhere.

Happily, an encouragingly high proportion of the big names of the pre-war era survived to present themselves for racing action once more when things began to get back to normal.

While the World Final was not revived until 1949, the British Riders Finals which filled the void contained more than a smattering of the golden favourites of the 1930's, still going strong.

Thus it was the revered figure of Eric Langton who topped the qualifiers for the 1946 Wembley Final with 81 points, and another veteran, Ron Johnson, was just a point behind.

Also well to the fore was Jack Parker, who had switched to Belle Vue. And Bill Kitchen, who moved in the opposite direction and joined Wembley, was another leading contender amongst the dozen riders who qualified from the National League rounds.

The four Northern League qualifiers included gnarled old-timer Tommy Allott, a 1928 starter now associated with Sheffield.

But it was Tommy Price who signalled the start of the new era. He cleaned up with a 15 point maximum on his own track. Most critical of his five rides came in heat six when an otherwise undefeated Parker tumbled.

But there was no denying the authority with which the Cambridge-born former grass track rider underlined his developing talents. A late starter – he was 25 when he joined the Lions in 1936 – Price had made one World Final appearance and a couple of international outings before the war. Yet only now was he beginning to enjoy a rating amongst the leading stars.

That victory undoubtedly gave him the confidence to go on to higher things. For several years his stylish and consistent accomplishments were a feature for both club and country.

In the first World Final to be staged for a decade, 38-year-old Tommy became the 1949 champion with a performance of impeccable character. Not rated among the 34 First Division riders who were exempt until the third round of the championships, he displayed increasingly impressive form as the season progressed.

When Price led the qualifiers for Wembley, his chances began to look very good indeed, especially as Vic Duggan and Ron Johnson – first and second in the British Riders Final a year earlier – were both absent because of injury.

But there was still the redoubtable Jack Parker to contend with. Price enjoyed a slice of luck when old timer Wilbur Lamoreaux packed up while in the lead in Heat 12, but two races later victory in the crucial battle with Parker put the Wembley man well on the way to the £500 first prize, and the distinction of being the oldest rider to annexe the crown.

Price was a phlegmatic character, and did not concern himself with the fact that the ballot had given him racing number 13, the same as that worn by Bluey Wilkinson in the last completed final. In fact, one of the few things that ever bothered Tommy was his tendency to suffer from hay fever.

An amateur radio enthusiast, he kept fellow 'hams' in touch with his racing achievements, and it was typical of the singular modesty of the man that he slipped away from the World Final celebrations so that he could share his joy and communicate the good news to a blind friend of the air waves.

Still a class performer four years later, he was recalled to the England team against Australia and inspired successive victories with 12 from the reserve position on his home circuit, followed by 14 at Birmingham.

After an absence of several years, Price was back on the speedway scene in 1964 as promoter of West Ham and England team manager. The following season he was the guiding light as the Hammers won the first British League title. Some seasons later, he popped up again as an executive of Standard Motorists Centres, recent sponsors of the Golden Helmet.

Another who promised much before the war and whose reputation rose sharply afterwards was Norman Parker, a year younger than his illustrious brother Jack and 34 times an England international.

Right: *Eric Chitty, wartime winner from Canada.*

A move to Wimbledon coincided with the most consistent spell of his career. His captaincy and tactical awareness made him one of the most respected riders in the business. Under his guidance several important new talents emerged later, such as Ronnie Moore and Barry Briggs.

Injury finished Norman's active career, though like Price, he became an astute team manager. The 1967 British League title win for Swindon owed much to his quiet, kindly influence.

Wimbledon boss Ronnie Greene had no reservations about re-building with experience to the fore. He gave Odsal the first £2,000 transfer fee to sign pre-war international Alec Statham, who was just a few weeks short of his 36th birthday.

Over at West Ham, the talents of Malcolm Craven caught the eye. His introduction to the sport had been as bag carrier and general dogsbody to former England skipper Colin Watson.

If his parents had had their way, Craven would have become a musician. But dreams of becoming a trumpeter were ended by a road accident in which he sustained a cut lip.

Norwich didn't think he had the ability to make the grade in speedway, but Wembley gave him a chance before the war. Afterwards, Malcolm became a hungry points gatherer and livewire personality.

There was no shortage of characters. Leg-trailing specialist Oliver Hart featured in each of the six wartime championship meetings at Belle Vue, and his Bradford team-mate Ernie Price had his moments, too.

Jeff Lloyd and his vastly experienced elder brother Wally were names to conjure with, and so too was George Wilks who in 1935 had cost Hackney Wick all of £25 in a transfer from Harringay.

After hostilities were over, he was solidly good value for Wembley. But those Lions, fast emerging as a team as potent and powerful as any of the pre-war giants from Belle Vue, were doing their bit by unearthing fresh talent, too.

Bill Gilbert came to the fore in 1948, scoring 13 against Australia at Harringay in his Test match debut, and nudging much more established names in the British Riders Final.

Left: *Belle Vue kept the sport alive in the war years, though they never knew who might turn up from one week to the next. Riders often arrived on leave from different parts of the country and spent Saturday afternoon building up bikes to ride in the evening. This is Norman Parker and Les Wotton, making preparations.*

A contemporary was Split Waterman, whose racing debut had been while he was serving with the Army in Italy, where he became the star turn at the Naples track. After demobilisation he was handed a regular place in the Wembley team and in next to no time was busily breaking records.

The following year he also won his first international recognition, and he made 30 England appearances in all. As chance would have it, Waterman, whose birth certificate showed his forenames to be Squire Francis, moved to his greatest performances following a £3,000 transfer to Harringay.

An intrepid joker, with piratical looks and a cavaliering spirit which surely belonged to an entirely different historical era, he was one of the most enduringly popular sons of the post-war period. Years later he was to make headlines of a different sort, with his involvement in tales of gold smuggling and other nefarious activities!

Waterman all but struck gold in the world championship, and was twice within a whisker of taking the title. He scored 12 points in the 1951 Final, and was placed second in the first three-man run-off required in the competition. Two years later, he won his first four races; but clutch problems caused him to arrive breathless and ill-prepared for the start of his last heat.

The race, and with it the title, was won by Freddie Williams . . . yet another of the crop of post-war Wembley discoveries, whose second championship win this was.

Williams was a dockyard apprentice in the industrial town of Port Talbot when he answered an advertisement to attend Rye House training school, then run under the auspices of Wembley. He shaped soundly and earned a contract – his first public appearance was also the first speedway meeting he had ever seen – yet such was the strength in depth of the Lions that it was a couple of years before he managed to secure a place in a team hit by injuries.

After that there was no looking back for this fast-starting, cucumber-cool Welshman. He became a Test match regular, and, in 1950, topped the charts in his first World Final, scoring 14 points. He bowed the knee only to old maestro Jack Parker, whose heat 14 victory was his solitary win of the night. A coachload of family and friends up from the Rhondda cheered the new champion.

Freddie was close to collecting a second title two years later, losing by inches to Jack Young after leading the eventual champion until the

Above: *Hyde Road, Manchester. Left to right: Jack Parker, Eric Gregory, Frank Varey and Bill Pitcher in wartime action.*

Right: *Wilbur Lamoreaux, durable American who rode in England before and after the war.*

last corner of their thrilling battle of wits. But he earned another title in 1953, when he dropped his only point to Waterman.

Apart from qualifying for reserve position in the following season, he was never again to be seen in a World Final; and although his brothers Eric and Ian (captain of Swindon when they won the 1957 National League title) followed him into the international arena, Freddie quit prematurely after Wembley closed for business.

When the Lions roared again for an all too brief return in 1970 and 1971, Williams was back in his beloved Stadium, acting as team manager. Today the visitor to Wembley High Road, just round the corner from the track, can see evidence of how wisely Freddie invested his peak year earnings in a flourishing motor car and motor cycle business.

So the Welsh had their champion, and Scottish fans, numerous and enthusiastic in these boom years, claimed their own in diminutive Tommy Miller. His exploits on behalf of Glasgow's White City team earned him the rating of the finest rider to appear north of the border.

Beginning with a six ride maximum against England in his first representative appearance, he collected 236 points for Scotland in 18 matches between 1950 and 1953. He rode for Great Britain and for England in full internationals, but faded from view after Glasgow, and Scottish speedway in general, went into a decline.

Meanwhile, England went on seeking a new champion to succeed Price, and to call their very own. Craggy Dent Oliver, who signalled his home international debut with 18 against Australia on his own Belle Vue track in 1948, was one of whom high hopes were held. Two decades later he was the man whose influence helped restore some of those traditional glories to Manchester.

Other northern stalwarts such as Bradford's Ron Clarke and Eddie Rigg also had plenty of admirers, yet did not quite reach the highest standards of top level achievement. Cyril Brine (Wimbledon) blossomed in 1950 with a succession of Test match tall scores.

World championship honours came the way of Louis Lawson (Belle Vue) who was third in

1949. Wally Green, recalled by West Ham from loan duty at Hastings, finished second in 1950 and two years later Wembley man Bob Oakley claimed a shock third place; for both of them, incredibly, this was to be their only World Final appearance.

Dick Bradley, a former grass track specialist, nursed by Second Division Bristol, made a sensational England bow at Harringay in 1952. Australia had won the first four Test matches of the series, but Bradley, riding at reserve, grabbed 16 points and inspired a 55–53 victory.

The first Second Division rider to represent England in post-war internationals, though, was Alan Hunt, a Cradley Heath discovery later to perform great deeds for Birmingham. A track crash in South Africa brought his career to an untimely end.

As more tracks opened up, there was never a shortage of home riders who were only too delighted to attempt the pursuit of fame and fortune. The Roger brothers at New Cross promised much, and Bradford came up with a teenage starlet in Arthur Forrest, soon to become the youngest rider to be capped by his country.

Yet, just as they had done in earlier days, the Australians still seemed to have that extra special knack of producing riders who were capable and exciting, and, every so often, something else besides.

Vic Duggan was one such. Indeed, nobody dominated the immediate post-war period more vividly or comprehensively than this one-time grocery delivery boy, who was sacked from his first job in Sydney . . . for speeding on a motor cycle and sidecar! As a young hopeful with Hackney, Bristol, then Wimbledon just before the war, he had hinted at impending stardom.

A clear indication of his potential came in 1939 when he was a double figure scorer in each of the five matches against England, and a World Final qualifier.

Wimbledon wanted him back in 1946, but transport problems, notably the high shipping costs, proved prohibitive. It was not until the next year that the Aussies started to flow back into British speedway and Vic, together with his brother Ray and Frank Dolan, made history by flying in to join Harringay.

Left: *Vic Duggan, 'as consistent as Huxley had been'.*

In that golden summer of 1947, while Denis Compton and Bill Edrich bestrode the cricket fields of Merrie England and established new scoring records, Duggan embarked upon a phenomenal sequence of success on the speedway track.

His total for the year was an all-time record. He scored 297 wins, 39 second places and three thirds in 348 races. He topped the First Division averages with 11.46.

Not surprisingly, Duggan was the hottest favourite of all time when the British Riders Championship was to be held. But after scoring maximum points in four qualifying rounds, he crashed out of contention at Wembley.

Fate decreed that Vic had to wait until a further 12 months had elapsed before he landed what was arguably the outstanding individual award of a career littered with successes. After losing to Alec Statham in his first race, he was unbeatable and duly stepped up to receive the awards and congratulations of the Duke of Edinburgh, who made the presentations.

At international level, Duggan collected 308 points in 29 appearances, and most of his outstanding performances were achieved in England. He scored three successive 18 point maximums, the first of them in the final Test of a 1948 series in which he had scored 74 points.

Ray Duggan was killed in speedway's only double fatality, a crash with Norman Clay at Sydney Showground in January, 1950. It was not so surprising, therefore, that Vic should make that his last year in England, going out with a deserved reputation as the most explosive scoring power since Huxley.

Aub Lawson, also from Sydney, had an even longer and barely less distinguished career. He, too, gave a foretaste of his talents before the enforced six year break.

A post office messenger who joined the Australian Army's display team, he was just 21 years of age when Frank Arthur, promoter at the Royale and the adjoining Sydney Sports Ground, suggested that he might try his hand at speedway.

Lionel Van Praag gave him every encouragement, and after the youngster had shaped up with obvious promise, brought Lawson to Wembley in 1939. After an invaluable month on loan to Middlesbrough, he established himself in the First Division and was soon hailed as the most spectacular and exciting discovery of the year.

Like Duggan, he was one of the unlucky 16 denied the chance of appearing in the 1939 World Final. Later Lawson was to make ten world championship appearances and chalked up an Australian record of 73 points in the competition.

West Ham cabled for him to help them in 1947, and this began a five year association with the club. When Aub changed from his old leg-trailing style to the more practical foot forward method, his returns and reputation began to climb steeply.

At Test match level he was a prolific performer, particularly Down Under where he needed only 29 matches to amass a record 386 points. In 1949–50, when seven matches were staged, he scored 117 points (and four bonus) out of a possible 126, and was well into three figures in the following series. Lawson took 60 Tests to score 581 points, compared

Right: *Ron Johnson, still going strong in New Cross colours.*

Far right: *Oliver Hart, last of the leg-trailers.*

with Wilkinson's previous best of 540 in 61 matches.

After missing a year, Aub joined Norwich in 1953 and remained with them until 1960, when he was still good enough to qualify for the World Final. It's said that he never did a better day's work than when he took the young Ove Fundin under his wing and arranged for him to embark upon a career at the Firs which eventually outstripped that of his mentor.

An almost automatic choice for Australia from just before the war, capped 39 times altogether and especially successful on his home tracks when the series was revived, cheery Bill Longley rejoined New Cross from Bradford. And even on that tricky little circuit, smallest in the land, he was always good for points.

The little fellow with the big heart had been a semi-finalist in the Australian flyweight boxing championships before taking up speedway.

What the Aussies really wanted, however, was a new name with the punch to emulate the title-winning performances of Van Praag and Wilkinson. At one stage, it looked as though Graham Warren, born in Fiji and a Royal Australian Air Force dispatch rider during the war years, might be that man.

On his arrival in England in 1948, flaxen-haired Warren joined Cradley Heath of the Third Division, and quickly enough was transferred to Second Division Birmingham. Largely thanks to his brilliance they won promotion, with Warren scoring an incredible 25 maximums. It seemed that there was no stopping this sensational youngster.

In 1950 he collected a dozen points in the Wembley Final, and was at the peak of an international career which earned him 304 points for Australia in only 30 matches.

But a fractured skull, sustained in a crash in New Zealand, took away a little of his dash and fire. The Blond Bombshell rode again, and even came back to assist Wolverhampton in the Provincial League a decade after his skills were at their height.

Instead of Warren, it was Jack Young who became the next Australian to win the world championship.

Young, from Adelaide, started on an old

Left: *Jack Parker – the grand old man of British speedway.*

road bike which had been the property of Wally, his eldest brother. Soon he showed promise which attracted the attention and subsequent encouragement of Grosskreutz.

Walthamstow wanted him, but it was Edinburgh who landed Young in 1949. He started with a maximum in each of his first two matches, and then missed the next five weeks following an emergency appendix operation. But he recovered to top the team's averages.

A year later, Jack showed marked improvement and followed fellow Second Division riders Doug McLachlan and the ill-fated 'White Ghost' Ken Le Breton into the Australian team. In 18 internationals in England, he was to race to 214 points in 18 matches. Only Duggan, 242 in 19, had gobbled Test match points at such a rate.

It was in 1951 that Young produced Duggan-like consistency in other directions. In each of ten Northern Shield matches he scored full points. In Second Division meetings, Jack claimed 339 out of a possible 348 points, 25 maximum scores in 30 matches. In all team matches, he grabbed 589 of 612 points available.

Above: *Parker, his 'pension', and Golden Helmet match race challenger Split Waterman.*

And he became the first rider from the lower section of the League to capture the world title. Young needed a run-off to defeat Split Waterman and Jackie Biggs after all three had scored a dozen points. He got away from the stomach-stretching tension by reading a book of poetry between races.

Second Division, and old-time Aussie international Clem Mitchell in particular, had taught him plenty. Mitchell, manager of Edinburgh, tended the Young machinery with expert, loving care. But it was inevitable that the First Division should claim a rider of such talent.

It cost A. D. Sanderson, the new boss of West Ham, a record £3,750 to secure his signature in the face of spirited opposition. In his new environment, Young was brilliant. Australia beat England 4–1 and he scored 75 points in five matches.

Then came the World Final, and another first as Young successfully defended his title. This time he scored 14 points, including one win from the back over Freddie Williams and Split Waterman which many observers rated one of the finest rides of all time.

He didn't stay to receive the plaudits of his own Custom House fans, preferring to return to Australia straight away. It was the first sign of the toll the pressures were exacting upon his outwardly easy-going nature.

The following year, Jack resigned his tenure of the British Match Race Championship. A nightmare, he described it. And at the end of the 1953 season he delivered an ultimatum to West Ham. Either they shortened their 440 yard circuit to something less demanding or else he would press for a transfer.

When Young returned, the track had been trimmed by the best part of 30 yards. He stayed. In 1955, though, the Hammers slithered to the foot of the League table. And Jack announced that this time, he was not coming back. It was speedway's depression time. West Ham pulled out of the sport.

To all outward appearances, Youngie had it all. He displayed technique, style, dash and a disarming nature. Eventually he was lured back by Coventry, and scored as enthusiastically for Australasia as in earlier years of traditional Test match action. Yet some of that early devil and ruthless consistency was gone forever.

Had he maintained those qualities, Young would probably have left Lawson's world championship record in ruins. Nevertheless, 70 points from eight World Final appearances pay eloquent testimony to his talents.

Jackie Biggs, whom fate pushed back from the brink of all-time recognition, could not give away the game so easily. He came to England in 1947 at the age of 25, though little more than a novice. He made rapid strides at Harringay, in an environment where the abounding Aussie accents alone must have made him feel at home.

When subsequent legislation dictated that National League tracks were to be permitted only two colonial riders, he was allocated to Odsal (Bradford) for a spell, only to return to race again for Harringay. It was in 1951, his comeback season, that he came so close to becoming champion of the world.

He won his first four races in the Wembley Final. Incredibly, he contrived to gain a last in Heat 19, then trailed in behind Young and Waterman in the decider for a title which minutes earlier had looked to be his for the taking.

Never again did Biggs come so near. He subsequently assisted a string of teams, among them Poole, Ipswich, Coventry, Newport and

Hackney, and represented his country 34 times, before taking himself back to Australia to settle again in his native Victoria.

Even then Jackie, expert tuner and dry humorist, had not lost his taste for the sport and eventually it claimed his life. At the age of 50, he was killed while racing at Bendigo, an up-country track.

Another ill-starred racer was Ernie Roccio, the only new American to suggest that he might develop the class to maintain the traditions of his pre-war examples.

Roccio was the star of a U.S.A. team which toured England, delighted the fans at Shelbourne Park, Dublin, where Wimbledon fielded a unique nursery team, and qualified for the 1951 World Final.

Sadly, this dark, engagingly good-looking youngster was killed in a crash while riding for Wimbledon at West Ham in 1952.

There were hints of change in the international field. In Scandinavia, new names were beginning to make their presence felt. Even in South Africa, there were reports of a revival of something approaching boom proportions.

Some of the most exciting talent emanated from Sweden, where Olle Nygren was the first rider to try his luck overseas when he had a spell with Harringay. In the following year (1952) the 18-year-old Dan Forsberg, signed by Birmingham, became the first Swedish rider to qualify for the World Final.

Henry Long of South Africa, recruited by Belle Vue, made it to the same meeting, and Norway's Leif (Basse) Hveem was a reserve.

Hveem was an especially colourful character who began a sequence of wins in his national championship as a 15-year-old back in 1937. When war broke out and German troops marched into Norway, the enterprising youngster dismantled his racing machines, and carefully parcelled each piece before burying the packages in various parts of his garden.

He fled to England, and joined the free Norwegian Army, taking part in the Normandy landings of 1944. Afterwards he returned home, dug up his spares and reassembled his bikes. On the resumption of racing, Hveem was a regular big meeting winner on the continent.

Above: *Alice Hart, first lady team manager, with Parker and Henry Long taking notice.*

Certainly things were stirring in Europe . . . and even further afield. Half way across the world, in fact.

The visit of several English stars to New Zealand demonstrated that there were several bright prospects coming to the fore in that hitherto virtually untapped source.

Trevor Redmond and Geoff Mardon led the advance party and Ronnie Moore became the youngest-ever World Final qualifier as a 17-year-old in 1950. It was the first sign that one of the world's most minute speedway nations was about to embark upon a remarkable sequence of successes at the highest possible level of competition.

THE NEW WAVE

After those great boom years of the immediate post-war period, came a speedway slump – redeemed by the emergence of a new wave of star riders. In the early 1950's, no fewer than four youthful discoveries appeared – three of them from nations where there had been little previous suggestion of star talent – and all were destined to dominate the sport during the next decade or so.

There had been some racing activity in New Zealand as far back as 1928, and names such as Stewie St. George and Wally Kilmister featured in early dispatches. But nobody could have foreseen that the least densely populated of all the countries to have staged speedway racing would become a spawning ground for future world champions.

Sweden, substantial in area but also thin on the ground as far as population goes, had been something less than lukewarm in accepting the sport. Yet the Swedes also emerged as a real power in world speedway in this era, and unearthed a rider whose sustained appetite for winning and breaking records put even the likes of Huxley and Duggan in the shade.

But it was Ronnie Moore who struck the first blow for emergent youth. In 1950, remember, speedway was still largely dominated by performers such as Jack Parker and Tommy Price, who had started their career before the war and even earlier. Even the most exciting of the post-war newcomers, Freddie Williams and Split Waterman for instance, were in the middle or late twenties.

For a boy of 17, in his first year of British speedway, to win international honours and qualify for the World Final, was quite unprecedented. Yet Moore, brought to Wimbledon by Norman Parker, did just that and much more.

As a schoolboy, he had assisted his father in a Wall of Death show which toured New Zealand and was a major attraction at country shows and circus events. This preparation apparently fitted Ronnie perfectly, for he was disarmingly cool and confident as he settled into his new environment.

The crowds and the inevitable publicity did not bother him. Nor did the prospect of competing against riders of long-established reputation. Fourth place in the World Final in 1951 and again the following year indicated that the 'teenage wonder boy' had only to continue to listen, learn, observe and progress before he could claim a title of his own.

In 1954, at the age of 21, Moore conquered a talented field at Wembley and recorded the first maximum in the championship since Price five years earlier. Incidentally, this was Tommy's last World Final appearance; defending champion Williams was only reserve, and, as if to emphasise the changing order, future champions Peter Craven, Ove Fundin and Barry Briggs all made their debut in this meeting.

Moore, however, continued to be a polished, consistently and increasingly respected performer. Whatever he did oozed class. Born in Tasmania, he represented Australia in 13 internationals, scoring 149 points, including 80 in the 1952 series, which equalled the pre-war record of Bluey Wilkinson. This included three of the four full scores he achieved against England.

When New Zealand were granted full international status, Ronnie opted to wear the Kiwi emblem. At Plough Lane, where everything he touched turned to gold, he got the series under way with 18 in the first Test match.

Opposite page: *Ronnie Moore, boy wonder lynchpin of Wimbledon successes.*

Right: *Brian Crutcher, the irrepressible 'Nipper'.*

In the Australasia v England matches, he was far and away the highest scorer on either side, with 260 points in 21 matches. No wonder he was dubbed 'Mirac', for Moore and miracles were synonymous.

His second scintillating world title success, like his first five years earlier, was achieved with maximum points and made a nonsense of injuries which required him to wear special leg protection on each occasion.

In 1960, the year in which his wife Jill, a former Windmill dancer, presented him with twin girls, Moore celebrated by becoming the first rider to top 100 World Final points. The target could have been achieved even earlier, but for the fact that he missed the 1957 championships because of a short-lived excursion into car racing.

As captain of Wimbledon, he further enhanced his reputation as a technician and tactical genius. Ronnie Greene, for years the South London track's supremo, rightly regarded Moore as the most glittering jewel in his array of talent which completely lorded it over the National League for years on end.

All sorts of superlatives were applied to the man, his sportsmanship and his captaincy before injury and illness hurried along a premature farewell to British speedway in 1963.

Half a dozen years later, Moore was to return, making two more World Final appearances which took his championship total to 143 points in 14 events; he added his talents to Great Britain teams in Test match and World Team Cup occasions, and displayed much of his old style when sharing in a World Best Pairs win.

No rider had shown so much talent so young, and England badly wanted to find a new white hope of similar potential. Inevitably, many of those who were acclaimed with great enthusiasm fell short in their bid to take the sport by storm. But the spotlight was on the kids.

Arthur Forrest, the immaculately turned-out 'Black Prince', was hailed as a champion in the making. A Bradford rider, he embarked upon a run of five successive World Final appearances, high point of which was a third place in 1956.

Rye House discovery Gerry Hussey, who went to West Ham, was another for whom great things were predicted. But after an initial flourish, he also had to get back to the basics, before chalking up a couple of World Final placings which preceded his untimely death while racing in Australia.

Still more meteoric was the rise of Brian Crutcher, who was discovered at the nursery track run by his uncle at Ringwood. He became an instant star of Poole's promotion-winning Third Division team at 17, and in the same season (1951) was capped for the England C team.

A year later the rise of the 'Nipper' and of Poole was continued. The Pirates won the Second Division, and Crutcher fought his way from the first qualifying round of the world championship to win a place in the Final.

This proved to be the first of five successive appearances at the track which he was also to grace in League racing. Wembley Lions signed him early in Coronation Year for a £2,500 fee.

The following season, Crutcher finished as World Final runner-up to Moore, and pundits confidently predicted that he would be the champion himself before he was too much older. In the event, he never was. Misfortunes seemed to stalk him on the big occasion. In 1955 and 1956 he was well in the running, but falls spelled disaster each time.

After the Empire Stadium closed for League business, Brian went back to his beloved south coast and rode for Southampton. But he reached the World Final only once more before prematurely giving away the game during the 1960 season.

For the best part of a decade, Crutcher had been a thrill merchant and spectacle provider of endearing, exciting quality. He captivated South African audiences in 1953–54, scoring 84 points in five internationals and leaving in the shade the performances of the much more experienced Freddie Williams and Bill Kitchen. In home encounters with Australasia, he was top man in three series and claimed 176 points in only 14 matches.

Yet somewhere along the line, that initial boyish enthusiasm drained away. Perhaps too much was expected of him, or maybe he expected too much of himself. But basically, Brian enjoyed the simple pleasures and he never made any secret of the fact that the travelling and its attendant pressures never did appeal.

So if not with a rider of such natural gifts, just where was England to find her next world champion? It was Peter Craven who provided the answer. This diminutive, curly-topped sprite from Liverpool, the same age as Crutcher, did not appear to have the same easy talent. His local track gave him an extended trial, but handed him a free transfer. Spells at Wigan and Fleetwood didn't prove especially productive, either. The problem with the wee fellow was that he simply could not stop falling off.

Below: *The Mighty Atom is what they called Peter Craven, wizard of balance.*

Above: *Barry Briggs, with a style all of his own.*

Craven, however, was never anything less than enthusiastic about his own prospects. Undaunted by early failures, he presented himself at Belle Vue, of all places. How the cynics laughed. But they were forced to change their opinion. With Johnnie Hoskins, no less, guiding his progress, little Pete began to establish himself as a First Division rider of developing promise.

That potential burgeoned into positive achievement and in 1955 he really upset the predictions by winning the World Final. Like Moore, a year before him, Craven was just 21.

For the next few seasons, he was always there or thereabouts. In 47 internationals Craven raced to 621 points and in 14 series, he was top scorer on ten occasions. Australasia, Sweden – all opponents came the same to him. But he reserved for the Poles the most vivid demonstration of his daring skills.

Almost twenty years on, they still talk of his unbelievable exploits in Poland, where his Test match scores were 17, 18, 17, 21, 21 and 17. A brilliant, winning ambassador, Craven feared nobody and his cheeky smile belied a healthy appetite for victory.

Crowds everywhere loved this pixie-faced wizard of balance, who was nicknamed 'the Mighty Atom' and shyly admitted to wearing pyjamas under his racing leathers. He looked to be in line for his second world championship title in 1960. Craven won his first four races, but faltered at the final hurdle, and eventually had to settle for third place after a run-off.

Wembley belonged to him after a typically spectacular performance had made amends and earned him the 1962 crown. Peter was at the height of his powers and the peak of popularity.

But tragedy was to rob British speedway and cost him his life little more than a year later. Belle Vue had been invited to Edinburgh for a challenge match, and Craven, naturally, was the star attraction. He died four days after crashing into the safety fence in what appeared to be an attempt to miss a fallen rider.

The record books list Craven as England's top world championship performer, with 96 points in ten appearances. What the statistics cannot convey was the impact he made upon the sport, the affection he generated, and the sense of loss which accompanied his death.

Ove Fundin, who succeeded him as world champion, was tall, sandy-haired, with almost aquiline features and a taste for winning more voracious than any of his predecessors or contemporaries, for that matter.

It mattered little to this former furrier from Tranas in Central Sweden that his ruthless pursuit of success sometimes upset British crowds. For Norwich fans at least he could do no wrong and his impact there was massive.

Fundin toured England with Filbyterna in 1953, made his world championship bow the following year, and, after wintering in Australia with Aub Lawson, joined Norwich in 1955. For ten seasons, he was the most consistent performer at all levels, as devoted to success in domestic competition as in international combat and, especially, the world championship.

From his first title win in 1956 to his fifth in 1967, Ove was always the man the others had to beat. In addition to those victories, he featured in the rostrum placings year after year. A total of 173 points in 15 World Final appearances illustrates his consistency, as did the tag of 'Mr Perpetual Motion'.

Incredibly, he failed to register a maximum in all of those appearances. He could have had one for the taking at Malmo in 1961, the first year the Final was staged away from Wembley. Fundin received the roar of the night when he knocked off to allow fellow-countryman Göte Nordin through to set up a Swedish 1–2–3. It was the first time in a dozen years that a country had achieved a clean sweep of the honours, and only the third in history.

When the F.I.M. awarded the Internationale to England, as a recompense for the loss of the World Final staging, Ove embarked upon another sequence of victories which suggested that he intended to make this new tournament almost as much his personal property as the world championship itself.

European champion five times, Swedish champion on nine occasions, he scored 18 points in four successive internationals against Great Britain. His record for Sweden against England amounted to a staggering 195 points in 13 matches.

Australasia, Poland and the U.S.S.R. were treated with similar disdain as Fundin became the first Swedish rider to top 1,000 international points.

A man to feature in any and every discussion on the world's greatest riders, he scored a maximum when Sweden scored the first of half a dozen World Team Cup Final wins. And his 11 at Wembley ten years later, in 1970, provided him with a fitting farewell to the British scene which, a few interruptions apart, he had adorned for so long.

Ove was rock-hard, determined and, some suggested, the world's worst loser. Certainly, he was speedway's best winner for a lengthy period, and yet the mechanics of the sport held little appeal for him. Such was his innate talent that if the mood was upon him – and it usually was – Fundin could ride almost anything and win.

Above: *Ove Fundin – was he the greatest of all time?*

He was 22 when he collected his first world championship and a year later Barry Briggs, also 22, kept up the amazingly productive record of this era by claiming a place on the growing list of title holders.

Like Moore, he had learned his speedway in Christchurch, and followed the same path to join Wimbledon. However, he was not the same instant hit. Briggo, encouraged by *alter ego* Trevor Redmond, such an inspiration in the development of New Zealand riders, found himself at home with Moore and the polished Geoff Mardon at Plough Lane . . . but looked anything but a champion in the making.

Whereas Ronnie had such style, smooth grace and self-confidence, the teenage Briggs crashed and banged his way out of the novice stage. Fortunately, he learned fast. After a year or two, enough of the rough edges had been knocked off for Barry to take his place in the world rankings.

His first World Final rostrum placing, in 1955, was typical. A 12 point total included victories over holder Peter Craven and Jack Young, twice a past winner. This was enough to earn Barry a place in the run-off for second and third place, which also featured Moore and Eric Williams. Although Moore won comfortably, Briggs got the next place by courtesy of a generous referee after he had crashed spectacularly with Williams on the last turn, but was the first to pick himself up and struggle over the line.

No other rider of the day had a more aggressive or attacking style. With it, Briggo seemed determined to revolutionise the accepted order as he attacked established traditions. On his own admission, hunger and determination drove him on. In 1957, the world title was his for the first time after he beat Fundin in another no holds barred run-off. Barry's belief in himself soared after this result, and he successfully defended the crown with a maximum.

At the end of that season, though, he decided to return to New Zealand and failure to agree terms with Wimbledon meant that he did not return for the start of the next year. The public clamour persuaded the promoters to club together to bring him back to see if Briggs could become the first man to win three successive championships. In the event, far from match fitness, he finished third.

Still, brilliant one day and unpredictable the next, he continued to feature prominently, particularly after moving on, via New Cross, to Southampton. And in 1964, now a Swindon rider, he claimed another world championship.

Monumentally effective throughout the year, he brushed aside all opposition and made light of atrocious conditions in Gothenburg. Another comprehensive winning performance at the same Ullevi circuit two years later was even more significant for the fact that he was flying the flag for the Czechoslovakian Jawa/Eso machine, introduced to regular British League racing the previous summer.

Not even Fundin or Moore have a world championship record to match that of Briggo. He made 18 Final appearances between 1954 and 1972, when injury may well have robbed him of the fifth crown he so keenly sought. Barry piled up 201 points, was only once un-placed, and set standards which may well remain untouched in the record books for another fifty golden years and beyond.

In international terms, he was the first British representative to score a World Team Cup maximum, and during the sixties was the mainspring in numerous Test matches, usually as captain and most notably as the inspiration when the World Cup was won at Wembley in 1968.

Wimbledon owed him much in their golden years. Briggs later helped Southampton to the National League title and Swindon to a British League success, followed by spells with Wimbledon again and Hull which brought his distinguished career to a graceful conclusion. In the British League alone, he topped 4,000 points in eleven seasons.

As a world-wide ambassador, Briggs has achieved a huge reputation, acknowledged by the award of the M.B.E. for his services to the sport. If you ask him to recall his happiest memories apart from the obvious examples in world championships and the international arena, Barry inclines towards the British League Riders Finals at Belle Vue. For the first six years of that tournament, he won the title, but, more than that, loved it all because it was 'real racing'.

That summarises the philosophy of enthusiastic enjoyment, as sharply defined when he became speedway's first tax exile as was the case when the 17-year-old newcomer without a penny in his pocket graced the Wimbledon ranks in a pair of home-stitched, cardboard-padded leathers!

Those were happy-go-lucky times for young riders. But the 'big four' of Moore, Craven, Fundin and Briggs collared so many of the major prizes for such a time span that many newcomers experienced difficulty in translating exciting potential into real achievement.

Nevertheless, new faces kept popping up, with a continued emphasis upon youth. South African 17-year-old Doug Davies (Birmingham) qualified for the 1955 World Final, only to have the misfortune to be struck down by meningitis a few days before the event. His chance came the following year, when Nigel Boocock, 18, from Bradford, was a reserve.

It was a few years before Boocock made a sustained impact as one of the most whole-hearted and durable of English riders. After Waterman, Crutcher, Forrest and their like, Ron How – yet another of the increasingly imposing Wimbledon side – emerged as the most likely-looking of the home prospects.

As a Harringay representative, he had made an inauspicious World Final debut in 1952, when he failed to score. Between 1957 and 1964, however, How qualified for every World Final, though injury ruled him out of the 1960 meeting.

So often How looked a class performer in domestic competition, and he was an England regular for several years. Somehow, he never quite managed to better the stars in the sport's premier individual event, double figures in his last such appearance being the high point. In the same year he helped Oxford to a National League clean sweep.

In 1965, while riding for England against the U.S.S.R. at Plough Lane, the Buckinghamshire publican-cum-farmer had his throttle jam open. How crashed into the safety fence, and never rode again.

Red-leathered Mike Broadbanks, a Rye House and Wembley discovery, later a key member of Swindon teams which won championship honours in 1957 and 1967, was another all-action, colourful servant of the England cause.

One of the most-capped internationals was Ken McKinlay, the tartan trier from Lanarkshire. He began with Glasgow White City, before distinguishing himself at Leicester, Coventry, and West Ham, where he captained the team which won the inaugural British League championship.

Including 26 appearances for Scotland, in which he totalled 263 points, John Robert Viccars McKinlay had over 100 Test match outings. Seven times a tourist to Australia, he scored 291 points in 34 internationals there, and his contributions were an important factor in the revival of the oldest of Test series.

In 1958, he collected 158 points in 14 internationals, a domestic record at the time. Hurri-Ken also emerged as the most regular of the home-bred World Final qualifiers; a reserve in 1955, he embarked upon a sequence of appearances which brought him 66 points in eight actual meetings.

Closest McKinlay came to a rostrum placing was in 1958, when he fell in a third place run-off in which old stager Aub Lawson beat Peter Craven. The small, neat, fast-starting Scot shared with Bob Andrews the rare distinction of achieving a double figure score in a first full World Final appearance.

Andrews, latest off the Wimbledon stockpile, saved his greatest day until 1969. By that time he was riding for New Zealand, where he had emigrated. In partnership with Ivan Mauger he became a surprised and delighted World Best Pairs champion in Stockholm's baroque stadium.

From Fundin on, the Swedes had begun to develop outstanding all-round strength and looked to have chances of producing another champion or two. But for a maverick nature which diverted his attention into some extraneous pursuits, including T.T. racing and Formula II motor racing, Olle Nygren must surely have carved out a greater slice in the record books.

Nygren, given a testimonial in 1976 when he completed thirty years in speedway, had been the first Swedish rider in British racing, at Harringay way back in 1951. Later he took his total of clubs to ten, most notable among them being Norwich and Wimbledon.

In Sweden, the title of 'Varg-Olle' said it all, for his association with the Vargarna club in Norrköping extended through most of this incredible career. Such an accomplished all-rounder, Nygren claimed 54 points in just five World Final appearances, and was third in 1954. Half a dozen years later, he scored a maximum in the first World Cup.

There is hardly a speedway nation in which he has not featured while clocking up over 100 international appearances. Now renowned as a tutor, married to an English girl and living in

Norfolk, the still sprightly veteran is uniquely qualified to pass on excerpts from the knowledge accumulated through a lifetime of adventure and rich experience.

Rune Sörmander, never too much of a success in England, still qualified for seven World Finals and was an international regular for many seasons. PeO Söderman and Arne Carlsson also impressed as candidates for the big time, but failed to make their Scandinavian reputation count for a great deal elsewhere.

It was in 1961 that the 'big four' became the 'big five' with the arrival at the top of the class of Bjorn Knutsson, from Norrkoping. After taking a chance on him a couple of years earlier, Southampton quickly discovered that it was one of the happiest signings they could have made.

On his World Final debut in Malmö, the youngster was consistently faster and more dashing than the rest and really should have taken the title. Unfortunately, he contrived to crash in his vital meeting with Fundin, whom he had relieved of the British Match Race Golden Helmet only a few days earlier.

In overall terms, Knutsson was the outstanding rider of the year. He earned more points in all competitions than any other and it was clear enough that here was a world champion in the making.

Though Fundin was the obvious example in international events, even his supremacy was being seriously threatened. In Britain, the combination of Knutsson with Briggs helped Southampton to develop as a major force and their combined efforts were all-important in the 1962 National League success, when at last Wimbledon's sequence of championship successes was halted.

In 1964, following the closure of Southampton, the Swedish star switched to West Ham and was as all-powerful as the likes of Wilkinson and Young had been before him.

Ironically, it was not until the following year that Knutsson at last fulfilled his ambition of winning the world crown, despite finding himself and the rest of the commuters banned from the first season of the new British League.

The following year, when machine troubles left him short of double figures for the first time in six World Finals, was also his last in the big time. His business enterprises claimed an increasing amount of his time and energy. But for this, Björn, who was four years younger than any of his superstar contemporaries, would surely have gone on to more heights.

It can only be a matter of debate, but the evidence does suggest that he would probably have added further individual honours. And in the World Team Cup, he was as consistent as anybody, with 70 points in seven finals, though in each of his last four such appearances a maximum always eluded him by a single point.

The dashing and debonair Göte Nordin stepped forward as a candidate for top honours. A third place in Malmö in 1961 signalled his quality, and in due course he delighted and dazzled British fans at Wimbledon, Newport, Poole and elsewhere.

Victory in the Internationale in 1966 and 1967 underlined just how much class Nordin had. Ill fortune dogged him in world championship events, though. On several occasions he was strongly fancied to emulate the title winning exploits of Fundin and Knutsson only to miss out.

Arne Pander, first Danish rider to make a post-war impact in Britain, was even more unlucky. Pander, associated with Oxford for a number of productive years, enjoyed a big reputation on the continent and lived up to it in National League action but, remarkably, did not once get through to the World Final.

Other Scandinavian countries were inspired by the Swedish influence, and Norway signalled intentions of challenging their tradition for monopolising the supply of front rank talent.

Henry (Stompa) Andersen won the European Final in 1955 on his way to a Wembley debut and the lively Aage Hansen was another promising prospect from Norway.

Then along came Sverre Harrfeldt, the outstanding product from the land of the fjords. Wimbledon signed him in 1963 as a replacement for the injured Ronnie Moore, and later in the same season the 26-year-old former long track racer from Oslo was building an impressive pedigree.

The Russians are coming! Igor Plechanov, **left**, *and Boris Samorodov,* **right.**

He narrowly missed victory in the Internationale, won in controversial circumstances by Fundin, and then collected ten points on his World Final debut.

In 1966, Harrfeldt, now a West Ham favourite renowned for his sweeping dashes which took him on the longest but most successful route round the big Custom House circuit, came closer still to a world crown. In Gothenburg, he was runner-up to Briggs, the only rider to head him all night.

Those who thrilled to his all-action exploits in this period will confirm that his limited taste of world competition did not do justice to a fine, sporting competitor, who survived a horrific European Final crash in Poland in 1968 and wrapped up his British career in some style at Wembley.

Though muted by comparison with its halcyon days, the colonial influence did extend beyond Moore and Briggs. The New Zealanders actually claimed their first World Final top three placing through Mardon in 1953, and erstwhile Belle Vue skipper Ron Johnston was a rider highly respected by his fellows and much under-rated by the catalogue of statistical records by historical collectors.

Australia had as a successor to Lawson and Young a sinewy, blond-haired youngster from Melbourne, Peter (Piccolo) Moore by name. Wimbledon (yes, again) plucked him from the obscurity of unfashionable Long Eaton, and turned him into a National League star.

Moore made five World Final appearances. Fourth place with 12 points in 1960 was the outstanding moment for this fast-starting, shrewd tactician who enjoyed his peak years in the days when Ipswich boasted a pacey 440 yard track.

Lovers of big, fast circuits from Eastern Europe were the Poles, who produced names of the stamp of Florian Kapala, Mike Polukard and Marian Kaiser to whet the appetite of western observers.

And the Russians, late starters maybe, looked to have plenty to offer. Igor Plechanov was their first trail blazer, a cheery, throttle-blipping extrovert who made the first of half a dozen World Final appearances in 1961.

He captained a series of tremendously popular Soviet touring teams and helped himself to second position in two world championships. His dash to overhaul Fundin in the run-off for second place at Gothenburg in 1964 was one of the sport's most breathtaking moments.

Boris Samorodov, with 11 at Wembley in 1963 and the same again a year later, also gave the established order plenty to think about.

The developing pace of the youngsters, Gennady Kurilenko in particular, boded well for the future. Suddenly, there seemed to be a very real suggestion that membership of the newly-formed British League, even widespread experience of speedway in the western world, was by no means a pre-requisite for success at the top flight.

As events of the next decade were to demonstrate, such prognostications proved to be well off the mark.

SCULT OF THE SUPERSTAR

The latest decade of speedway racing has witnessed the development of the cult of the superstar. A handful of the old stagers had enjoyed some sort of stature in their own time, and big names, unforgettable personalities oozing skill and outstanding accomplishment, contributed to the rich fabric of those early years. Yet none of them developed to such a fine art the high speed, jet-setting, race in any continent on any day of the week routine of the stars of the seventies.

International frontiers have been pushed back by the ease of travel, and top riders can often command appearance fees of mouth-watering proportions. Thus no rider is limited to the number of meetings he can do, other than by the number of days in the week. And a booming continental set-up offers plenty of racing and earning opportunity if British League commitments are slack.

Small wonder, then, that the riders in greatest demand can earn at something better than prime ministerial rates, and will not have to fret too much to pay the mortgage even if home is a six-bedroomed mini-mansion set in a select acre or two. You can almost guarantee that the car outside the front porch will be something exotic, a Mercedes or a BMW perhaps.

Manners rather than the trappings of success still maketh man. But nobody will begrudge the improvement in life style and image of the leading riders. Any top performer in the field of entertainment is entitled to ask for the going rate for the job. And the clean-cut, elegantly tailored speedway stars can rub expensive shoulders with sporting colleagues, media people, and folk from every facet of life without being thought of as anything but first-class citizens.

Not that it is easy to achieve such a position of eminence. It is, as it has always been, hard work. Plenty aspire to the heights, and plenty fail to make it. Speedway racing has always been a hard business, the competition tough. For all that veneer of fun and games, it's as demanding and punishing as any other professional sport.

Ivan Mauger has demonstrated that, if you try hard enough, all things are possible. His has been a schedule of determination, hard work, resolute application and preparation down to the last, most minute detail. He has epitomised the very word 'professionalism'.

Descended from an Anglo/French family which emigrated from the Channel Islands in the last century, Mauger grew up in Christchurch, New Zealand, at the time Ronnie Moore and Barry Briggs were starting to make the speedway world sit up and take notice. In this pair and in Ove Fundin, surely the greatest of their contemporaries, Ivan had men who provided the ideal example and inspiration.

Today, there are experts who are ready to claim Mauger as the most successful speedway rider there has been. Certainly, he must qualify as one of the most travelled. Without doubt he has been amongst the most handsomely rewarded. Sponsorship and racing contracts all round the globe have made Mauger a rich man who has helped the sport to haul itself out of the somewhat impoverished image which attended its difficult years of the late 1950's and mid 1960's.

Incredible as it now seems, though on reflection it may well be significant, Mauger was a child of those slump years. He arrived in

England as a 17-year-old hopeful in 1957, eager to emulate the performances of his illustrious Kiwi predecessors, but apparently ill-equipped to do so.

After a couple of years, he returned to the southern hemisphere to re-think and learn the trade. When Mauger came back, to Provincial League Newcastle in 1963, he had developed a new cutting edge. The formation of the British League a couple of seasons later provided Ivan with the platform from which to prove to the doubters that his experiences had been beneficial.

Where better to prove the point than in the world championship? In 1966, Mauger won the European Final, and qualified for a World Final for the first time. He finished fourth in Sweden, third at Wembley a year later, and in 1968 embarked upon a ten-year cycle of devastating triumph which was to bring him five titles.

His first win in Gothenburg was smooth and stylish and his next, at Wembley in 1969, no surprise. Yet Mauger rated his third success, in Wroclaw, Poland, even higher. The Eastern Europeans, and the Poles in particular, had given the visiting British a few knocks – none more so than a World Team Cup walloping on this very track four years earlier – so to actually succeed in Poland was sweet and significant.

He equalled Briggo's record of four titles in 1972, and in 1977, a month short of his 38th birthday, showed that he was still far from finished with winning. That victory in Gothenburg put Mauger up alongside Fundin and owed much to the ice-cool temperament for which he had become renowned.

Generally believed to be a declining force, he had struggled through to the Final with some difficulty. But in the traditional slush and mud of Ullevi, he hung on, and arrived at his last race as the outsider. Ole Olsen and 18-year-old Michael Lee were also in with a chance and it looked as if Ivan was going to have to settle for third place.

But heat 18 was smothered in drama, with race leader John Boulger and Olsen both falling. After much delay and another false start, Mauger jetted from the tapes to win the re-run. His normally placid exterior cracked as he emotionally thrust five fingers to the night sky – perhaps just a couple of them for the numerous critics who had written him off.

Below: *The galloping Ivan Mauger – the epitome of professionalism.*

Above: *Ole Olsen, telling how it is after winning the 1975 World Final.*

Below: *Antoni Woryna, such polish from Poland.*

Anybody with a record like his can stand the criticism, just as Fundin always could. In fact Mauger, M.B.E., has under-scored his versatility with a couple of world 1,000 metres long track titles, World Best Pairs wins with Bob Andrews and Ronnie Moore, four European titles, three Internationale successes, a couple of British League Riders Final wins and a League record which more or less surpasses description.

From 1968 to 1972, he topped the First Division averages, a position he repeated in 1975. In each of the intervening years Ivan was no lower than second. Rather more than that, he was the inspiration as Belle Vue became the first side to win three successive British League championships, and after a much-publicised transfer to Exeter in 1973, was similarly influential and transformed a previously unfashionable club into one of championship pedigree within a year.

Hull paid £12,000 and agreed a fat three-year contract to capture him in 1978, and will doubtless be hoping for similar things to happen. So much respected by other riders, Mauger has not always appealed to the fans and even some of his best friends would describe him as aloof. There are some promoters whose kindliest comment about the man is that he is expensive.

There was never any danger that, having made his mark, Mauger would go the way of some of the old-timers, whose ability to earn was not matched by the acumen to hold on to their pickings. But if he has lacked some of their charismatic charm, Mauger has set new standards, a pinnacle of excellence which defies challenge in the immediate future.

Nevertheless, his example has been an inspiration to several other would-be superstars, who on their day have had the measure and even the beating of Ivan. All have learned that similar drive and dedication can bring its own rewards, and Ole Olsen is an illustration of such a rider with the ability to make significant inroads into the record books.

Mauger was for a while Svengali to Olsen, and took him under his wing at Newcastle. The pupil learned so well that he became a phenomenally successful performer, and over the last few years the Dane has been the closest of Ivan's challengers. During the 1970's Olsen, far and away the finest rider his country has produced, can point to World Final victories of undeniable excellence in 1971 and 1975, both times with a maximum. His 73 points in seven championship appearances is only a decimal point or two behind Mauger's own incredible striking rate of 154 in twelve.

Coming from one of speedway's minor nations, Olsen has not enjoyed the same number of other international opportunities. But he too has won the long track championship and his 1977 British Riders Final win was his third at Belle Vue. His exploits and initiative have coincided with a considerable upsurge in Denmark.

In half-a-dozen years as a Wolverhampton rider, Olsen broke virtually all of their scoring records, before a big transfer deal took him to Coventry, a track whom he had hankered to represent for some time.

Olsen is one of those aggressive, exciting personalities the very mention of whose name draws crowds by the thousand. Though not without his skirmishes with officialdom, he is held in world-wide high regard.

If the 1977 world championship had been decided over a series of meetings, a method he has championed in preference to the time-honoured one-off system, he would probably have won the title by a mile. As it was, his catalogue of individual successes in the year included victory in the Grand Prix – even though he had missed one of the qualifying rounds.

Can Olsen make up the leeway and join the greats such as Mauger, Fundin and Briggs in the world championship catalogue of fame? No matter what direction top flight international speedway takes, Ole has talked of quitting the British League scene within another year or two, and that would probably impair his chances.

Nevertheless, he is a racer of very special ability, the sort of talent which comes along only at intervals. The road to super-stardom is a rocky one, and for the British, the search for a top performer to succeed Peter Craven turned out to be an especially tortuous and difficult business.

Nigel Boocock, for an incredible 18 years the idol of Coventry fans, was perhaps the best beloved and most durable England international during this time. Nigel wore the Great Britain body colour 54 times, represented England on 51 occasions and was capped 59 times as a British Lions tourist.

Left: *Steady Eddie (Edward Jancarz).*

The blue-leathered Yorkshireman enjoyed some of his most productive series against the Russians, hard but eternally optimistic opponents who mirrored Booey's own attitude. Australian crowds found nothing effete about this nuggety Tyke who shrugged off a lifetime's bumps and bangs as if they were nothing.

He scored his 1000th Test match point in Australia, where the most prolific series of the eight he undertook yielded 88 points from seven matches in 1970–71. It was the best performance by a visitor since Jack Parker 20 years before.

Nigel collected over 400 League and Cup points in each of the first five years of the British League, and piloted his Bees to the title in 1968. The following summer, ten points in the World Final at Wembley earned fourth place, which constituted the best of his eight appearances, plus a couple as non-riding reserve.

A spirited battler after the old school, Boocock was the first Englishman to win the F.I.M. Internationale, and could always be relied upon to fly the flag. But there was a younger brigade on the march and eager to make a contribution.

Nigel's kid brother Eric stimulated Halifax, whose re-opening coincided with the start of the British League. A year later, the Dukes were champions and Boocock junior was a tower of consistent scoring strength.

When England teams came to be selected, Eric was always there or thereabouts. He had pace, polish and was more technically gifted than Nigel. At home and abroad, there was this reassuring adaptability about him. Somehow, though, the major awards eluded Eric.

Then, in 1974, his efforts received an overdue reward, and he became British Champion. Injuries were a factor which influenced a premature retirement all too soon afterwards, and the following year Eric took over as manager of Belle Vue.

It was Ray Wilson who emerged as the rider most likely and most determined to restore the stock and reputation of the English. In 1971, he split Mauger and Olsen at the top of the First Division averages, finished a creditable fourth in the World Final, and became the first Englishman to score a maximum in the World Team Cup – in Wroclaw, of all improbable places.

Right: *Extrovert Zenon Plech.*

The following year, Wilson and Terry Betts lifted the World Best Pairs title in Boras, Sweden. It was not the individual title for which the faithful fans had been waiting for years, but at least it was a taste of the big time.

In 1973, Wilson became the first Englishman since Jack Parker 26 years before to collect the British title. Colonials had monopolised the competition in between times.

And he struck another blow in the international arena by leading England to the Daily Mirror International Tournament and then headed an all-English team which won the World Team Cup.

A rock at Leicester, where he was to all intents and purposes the local boy made good – though born in Surrey, he had moved to the midlands city while still in short trousers – Wilson was a lion heart for club and country.

Betts and Martin Ashby were soldiers of similar durability. The fair-haired Betts, a sunny personality who must rank as one of the most popular of riders, waited a dozen years before leading King's Lynn to their first national honour, the K.O. Cup in 1977.

Ashby's reward for providing Barry Briggs and Mike Broadbanks with the support necessary to earn Swindon the 1967 British League title was to be posted off to Exeter for three years by Rider Control, the sport's latter-day Robin Hood committee.

Both could point to international records of some substance, with close on 100 Test appearances. Betts achieved the rare distinction of scoring a maximum against all of the major speedway nations.

Trevor Hedge (Wimbledon) was like Betts a one-time Norwich discovery who became a ten-year club servant elsewhere. He also had sufficient quality to have won the Internationale in 1969. Yet for no particularly good reason, each of this talented trio managed just one World Final appearance apiece. The prospect of an English world champion seemed as remote as ever.

Suddenly, in 1972, John Louis, a 31-year-old former scrambles rider, in his first season of senior track racing with Ipswich, his home town team, battled through to the World Final – and finished fourth at the first attempt.

In 1975, he did even better, beating Mauger in a run-off for third place. For the first time in 13 years, England had produced a rider on the World Final rostrum.

It is one of the modern imponderables as to whether Louis might have made an even greater impact but for spending the first half of his motor-cycling life as a moto cross rider. Gutsy, ebullient, and enthusiastic, he was quickly nicknamed 'Tiger' and dressed in matching gold and black. The man learned so quickly, and emerged to play the key role in an Ipswich team which won two successive British League titles, the latter as part of a 'double' in 1976.

Louis has featured in three of England's World Team Cup wins and scored a maximum in Wroclaw. He was also the dominant partner with Malcolm Simmons in Eskilstuna when the World Best Pairs title was won. His appetite for international success was at a peak when he scored 84 points and three bonus from a possible 90 in five Test matches against Sweden in 1975.

But if Louis came too late upon the speedway scene, Peter Collins got his timing absolutely right. A former grass track discovery, this disarmingly modest lad from Lymm, Cheshire, was one of Dent Oliver's prize pupils at the Belle Vue training school. From the start, it was clear that Peter had everything.

The habit of World Final qualification came easily to him, and in 1976, his ambition of winning the championship was realised. It was a decisive, positive display, wholly in keeping with the dashing style which had already earned him the tag of his country's best in more than a decade. At a time when slick tracks, quick machinery and improving standards all round were a feature of the sport, Peter seemed capable of beating anybody and everybody, from the back as well as on those seemingly rare occasions when he made the gate.

By this time, Collins had already piled up a stack of achievements. The youngest rider to make 50 Test appearances, he reached this landmark during 1975, a year in which 14 internationals yielded 186 points and 14 bonus, far and away a new English record. In the previous winter in Australia, he collected 97 points from seven matches.[1]

Above: *Peter Collins, savouring the sensation of his first world title.*

[1] In the 1977–78 series in Australia, Collins scored 108 points . . . just three short of Jack Parker's 1950–51 record.

He had really begun to come to the fore a couple of seasons earlier, as a 19-year-old. When England and Sweden drew in the International Tournament Final it was Collins, on his Wembley debut, whom team manager Len Silver nominated to face the much more experienced Anders Michanek in the decisive run-off. And he again showed his liking for Wembley a few weeks later, breaking the track record on his way to a maximum in the World Team Cup Final.

Peter rounded off that year with a remarkable victory over Michanek which brought the Speedway Star K.O. Cup to Belle Vue. After 26 races had failed to separate the Aces from Reading, a run-off was ordered and Collins, with his throttle and clutch at the left hand as his right wrist was broken and encased in plaster, produced another breathtaking solo show.

In 1974, he won the European Final, beating Mauger and Olsen in a run-off at Wembley. But Peter missed the starts so consistently in Gothenburg that even his talents could not compensate. Still, he had another World Team Cup maximum, and a British League average of more than 11 points indicated that he was on his way. Victory in the B.L.R.C. at Hyde Road rounded off the year with a timely message to his rivals.

Sentimentally, he was reckoned to be the outstanding hope for the next Wembley Final. But despite all expectations, it was anything but third time lucky for Collins. He won his first two races in the manner to which Wembley watchers had become accustomed. An impromptu watering session which failed to lay the rising dust also caused the first turn to take on the texture of a skating rink. P.C., on the outside grid, found himself filled in, and the shadows of Michanek and Mauger were no longer there for the chasing. Olsen rode unchallenged to the title.

This was the first major setback Collins had suffered. There was a hint of a crack in that normally unflappable, easy-going exterior. His helter-skelter charge to the top of the speedway world had not bargained for such an acute disappointment, which is how it seemed at the time; another B.L.R.C. victory and the inevitable 12 points in the World Team Cup Final provided scant consolation.

The only possible salve to Peter's hurt feelings was the ultimate prize – the world title. On September 5, 1976, at Katowice (scene of his championship debut three years earlier) Collins at last ruled the world with a typically gritty winning show.

In a wholly memorable year, he was the outstanding rider. He won the Inter-Continental Final, the Daily Mirror Grand Prix and a fistful of other titles along the way. Later he was to receive the unique accolade of the Segrave Trophy, a motor sport award without parallel – the first speedway racer thus honoured.

Daring, athletic and the biggest drawcard in the business, Peter looked a clear-cut favourite to retain his title. But a freak accident, half-a-dozen days before Gothenburg 1977 made all the difference. A cracked and badly gashed leg caused him excruciating pain. Although he defied medical opinion and maybe even common sense to score 13 points, thanks largely to the most inspired starting of his career, it was not quite enough.

Yet already, Collins has acquired sufficient reputation to convince all and sundry that he has it within his grasp to go on to challenge the likes of Ivan, Ove and all of the all-time great ones. He just loves to race, has tremendous natural ability, and even in these increasingly competitive times, has the knack of being able to beat the world's best from the back.

Is it indicative of the changing times and swing in international supremacy that once again the English are coming to expect to see its top riders challenge the world? Malcolm Simmons, always so talented but such a late developer, grabbed runner-up spot behind Collins in Poland, and had a share in the World Best Pairs crown with him in 1977, the second year running in which he had climbed the winner's rostrum in the competition.

Simmons, former grass tracker from the Medway towns in Kent, had spells with Hackney, West Ham and King's Lynn before a move to Poole coincided with the best form of his career.

Who is to say that Michael Lee, at 18 the youngest to win the British title and fourth in his World Final debut, cannot add to the ever-growing reputation of the English? On his King's Lynn debut, ten days out of school, he beat the then England skipper Ray Wilson from the back and his precocious talents have matured excitingly since then.

Lee looks to be at the head of another coming wave of home-bred talent, in which the Reading and England pair of Dave Jessup and John Davis and Gordon Kennett, captain of 1977 champions White City, may also prove to be front runners.

All of this has tended to deflect attention from the overseas riders, who in another era might have been expected to dominate the British scene which had so welcomed them for so long. As a source of additional colour and interest, the Swedes were massively significant contributors for a long while. Optimistic promoters, ever eager to unearth another Fundin or Knutsson, were usually prepared to chance their arm on an unknown with the potential to become a big name in double quick time.

Diminutive Sören Sjösten, who embarked upon a long and fruitful association with Belle Vue in 1962, twice aspired to the heights of a place on the World Final rostrum but got no further. Never better than when he won the British/Nordic title at Coventry in 1970, he seemed destined to be cast in the role of entertainer rather than championship winner.

For years, Sjösten rated as one of the most spectacular riders in the business. He helped Belle Vue to their three successive British League championships, and it was on his hallowed and favourite Hyde Road circuit that he helped Anders Michanek to lift the 1974 World Pairs crown.

It was in the same year, when the majority of his fellow countrymen were outlawed from the British League – Sjösten stayed as he was married to an English girl – that he produced his most electrifying form in the international arena. Highlight was his performance in a Test series against England, when he carried a largely inexperienced side almost single-handed.

As Swedish reputation in the late 1960's suggested a continuation of the strength of the preceding decade, Bengt Jansson emerged as another candidate for the top flight. When he narrowly lost the 1967 world title to old maestro Fundin, it seemed to be only a matter of time before Jansson took over the mantle of greatness.

Above: *Tommy Jansson, for whom the Swedes had such high hopes.*

A superbly balanced stylist with a most adroit racing brain, the ever-smiling 'Benga' rarely failed at the top level, but never again did he come so close to winning the world championship. His best times in England were with Hackney, whom he took to within a decimal place of a League championship and, later, two Cup Finals, one successful.

Slim, fair, eternally good-natured, Jansson was if anything too much of a nice guy. But few riders of his time displayed greater technical ability.

Bernie Persson was another who came desperately close to a world title – in 1972, he was beaten by Mauger in a run-off at Wembley after both had scored 13 points. Spotted by the then Edinburgh boss Ian Hoskins – son of the redoubtable Johnnie – Persson became a big favourite in Scotland before moving down to serve Cradley with distinction.

Solid consistency was his forte, and SVEMO officials long nursed the hope that Bernie might produce that something extra, that spark of inspiration necessary to conquer the greatest heights.

Hasse Holmqvist was a big, strong, flamboyant discovery whose devil-may-care talents promised plenty but ultimately disappointed, and Törbjorn Harrysson, tiny, brisk, perky and so good to watch, certainly never lacked panache.

Harrysson, from the Baltic island of Gotland, emerged from nowhere and was the best-placed Swedish rider in Gothenburg in 1966. His World Final debut came at the end of his first full season. Serious injury sustained in the corresponding event three years later put an end to all that.

World champions need something more than consistency or dash. Anders Michanek eventually proved to be the man who supplied that extra ingredient. Although associated with a variety of British tracks since 1967, and a member of the Reading team which won the League title in 1973, it was not until the following year, when he missed the commuting routine, that Anders finally topped the world.

If only he could have persuaded himself of his ability to be a winner, instead of adopting the mantle of 'always the bridesmaid', it could have happened that much earlier. Anders displayed splendid consistency in the Swedish League and its British counterpart. At international level, too, he was the man who could always be relied upon.

The spark which separates the good from the outstanding had been in evidence for a while. Michanek always could look after himself in tough situations. And yet his World Final triumph, when it came, caught some people by surprise.

Anders was nudging 31, after all, hadn't contested the English season, and thus seemed to lack the sharpness of many more favoured candidates. He had gone to Katowice 12 months earlier as one of the all-time hot favourites, and blew it. Was his chance gone?

In the event, he was a comprehensive 1974 winner in Gothenburg, slashing huge chunks out of the track record – in spite of the traditionally wet conditions – and at the same time giving the new ERM four-valver a glittering advertisement. In analysis, he reckoned that it was most significant that the pressure had been off at last. He had had time to be a family man and, at times, a gentleman of comparative leisure.

When Anders said that he could do without the helter-skelter existence of the commuter, he genuinely meant it. That was a major symptom of the big man's eventual disappearance from the British scene.

His record, nevertheless, bears scrutiny. Twice with Tommy Jansson, once with Sjösten, he won the World Best Pairs title. Add to this a European title, Swedish championship, and seven years in which his British League average was well into double figures. His international scoring rate was second only to Fundin, and never better than when Sweden undertook an inaugural tour to Australia where he revelled in the big tracks.

Michanek put together ten World Final appearances, including one as reserve, which yielded 89 points. Only five riders have bettered that. In the World Team Cup, invariably a speciality, ten outings produced 81 points, second only to Ove (83). And for good measure, Anders won the 1977 long track title.

Christer Löfqvist, a carbon copy of Harrysson, was a flamboyant but ill-fated arrival. West Ham introduced him to British League racing and after their demise, he switched to Poole with whom he made it to his first World Final in 1972, scoring 11 points.

Unfortunately, the little fellow from Visby, son of a former racer who lost his life in a track accident, died in 1978 at the age of 33, following a long illness.

Tommy Jansson, almost ten years younger, also died prematurely. On May 21, 1976, he was killed instantly in a Stockholm track crash which threw a great pall of gloom over the whole of Swedish speedway and sorrowed many others around the world.

Tommy had the dash and verve to become one of the great names. That much was evident from the first time he rode at the picturesque Eskilstuna track, managed by Joel Jansson, his ex-international father. Wimbledon offered Jansson the opportunity to take on the role of their top man, and past incumbents such as Ronnie Moore and Barry Briggs had every confidence in the youngster's ability to emulate their efforts.

A clean-cut, good-looking boy with so much to offer, Tommy had tasted success early. He was national junior champion at 17, a World Final qualifier the following year, World Best Pairs champion before he was 21, Swedish champion a season later.

Tall, upright, so easy on a bike, he looked to be the natural successor to Michanek, a figurehead to inspire the latest brigade of emergent Swedish racers. In 45 international appearances, he had already hustled together 346 points, with 164 in 15 matches in the hectic summer of 1975.

His loss, cutting down the one world class prospect they had, may yet be seen to have put back Swedish speedway by a few years.

Whatever else happens, the other Scandinavian countries look to be catching up. Denmark, in particular, owe much to Olsen and his influence. With prospects such as Finn Thomsen, fifth on his World Final debut, they could take over from Sweden as the dominant international force in that part of the world.

The Norwegians have if anything gone back, especially after the very promising Dag Lovaas, their brightest prospect since Harrfeldt, surprisingly decided to retire at the age of 25.

There have been signs of more rapid development in Finland, from their elegant ambassador Matti Olin. An increasing number of their riders have been catching the eye in Britain, none more so than Ila Teromaa, whose first three years with Leicester stamped him as a world class hope.

Incidentally, there has been no better on-the-spot measure of progress amongst the young Europeans than the improvement of those who make an annual pilgrimage to training schools run by Olle Nygren. The veteran Swede, a trail-blazer for post-war continentals, now emerges as an equally important figure in his role of tutor.

Recruitment from Australia and New Zealand continues to appeal to British promoters, though. The promising youngster from Down Under can always try his luck first in the National League – still effectively the Second Division, whether its officers and afficionados admit it or not – whereas even our European Economic Community 'brothers' are denied access to that competition.

The New Zealand influence has diminished considerably. The Kiwis have had little joy in finding a possible successor to their world title-winning superstars. But the Australians, especially latterly, have been reviving.

Their situtation at the inception of the British League seemed to be promising. Droll Charlie Monk stepped out of the Provincial League shadows to win the 1965 Internationale, and rubbed shoulders with the top names for three or four years, without ever quite making the jump.

The voluble Garry Middleton hinted at big things but failed to live up to his own publicity and it was Jim Airey who ended a barren spell by becoming the first Australian to qualify for a World Final in eight years. That was in 1971.

The four-times national champion, almost invincible at Sydney Showground, captained Australia 25 times in his 41 international appearances, and in his own country alone Airey rattled up 313 points in 22 Test matches. However, he quit prematurely at the age of 30 and has concentrated on business.

John Boulger, from Adelaide, has proved to be much more of a stayer. Signed by Long Eaton in 1967 on the recommendation of Ray Wilson, he started with a paid maximum, then did not collect another full score for two years. Nevertheless, solid improvement brought him a succession of notable results including two national titles, victory in the first Australasian Final of the world championship, two World Final appearances, and many good years with Leicester.

Boulger has also a modern-day record of more than 70 international appearances for

Australia, often as skipper, and most notably in the 1976 World Team Cup Final which produced a first-time victory. With 111 points in seven Test matches against the 1972–73 Lions tourists, J.B. came closer to Aub Lawson's long-standing series record than any other rider.

With time on his side, Phil Crump, from Mildura, Victoria, could go even further. A Second Division Riders' Champion while with Crewe, he enjoyed three phenomenally successful seasons at Newport, and, with father-in-law Neil Street (himself a former international with 20 years or more of British racing experience) amply proved the qualities of the new SR4 four-valve conversion.

He scored 103 points in seven Test matches in 1974–75, collected double figures on his World Final debut a few months later, and in 1976 collected third place in Katowice. After another couple of weeks Crump, Boulger, and promising Sydney youngsters Billy Sanders and Phil Herne collected the World Team Cup for Australia.

That result, at London's re-opened White City, must have brought moisture to the eyes of many of the old-time pioneers as well as suggesting evidence of a national revival.

Even in its increasingly healthy state, British speedway may never be immune from the challenge of overseas nations, eager to get in on the act. And that includes Eastern Europe.

In view of the painstaking manner in which sports officials from behind the Iron Curtain pursue excellence, it is perhaps surprising that they have not made greater inroads into the modern speedway scene.

The latter-day Soviet riders have flattered to deceive. Despite good World Final placings for Gennadi Kurilenko, Vladimir Gordeev and Grigori Chlynovski, none have demonstrated the same sort of dash as that of predecessors Plechanov and Samorodov. Closest suggestion of such calibre came from Chlynovski, who displayed fine consistency on a 1974 visit to Britain which produced 65 points from five internationals and a sixth which was rained-off.

It was a huge blow for the Russians when Valeri Klementiev, the 1969 European champion from Tbilisi, Georgia, was killed while practising a couple of years later. This enthusiastic youngster had looked to have the qualities necessary to become an influential performer at the highest level.

Encouraged by their international displays, Poland nursed high hopes of starting the 1970's with their own world champion. The granting of the chance to stage a World Final in Wroclaw seemed to be the ideal opportunity.

Edward Jancarz, third in the 1968 championships, was out of the running because of injury; but stylish Antoni Woryna – third in Gothenburg in 1966 – and Pawel Waloszek, a track-crafty and vastly experienced campaigner, were both strongly fancied.

As things turned out, Mauger proved to be something of a spoilsport on the day. Waloszek was beaten only by Ivan and Woryna made the rostrum again, but it was not quite what the Poles had hoped for.

Three years elapsed, and then the Poles did have their own world champion, though hardly the one of their choosing. Jancarz was fit again for Katowice's first World Final and rapidly adding to his reputation as the most polished and technically gifted performer since Woryna at his prime. And the exciting new talents of Zenon Plech were about to be released upon western observers who were quite unprepared for such extrovert throttle-thrashing.

But both were up-staged (Plech had to settle for third place) as the 130,000 in the Slaski Stadium roared a salute to Jerzy Szczakiel, an unassuming 24-year-old whose only previous World Final appearance had failed to produce a point. This time, however, he confidently rattled up 13 points and in a decisive run-off against Mauger, kept his cool and won the most remarkable championship victory.

Szczakiel had previously partnered the sound and consistent Andrzej Wyglenda to the only maximum win ever achieved in a World Best Pairs Final, so his ability was not quite a one-off happening. Yet this was the biggest upset the World Final had known; one sensed a certain embarrassment from PZM officials and that in itself cannot have helped the fellow, who never showed the stomach or the

temperament for the role of world champion.

If nothing else, it was a demonstration that the predictable does not always happen. And his shock win must have given heart to the riders and statesmen of lesser speedway nations – the likes of the U.S.A., Czechoslovakia and West Germany were all renewing a bid for a place amongst the world rankings, with World Final qualifiers to emphasise the spread of internationalism.

Nobody showed greater potential than Egon Müller, the lightweight West German – first to qualify for world recognition since Josef Hofmeister's four Final appearances between 1957 and 1960.

Most of Müller's time is devoted to the lucrative long track scene, in which he has already claimed a couple of world titles. Yet he seems as plausible a candidate as any for future honours, and, in this era of the superstar, fully fits the part.

Club entertainer, pop singer, and a personality in his own right, Müller is dismissive about his own chances in the speedway world, but others are not so sure.

The extent of his future involvement in British speedway could be the key. For fifty years, this has been the world's most important stage. And there is no sign that this state of affairs is likely to change in the foreseeable future.

Above: *Michael Lee – at 18, the youngest British Champion, and fourth in his first World Final. Surely one for the not too distant future.*

JEUX SANS FRONTIERES

While most of the legendary names recorded and great deeds chronicled in these pages have emphasised the British connection, it would be unforgiveably insular to ignore development in other quarters of the world.

It is true to state that no other country has produced so many riders, mounted as many speedway promotions, or been responsible for a more comprehensive or enduring system of domestic competition.

Nevertheless, speedway enjoys a considerable place in the sporting consciousness of countries in both the northern and southern hemispheres. It has been staged with a varying degree of success in something like three dozen nations.

Australia, where it began to take off, has known plenty of ups and downs. Interest remains high at the major state centres, especially if there is a big national or even international event being staged. And as ever, a number of country tracks have enjoyed a fair measure of support.

The vast distances from one another has dictated the lack of team competition Down Under, though there was an attempt to introduce regular league racing in 1948, and a full-blown inter-state series a quarter of a century later.

But it takes hours to fly, and literally days by any other means of transport, to travel from the imposing Sydney Showground of fond memory to the 641 yard Claremont Speedway in Perth, Western Australia, proudly claimed by extrovert boss Con Migro to be 'the greatest show on earth'.

It is almost as far from Adelaide or Melbourne up to Brisbane. Thus, although there is regular interchange of riders between the different states, regionalised team competition has never really been a practical possibility.

The format of most meetings in recent years has seen to it that solo racing has had to take its place alongside speed or midget cars, stock car events and the sidecar fraternity. Usually the bikes share the programme, with major championships or Test matches providing the exception to that state of affairs.

Few pastimes are more popular than the time-honoured sport of 'Pommy-bashing' and when Test teams from the old country provide the opposition, the local wits are rarely short of repartee. But in general, the Aussie fan is happy to lounge on the grass bank clutching his can of lager and enjoying the spectacular talents of car colossus A. J. Foyt – it takes something like Crump v Collins to provide equal excitement when the solos appear.

Nevertheless, those international exchanges have probably done as much for the genuine speedway scene Down Under as any of the domestic competitions. Until the British Lions came back to a 35,000 crowd at Sydney in 1967–68, the same old mish-mash of scratch races and handicap events provided a pattern little changed from the earliest meetings of Hoskins, Hunting and company.

Not all of the punters favour the all-round form of entertainment on the same programme. The out-and-out speedway devotee regards himself as something of a purist, and it is a curious fact that it is more likely to be at one of the country circuits – some of them little more than training tracks in the bush – where the bikes hold exclusive sway.

Nevertheless, there have been some profitable hunting grounds for emergent talent in recent seasons, when Australia has nurtured hopes of regaining the position of eminence earned back in the halcyon days.

Those original superstars such as Frank Arthur, Vic Huxley, Max Grosskreutz, and world title winners Lionel Van Praag and Bluey Wilkinson set standards of brilliance which have been approached at times, but never bettered.

Jack Young, first man to win two successive world championships, was an outstanding post-war ambassador; Vic Duggan, Aub Lawson and Peter Moore were notable contributors to the story, and then came a barren period between 1961, when Ray Cresp was a World Final qualifier, until ten years later when Jim Airey finally broke into the top class.

But indications are that the new brigade of riders, such as Phil Crump and Billy Sanders, can help to re-vamp the Australian image and reputation. Since the F.I.M. granted the Aussies separate recognition in 1974, their international stock has improved, and for the first time, world championship qualifying rounds have been staged in the southern hemisphere.

Somewhat surprisingly, in view of their relative proximity, the New Zealanders have not had a great deal of contact with Australia. Yet those Rickety Rackety Isles have the distinction of providing three of the greatest riders the sport has known.

When Ivan Mauger won his fifth world crown in 1977, he equalled the all-time record of Ove Fundin (Sweden) and hauled himself one ahead of Barry Briggs, his illustrious Christchurch counterpart. And both are quick to acknowledge that Ronnie Moore, the world's number one in 1954 and 1959, was their inspiration.

Stewie St George, one of the 1928 pioneers, was the first New Zealand rider to cut a dash in England. The next to make an impact was Wally Kilmister, who won the 1936 national championship.

However, the free-lancing activities of British visitors such as Gil Craven, Norman Parker and Freddie Williams eased Kiwi speedway out of the shadows after the war. Their example enlivened many a domestic meeting and gave the locals something against which to measure their developing skills.

Trevor Redmond, jovial joker Bruce Abernethy, and Moore were leading members of the advance party in England, but those three world champions rightly belonged to an exclusive club. While Briggs and Mauger, in particular, raced relatively little in their own country in recent years, the example they set is bound to remain as an inspiration to all hopeful youngsters for generations to come.

In reality there are few tracks and fewer opportunities, but a handful of hard workers have kept the solo scene alert and alive. Like the Australians, the New Zealanders have begun to enjoy an increased amount of self-government, too.

Traditionally, their affairs were handled by

Below: *Australian speedway in the modern idiom as Jim Airey leads Sören Sjösten at Sydney Showground.*

Above: *They came from everywhere – New Zealand, for instance. This is Wally Kilmister.*

Below: *Good game? Andrzej Wyglenda (Poland).*

the Speedway Control Board in London, but this is no longer so. And not everybody today is completely scornful of suggestions that the world championship itself could be staged Down Under within the next few years.

Colonial riders had been included in British qualifying rounds from the outset right up until 1975, whereas now, in theory at least, a rider can qualify for an advanced stage of the tournament without having to travel half way across the world. The reality is that the World Final has not been taken out of Europe . . . yet.

Times do change. One day, perhaps, the teeming millions of the Far East may take to speedway. In recent times, there have been attempts to introduce the sport in Singapore. Barry Briggs has even sampled racing in Japan, whose two most notable travelling exponents have been Junicho (Jimmy) Ogisu, who appeared in the Internationale in 1970, and the lady rider Nanae Okomoto, who was quite a star turn on Australian tracks a few years earlier.

Even more recently, Australian riders have demonstrated their skills in Papua-New Guinea. First Pacific activity, though, was as far back as the 1920's, when the unforgettable Billy Galloway took a team to Fiji. The island's only subsequent mention was as the birthplace of Graham Warren, an Australian international of the post-war era.

In retrospect, it is surprising that the Americans did not exert more of an influence upon the development of the sport, especially after Eddie Brinck, Sprouts Elder and then the 1937 World Final place men Jack Milne, Wilbur Lamoreaux and Cordy Milne had shown such prowess.

The flavour of international speedway today can envisage no more dramatic influence than the revived, and increasing participation of the United States. The Americans have always been famed for their enthusiasm for bikes; there are those who argue that the origins of dirt-track racing owe as much to America as to Australia.

Despite the variety of motor cycle sport across that vast land, speedway, or short track racing as it is more widely known there, has only really flourished on the west coast. California before and after the war was its focal point.

A couple of American teams have toured England – the most recent was in 1951 – but for many years afterwards, there was little or no activity. Then Mauger and Briggs went out to conduct a series of training schools and interest was stimulated once again.

Soon, some lively local talent began to appear, notably the Bast brothers, Rick Woods, and Scott Autrey, who qualified for the 1976 World Final, the first American to get

Above left: *Jochen Dinse, first East German in the World Final, 1967.*

Above: *Czech pupil Jiri Stancl and master, Antonin Kasper.*

that far for a quarter of a century.

Now there is a thriving, albeit miniature league, based around Costa Mesa. A few meetings have been staged indoors, at Houston Astrodome for instance, which brought the sport to the attention of a new section of the American public. The prospects look interesting, to say the least.

To the north, in Canada, there is some scanty evidence of racing activity in the 1930's. Outstanding performers such as Eric Chitty and Jimmy Gibb had to seek their fame elsewhere, in the States at first, and then in England.

Toronto-born Chitty once sought recognition for England, on the grounds that his father hailed from Hammersmith and his mother had been born in Birmingham! He lost the argument. But he was a redoubtable performer, three times British wartime champion.

Below: *Valeri Klementiev, tragic young Soviet prospect.*

Attempts to organise speedway in Canada have met with little success, though there have been spasmodic promotions.

South of the border, down Argentina way, there was more activity, especially during the early days of the sport. The visit of a party organised by Sprouts Elder and including several leading riders of the day did attract some interest. Juan Salatino was the undisputed national champion for four years up to the war, but things did not progress.

Twenty years later, more adventurers from England participated in a pioneering visit to Venezuela. But the venture was an ill-advised, short-lived affair and its grandiose plans quickly collapsed.

The time may well be ripe for further attempts to popularise the sport in that part of the world. Road racing has captured the attention in some South American countries; the 1977 F.I.M. autumn congress was held in Caracas. There have even been rumours of a bid to stage speedway in Brazil.

Temperamentally, though, speedway has always lent itself more appropriately to a European stage. While the British were quick to appreciate the possibilities, many of their near neighbours (later to become political and economic partners) also had an opportunity to sample the sport in its formative years.

The old record books suggest that France was the first country to stage its own domestic championship. Charles Bellisent, the first winner, was still accomplished enough to lord it over his fellow countrymen two decades later, in 1948, while his son Pierre was described as a coming force.

In between times Fernand Meynier was a big name, well to the fore when events billed as a world championship and including star performers from across the English Channel took place in the early 1930's.

The post-war activity, encouraged by promoter Arthur Westwood, promised much but failed to progress. The Claude Boston troupe kept the flag flying but other branches of motor cycle sport, notably moto cross, have tended to command much more traditional appeal.

George Kay took over a Harringay team including Vic Duggan with a view to

Left: *The brothers: Valeri and Vladimir Gordeev.*

popularising speedway in Switzerland in 1949. The Swiss made a later start than their neighbours because of a post-war shortage of cinders. For one reason and another, they never did catch up, and interest faded.

Belgium was also staging a few meetings around this time, but things did not take off. But in Holland, there was some healthy action. Few did more to generate enthusiasm than Gerrit Kops, winner of his first Dutch title in 1938, and still going strong a quarter of a century later.

Jimmy Baxter can lay claim to providing the foundations of speedway in the Netherlands. He opened a track in Rotterdam in 1935, and one of the regular visitors in ensuing years was Stan Greatrex of New Cross.

But the Dutch riders, such as post-war stars Henk Steman and Tinus Metzelaar, kept themselves fully occupied on the continent. At least there was always a ready welcome for visitors, and annual Golden Helmet meetings featuring many invited foreign riders proved consistently popular.

There was a League in operation for a while, with Feyenoord Stadium attracting crowds which sometimes topped 50,000. Then interest waned, and it was not until recent times that Holland produced a rider of significant class in Henny Kroeze, a British League favourite with Halifax from 1974 to 1977.

Another contemporary performer with the ability to compete with the best in the world is Egon Müller, of West Germany. But for his involvement with long track racing, so popular on the continent, Müller could have conquered the stars on speedway.

World champion on the 1,000 metre tracks in 1974 and 1975, he qualified for the World Final in speedway in each of the next two years. Despite doing little more than flirt with the shale sport, blond-haired Müller, from Kiel, showed qualities compatible with regular performances at the highest level.

He may well go on to emulate the performance of Josef Hofmeister, who came to Wembley for four successive World Final appearances between 1957 and 1960 and performed with distinction in Poland, Sweden, Czechoslovakia and elsewhere.

Manfred Poschenreider dominated the next few years and he, too, possessed great ability and fine temperament. Barry Briggs, who raced against him often enough on the continent, declared that it would have been no

Above: *Racing in Leningrad – the 1970 European Final. From the left: Trevor Hedge, Viktor Kalmykov, Hans Jurgen Fritz, Ivan Mauger.*

Opposite: *Sverre Harrfeldt, the wonder Norse.*

trouble for Poschenreider to have become an equally big star in Britain.

The real step forward, though, has been the formation of a West German League, which is developing fast. While the competition is not yet of a particularly high standard, it may well provide a platform for the Germans to emerge as one of the coming nations of the future.

Yet speedway there can go back the best part of fifty years. Big crowds were reported in 1929, when Spencer (Smokey) Stratton, a livewire New Zealander, was a big favourite. So were Arthur Jervis and Ginger Lees, who held the Hamburg track record.

Max Grosskreutz and Dickie Case were among those who attempted to bring about a revival a few years later, but the locals did not show any great aptitude. Nevertheless, Gustav Kellner, Sebastian Roth and Alfred Rumrich all appeared in League racing in Britain before the war.

After 1945, tracks were quick to re-open, especially in the south, a traditional stronghold. Hermann Gunzenhauser, expert on big tracks or small, held sway and lost nothing by comparison with foreign visitors.

One such was Fritz Dirtl, a pioneer of modern activity in Austria. He still ranks as arguably the finest rider produced by that country, though the Speedway Riders Association refused him a work permit when a National League track tried to sign him in 1952.

The real architects of the sport in Austria were the Killmeyer brothers, Leopold (who rode for Plymouth in 1933) and Karl. At home and abroad, they regularly spread the speedway gospel for many years.

Josef Bossner sustained the same sort of effort for a long spell, both as a rider and administrator. Rewards have come in the last two or three years, with representation in the World Best Pairs Final and the first Austrian riders in British League action.

Italian speedway, far less prominent, was at its busiest at the end of the war, with Trieste a centre of some importance. British Army personnel were responsible for the opening of several tracks, but development was limited.

Further attempts to broaden the scope of racing were made in the 1960's, but it was not until 1976 that reigning champion Guiseppe Marzotto became the first Italian to sample British League racing. He did enough in a brief stint with Wolverhampton to suggest that given a similar opportunity ten years earlier, he could have been something of a trail blazer.

In its early days, King Alfonso of Spain was an avid speedway follower. Naturally enough, he did his bit in an attempt to introduce the sport to his own country, and tracks in Madrid, Barcelona and Seville were reported to be well up to standard.

A Spanish team, including the Poto brothers, the leading exponents, visited Wembley in 1930. Development was limited, however, and apart from a small revival almost twenty years later, little more was heard from this part of the world until Ian Hoskins (son of Johnnie) and former Wimbledon and England rider Reg Luckhurst took off to Majorca in 1972.

Their reasoning was impeccable. There was plenty of interest in motor cycle sport, fanned by the role played by Bultaco machinery. The ingredients of excitement and competition were there. Unfortunately for the promoters, the locals and tourists alike preferred the beaches to the speedway.

Egypt featured early in the annals of the sport, when a group of Australian and British riders tried their luck there in 1928. This didn't come to much, though there was some further activity, again involving British enthusiasts, at the end of the war and afterwards. There were circuits in Palestine and Aden, too.

Israel finds an entry, a much more recent one, for it was in 1975 that the World Champions Series, organised by Briggs and Mauger and featuring Fundin on one of his comebacks, staged a few meetings there.

To the north, there have been more regular rustles of activity from countries such as Bulgaria, Yugoslavia and Romania.

The Bulgarians have dabbled in World Team Cup qualifying rounds and in 1969, produced an entertaining and spectacular little cameo in the World Pairs Final. Peter Perko and Peter Iliev displayed antics on this occasion which persuaded even the phlegmatic Fundin, who must have seen it all in his time, to vacate his position at the back of the pits and watch their enthusiastic but generally unproductive efforts on the track.

Certainly the Pairs Finals, more than any

other event, have given world observers a glimpse of a few hitherto unknown names. While long track is the majority interest, Yugoslavia have thrown up some interesting customers, notably Stefan Kekec who has attracted the attention of British League promoters.

Of all the eastern European nations, though, none has a more distinguished pedigree than Poland. In 1947 the Polish Union of Motor Cyclists sent a representative to England to obtain first hand knowledge of the sport. A report was submitted and within a year, under the direction of the State Office for Physical Culture, five huge stadiums were constructed, together with several small tracks, and a nine-team league formed.

British JAP bikes were imported, riders from Czechoslovakia and Sweden hurried things along, and by 1949 Poland entered the international arena, and beat Holland 82–64 in Warsaw in the inaugural Test match.

Alfred Smoczyk, the first Polish champion, was a natural. Florian Kapala, only rider to win the national title four times, kept up the standards and in 1959, Mieczyslaw (Mike) Polukard was their first World Final qualifier. Since then, with one exception, Poland has always had at least one representative in the final stage of the championships.

A soundly organised League competition has provided a steady flow of talent. At times, bravery rather than technical expertise seemed to be the guiding factor, but three World Team Cup successes and a third place for Polish riders Antoni Woryna in the 1966 World Final, emulated two years later by debut maker Edward Jancarz, reinforced their claims to be allowed to stage the sport's premier event.

At Wroclaw in 1970, their ambitions in this direction were realised, and since then, there have been two World Final stagings at Katowice. The 1973 event not only attracted a 130,000 crowd but also provided the greatest shock in championship history. Poland had a winner for the first time, the unfancied Jerzy Szczakiel from Opole, who beat Ivan Mauger in a sensational run-off.

Spectacular youngster Zenon Plech and the stylish Jancarz, his Stal Gorzow team mate,

Opposite: *More brothers: Jan and Vaclav Verner.*

Left: *Egon Müller, darling of West German fans.*

have done much to uplift the stock of Polish speedway, as leading representatives in British League racing.

Overall standards had fallen back when four-valve machinery was introduced. The Poles, not for the first time in their history, were short of competitive bikes, but having surmounted that problem, they look to be back in business as an international force.

Czechoslovakia, where the Jawa machines are manufactured, are also on the up-grade. There was racing on the 1,000 metre trotting track at Marianske Lazne in 1924, and speedway in more conventional fashion in 1932, yet Czech history has been remarkably chequered.

The annual Golden Helmet stagings in Prague and Pardubice have attracted the cream of the world's riders for years, with Tommy Croombs (before the war) and Bill Kitchen (afterwards) among those who were popular visitors.

But despite the dominance of Hugo Rosak, they failed to produce men capable of challenging on foreign circuits until Lubos Tomicek, Antonin Kasper, and, latterly, the Verner trio.

Vaclav Verner and his younger brother Jan have shown their capabilities in Britain. In 1977, Jan Verner established a unique record by appearing in five world championship finals – speedway, long track, best pairs, World Team Cup, and ice-racing.

The Czechs have proved especially accomplished on the ice – Antonin Svab won the title in 1970, the first rider other than a Russian to do so. And young Milan Spinka, four years later, emulated this performance.

In pure speedway terms, though, Jiri Stancl is perhaps their most talented rider so far. Already he claims a fistful of national titles, and was only 21 when he first qualified for a World Final, in Sweden in 1971.

So often a chopping block in World Team Cup Finals down the years, Czechoslovakia have exciting new strength in much greater depth than before.

If there is one nation which has shown limitless potential, but failed to do more than scratch at the surface of real lasting success, it is the U.S.S.R. Their sportsmen have excelled in so many areas, and in moto cross alone have conjured up many world class riders.

Yet in spite of a great deal of enthusiasm and a full-blown League system, Russian speedway has not fulfilled its promise. Northern ace Clem Beckett – later to be killed fighting in the Spanish Civil War – took a tour party to the Soviet Union in 1932. But to all intents and purposes, there was no real speedway development there until 1959.

Then Czech and Polish riders were invited to help with the introduction of the sport. In next to no time, it was reported that there were twenty tracks in existence.

Igor Plechanov, Boris Samorodov, Leonid Drobjasko and Farid Szajnurov all rubbed shoulders with European counterparts with some success. Plechanov, whose cheery, hustling style endeared him to western fans, qualified for the World Final at Malmö in 1961, riding a Jawa/Eso. And his subsequent successes in international competition were outstanding, including runner-up spot in two successive World Finals.

Samorodov also put the cat among the pigeons at times, never more so than at

Wembley in 1963 when he was excluded from his first World Final ride after a clash with Ron How. The meeting was held up for some time and a major diplomatic incident looked to be on the cards! Eventually Boris was led away, protesting bitterly. The manner in which he blasted to 11 points from four remaining rides showed what might have been.

Gennadi Kurilenko and Vladimir, elder of the Gordeev brothers, also scored double figures in World Finals though Gordeev was subsequently banned for using a prohibited nitro additive.

Valeri Klementiev, the European champion in 1969, was a rider of infinite promise who met a premature death in a training accident a year later, just as he was promising to be a real successor to the old guard.

And hard-riding Grigori Chlynovski, had a 1973 experience at Katowice which was not altogether dissimilar to that which had befallen Samorodov ten years before. He suffered disqualification after apparently winning his final ride, which would have given him 13 points.

En route, however, he had tangled with Plech, and the multitudes roared their disapproval. It was after the longest hold-up of several which have littered world championships that Chlynovski was disqualified.

In international competition, the Soviet riders earned a reputation for their optimism and all-out effort. But they simply lacked the refinement necessary to conquer the world. The rough edges remained.

The tale of disappointment in Soviet speedway reached such a crossroads in 1977 that they were noticeable only for their absence from major events. Whether this is a time for complete re-appraisal, or the end of the road, remains to be seen.

But it is hard to believe that a nation of such dogged determination, a country indeed which had made overtures to stage a World Final, should withdraw from the scene. A re-vamped new brigade seems altogether more likely.

The Soviet centres stretch from Leningrad to Vladivostok and the opportunity for producing, training, and encouraging riders is there. In theory, nobody has a better

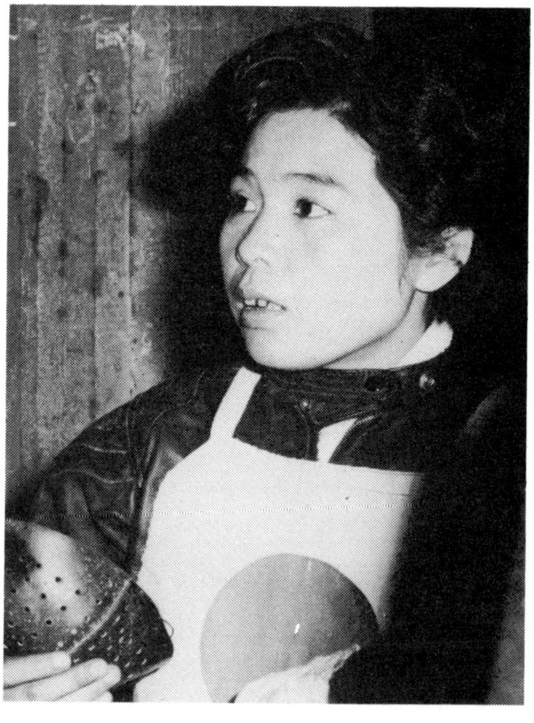

We are Japanese, if you please. Junicho (Jimmy) Ogisu, **right**, *and Nanae Okomoto,* **far right**.

chance of getting it right. If the U.S.S.R. controllers would concede that at the present, others know best, they could be taking the first step towards establishing themselves as a huge force in speedway racing.

One keeps expecting the East Germans to emerge, as well. They promised plenty in the 1960's, with Jochen Dinse qualifying for a World Final in 1967, followed four years later by the impressively athletic Hans Jurgen Fritz. Despite attempts to build up a league system, they have faded.

Hungary has featured one or two riders in international events, with Pal Perenyi and, more recently, Janos Szoeke, impressing observers. The most successful rider, however, was Sandor Levai, a former freedom fighter who fled to England after the 1956 uprising, and established himself as a character of considerable flair with a number of British League clubs.

Political history has played a part in restricting the contacts between several would-be speedway countries. And South Africa, once closely linked with Britain, has declined as a force in the speedway world since those other ties were cut.

Quite apart from those reports which make Pietermaritzburg in 1907 the claimed stage of the first-ever dirt-track meeting, there was plenty of activity there from 1928 onwards. Tracks were laid round several of the prominent rugby grounds, especially in the Transvaal.

British visitors were regulars in the late 1920's and early 1930's, among them Phil Bishop, who twice won the South African championship, Wally Lloyd, Nobby Key, and those remarkable ladies Fay Taylour and Eva Asquith.

The emergence of Buddy Fuller before the war, Henry Long, Doug Davies and the Serrurier brothers after it, signalled an important step forward. Both Long and Davies made World Final appearances, and teams from England, New Zealand, Holland, and a European Select came out regularly for series of representative matches.

Since the Union withdrew from its previous Commonwealth connections, there has been very scanty activity. A meeting or two here or there, the occasional appearance of itinerant free-lancers, but little else.

Rhodesia showed interest for a while, and there was a short-lived bid to bring back speedway there around 1970.

But as in Mozambique, Uganda and Kenya, these efforts failed to evoke much local response. In the light of much more recent legislation, though, it is fascinating to record that in Nairobi in 1951, where there was a spurt of interest, the A.C.U. amended its rules to allow the many Sikh riders to compete while wearing their turbans, rather than the usually mandatory crash helmets!

The dark continent has opened up very little, and probably never will. The real growth area, especially in recent times, has been Scandinavia.

Sprouts Elder and Ray Tauser included Denmark and Norway on their list of calls way back. Morian Hansen, first continental to make his mark on the world rankings, reigned supreme as the Danes developed their talents. Basse Hveem enjoyed a similar reputation in Norway, and Torsten Sjöberg

Below: *Influential Scandinavian forward thinkers, Tore Kittilsen (Norway) and Charles Ringblom (Sweden) are regulars at big F.I.M. events.*

was in a class of his own in Sweden's early days.

Yet none of these nations took off until after the war. Then it was Sweden, who had once banned the sport which its opponents claimed was too dangerous, emerging later as far and away the outstanding breeding ground for talent.

League racing was introduced in 1948, with tracks opening in many new centres. The British influence was evident, with several National League tracks paying a visit, but quite the most significant movement was in the opposite direction when Olle Nygren and Bertil Carlsson came to England for the first time to ride in the re-introduced world championships.

Two years later, in 1951, Nygren became the first Swedish rider to join a British club. During the mid-summer break, he scored 76 points in ten appearances for Harringay.

Dan Forsberg had 28 outings for Birmingham in 1952, scoring 184 points, and became the first Swedish representative in the World Final. The 18-year-old debut maker scored nine points, including two race wins.

Nygren, not to be outdone, remained the favourite candidate for world honours and in 1953, after scoring 12 points at Wembley, fell on the last lap of a third-place run-off with Geoff Mardon. The next year, Olle was back again, beaten by Brian Crutcher in another run-off but rewarded with third place overall.

It was in the same Final that Ove Fundin made his first championship appearance. He scored two points and finished at the bottom of the field.

By the time he made his 15th World Final appearance in 1969, Fundin had helped himself to five championship wins, was runner-up three times and third on another three occasions. It was a record of consistency which acknowledges his place among the all-time greats.

British promoters were quick to regard Sweden as the obvious place to look for reinforcement. Charles Ochiltree, for 30 years the man in charge of Coventry and former British Speedway Promoters Association chairman, believes that their inclusion saved the sport in this country.

The inclusion of many colourful riders in British teams has certainly been a controversial topic but most people would argue that the Swedes have done more good than harm. Whether they would have been able to make quite such startling progress in the international field is debatable, but the roll of honour does them credit.

Björn Knutsson and Anders Michanek have also won individual titles; such technically accomplished performers as Nygren, Göte Nördin, Bengt Jansson, Sören Sjösten and Bernie Persson have all come close.

And these have been prominent members of a succession of Swedish teams whose Test match and World Team Cup exploits frequently reached the heights. With a flourishing junior competition and a league comprising three divisions, Sweden was not going to go short of a continuing supply of riders.

It was a tragedy that Tommy Jansson, their outstanding discovery in years, was killed in a world championship qualifying round in Stockholm in 1976. Son of a 1958 World Finalist, he had emulated his father as an 18-year-old, and looked to be on the threshold of great things. Tommy's club team, Smederna of Eskilstuna, had also emerged as the country's most accomplished team as well as being the best supported.

In earlier years, Nygren had been associated with Vargarna through a series of successes, while in all-time terms, Getingarna claim eight First Division titles, including five between 1963 and 1967.

This strong domestic situation provided riders who sharpened their talents elsewhere to such good effect that Sweden achieved six World Cup wins between 1960 and 1970. And they have won three World Pairs titles in the last five years.

This is evidence enough of the stylish manner in which the Swedes gave a new dimension to post-war speedway racing.

Latterly, their cousins in the area have been sitting up to take notice. Denmark are about to embrace professionalism, and maybe the surprise is that it has not happened earlier. Tommy Price, Bill Kitchen, Freddie Williams and Jack Parker were 1950 visitors who commented upon the good standard of several Danish riders. Orla Knudsen, champion for four successive years after the war, proved to be a sound successor to 1937 World Final history maker Morian Hansen. And the unlucky, underrated Arne Pander enjoyed some splendid years with Oxford in the National League's declining years.

Ole Olsen, though, was different class. The former motor mechanic from Haderslev learned the rudiments of the speedway craft from Ivan Mauger, his erstwhile colleague at Newcastle.

'I taught him too much' was Mauger's rueful comment when Olsen relieved him of his world title in Gothenburg in 1971 with a performance of the highest quality. Four years later Ole again ruled the world, and his example has proved an incalculable inspiration to his fellow countrymen.

Though the league system there is small-time, a number of promising Danes have followed Olsen into British League racing in the last few seasons. Experts believe that they could be the next coming force in international terms.

The Norwegians, like Denmark, staged speedway as far back as 1929. Basse Hveem was the first rider to put Norway on the map, and after the war he was rated as the country's top sports personality.

In 1949, when the world championships were revived, there was an official oversight and no places were allocated to Norway. This prompted the delivery of a haughty letter to the Foreign Office's Embassy in Oslo. Soon afterwards, Hveem and Lief Samsing were told that they had been found qualifying rounds after all.

Hveem went on to enjoy a highly popular little spell with West Ham, and a dozen years later the dashing Sverre Harrfeldt became one of the all-time Custom House favourites. Runner-up position to Barry Briggs in the Gothenburg World Final of 1966 illustrated his capabilities.

Reidar Eide and Dag Lovaas followed him into the British League top rankings, and there have been several more extremely useful Norsemen who have made an impression.

Finland has begun to make an exciting impact in recent years. Motor cycle sport started there in 1922, but there was no speedway racing until after the war – and even then, it did not rate especially highly.

Ebullient Antti Pajari collected three national titles and impressed with Coventry but little more was heard until the 1970's. The outstanding performer thus far is Ila Teromaa, who arrived at Leicester in 1975 and quickly shaped in a manner which suggested potential of a high standard.

His success has encouraged further Anglo-Finnish exchanges, thus illustrating the fact that almost any rider who hopes to make any real progress in the sport is well advised to come to England sooner or later.

That much said, speedway in general has been enriched by the presence and eager participation of so many nations. It will be interesting to see how the pendulum of power and prestige swings in the next few years – and, indeed, to speculate upon the possibility of even more countries writing their own page of history.

Below: *Ove Fundin forges the Kaparna colours into the lead.*

BRITISH SPEEDWAY TRACKS

Every effort has been made to authenticate facts and figures, though many pre-war records are difficult to verify. Leading Appearances and Points Scorers are for post-war League racing only. Dates shown for riders indicate the season of their first and last appearance for a particular club, though in some cases they did not ride in all of the intervening years. Unless track length has been significantly altered, the dimensions shown are those most commonly used.

ALDERSHOT
Aldershot Stadium, Tongham, Aldershot, Hampshire.
Years of Operation: 1950–51 (National League, Third Division); 1952 (Southern League); 1954 (resigned in mid season); 1957 (Southern Area League); 1960 (Open Licence).
Track length: 303 yards.
Nickname: Shots.
Highest League position: 5th in Third Division, 1950.
Most points: 37 out of 72, 1950.
Promoters and Managers include: George Saunders, N. E. Cartlidge, Freddie Millward, Ted Payne.
Leading appearances: Basil Harris, 104 (1950–52); Doug Papworth, 93 (1950–52).
Leading points scorers: Basil Harris, 813 (1950–52); Trevor Redmond, 686 (1950–51).
Other leading riders include: Geoff Mardon, Ivor Powell.

ASHFIELD
Saracen Park, Hawthorn Street, Possilpark, Glasgow.
Years of operation: 1949–52 (National League, Second Division); 1953 (Open Licence).
Track length: 355 yards.
Nickname: Giants.
Highest league position: 7th in Third Division, 1952.
Most points: 41 out of 88, 1952.
Promoters and managers include: Johnnie Hoskins, Norrie Isbister.
Leading appearances: Willie Wilson, 142, (1949–52); Merv Harding, 101 (1949–51).
Leading points scorers: Willie Wilson, 896 (1949–52); Merv Harding, 836 (1949–51).
World Final qualifier: Ken Le Breton, 1949.
Other leading riders: Bruce Semmens, Keith Gurtner.

BARROW
(1) Holker Street, Barrow-in-Furness, Lancashire.
(2) Park Road, Barrow-in-Furness, Cumbria.
Years of operation: (1) 1972*–74 (British League, Second Division);
(2) 1977 (Open Licence); 1978 (National League).
Track length: (1) 415 yards; (2) 300 yards.
Nickname: (1) Bombers; (2) Furness Flyers.
Highest league position: 9th in Second Division, 1972.
Most points: 34 out of 72, 1974.
Promoters and managers include: Wally Mawdsley, Peter Oakes, Ivan Mauger, George Graham, Cliff Hindle.
Leading appearances: Tom Owen, 83 (1972–74); Chris Roynon, 83 (1972–74).
Leading points scorers: Tom Owen, 593½ (1972–74); Mike Sampson, 503 (1972–74).
Other leading riders include: Joe Owen.

* Barrow took over from West Ham during 1972.

Note – Mike Sampson's record includes his appearances for West Ham in 1972.

BELLE VUE
(1) Greyhound Stadium, Hyde Road, Manchester.
(2) Zoological Gardens, Hyde Road, Manchester.
Years of operation: (1) 1928 (Open Licence); (2) 1929 (English League, resigned); 1930–31 (Northern League); 1932–39 (National League); 1940–45 (Open Licence); 1946–64 (National League); 1965 to date (British League).
Track length: 418 yards.
Nickname: Aces.
Honours: Northern League champions, 1930, 1931; National League champions, 1933, 1934, 1935, 1936, 1963; British League champions, 1970, 1971, 1972; National Trophy winners, 1933, 1934, 1935, 1936, 1937, 1946, 1947, 1949, 1958; A.C.U. Cup winners, 1934, 1935, 1936, 1937, 1946; Britannia Trophy winners, 1957, 1958, 1960; British Speedway Cup winners, 1947; North Cup winners, 1931; Speedway Star K.O. Cup winners, 1972, 1973, 1975; Inter-Divisional K.O. Cup winners, 1975.
Most points: 63 out of 68, 1972.
Promoters and managers include: E. O. Spence, Alice Hart, Johnnie Hoskins, Ken Sharples, Harold Jackson, Dent Oliver, Jack Fearnley, Frank Varey, Eric Boocock.
Leading appearances: Sören Sjösten, 318 (1962–75); Dick Fisher, 258 (1953–66); Jack Parker, 223 (1946–54); Alan Wilkinson, 221 (1971–77); Ken Sharples, 220 (1948–56); Peter Craven, 218 (1952–63); Louis Lawson, 210 (1946–53).
Leading points scorers: Sören Sjösten, 2864 (1962–75); Peter Craven, 2318 (1952–63); Peter Collins, 1900 (1971–77); Jack Parker, 1840 (1946–54); Ron Johnston, 1725 (1950–61); Dick Fisher, 1669 (1953–66); Cyril Maidment, 1567½ (1962–68) Ivan Mauger, 1517 (1969–72).
World Champions: Peter Craven, 1955, 1962; Ove Fundin, 1967; Ivan Mauger, 1969, 1970, 1972; Peter Collins, 1976.
World Final qualifiers: Eric Langton, 1936, 1937, 1938, 1939*; Bob Harrison, 1936; Frank Varey, 1937, 1938, 1939*; Bill Kitchen, 1937, 1939*; Joe Abbott, 1937; Louis Lawson, 1949, 1951; Dent Oliver, 1949, 1950; Jack Parker, 1949, 1950, 1951; Henry Long, 1952; Peter Craven, 1954, 1955, 1956, 1957, 1958, 1959, 1960, 1961, 1962, 1973; Ron Johnston, 1955, 1957, 1958, 1960; Dick Fisher, 1956, 1963, 1964; Sören Sjösten, 1962, 1960, 1970, 1971, 1974; Cyril Maidment, 1964; Ove Fundin, 1967; Ivan Mauger, 1969, 1970, 1971, 1972; Peter Collins, 1973, 1974, 1975, 1976, 1977; Chris Morton, 1976.
Other leading riders include: Tommy Allott, Frank Charles, Max Grosskreutz, Bill Pitcher, Ernie Price, Oliver Hart, Eddie Rigg, Gordon McGregor, Chris Pusey, Eric Broadbelt.
*Final not staged.

BELLE VUE II
Years of operation: 1931 (Southern League, replaced Harringay); 1939* (National League, Second Division, replaced Stoke); 1968–69 (British League, Second Division). In the Provincial League of 1937, Liverpool moved to Belle Vue.
Nickname: Colts.
Honours: Second Division champions, 1968, 1969; K.O. Cup winners, 1969.
Most points: 47 out of 60, 1969.
Leading appearances: Ken Moss, 42 (1968–69); Taffy Owen, 39 (1968–69).
Leading points scorers: Eric Broadbelt, 342 (1968–69); Ken Eyre, 330 (1968–69).
* Took over from Stoke.

BERWICK
Shielfield Park, Tweedmouth, Berwick-on-Tweed, Northumberland.
Years of operation: 1968–74 (British League, Second Division); 1975 to date ((New) National League).
Track length: 440 yards.
Nickname: Bandits.
Promoters and managers include: Danny Taylor, Liz Taylor, Ken Taylor.
Leading appearances: Willie Templeton, 202 (1972–77); Graham Jones, 202 (1972–77); Andy Meldrum, 118 (1969–73); Dave Gifford, 104 (1975–77).
Leading points scorers: Willie Templeton, 1270 (1972–77); Graham Jones, 1260 (1972–77).
Other leading riders include: Doug Wyer, Robert Hollingworth.

BIRMINGHAM
(1) Alexander Sports Stadium, Perry Barr, Birmingham.
Years of operation: 1928 (Open Licence); 1946 (Northern League); 1947–48 (National League, Second Division); 1949–57 (National League, resigned in mid season*), 1960 (Open Licence).
Track length: 402 yards.
Nickname: Brummies.
Honours: Midland Cup winners, 1953, 1954, 1955; Anniversary Cup winners, 1948.
Highest league position: 2nd in First Division, 1952; 2nd in Second Division, 1948.
Most points: 46 out of 72, 1952.
Promoters and managers include: Les Marshall, Doug Ellis.
Leading appearances: Graham Warren, 188 (1948–55); Ron Mountford, 183 (1950–57); Eric Boothroyd, 167 (1951–57); Arthur Payne, 161 (1948–54); Alan Hunt, 151 (1951–56).
Leading points scorers: Graham Warren, 1543 (1948–55); Alan Hunt, 1469 (1951–56); Ron Mountford, 1272 (1950–57); Arthur Payne, 1001 (1948–54).
World Final qualifiers: Graham Warren, 1949, 1950, 1952, 1953; Wilbur Lamoreaux, 1949; Arthur Payne, 1950, 1952; Alan Hunt, 1951, 1953, 1956; Dan Forsberg, 1952; Eric Boothroyd, 1956; Doug Davies, 1956.
Other leading riders include: Phil Hart, Stan Dell.

* Bradford took over Birmingham fixtures, 1957.

BIRMINGHAM
(2) Perry Barr, Walsall Road, Birmingham.
Years of operation (as Perry Barr): 1929–30 (Southern League, resigned).
(as Birmingham) 1971–74 (British League, Second Division); 1975 ((New) National League); 1976 to date (British League).
Track length: 350 yards.
Nicknames: Blues, Brummies.
Honours: Second Division champions, 1974; New National League champions, 1975; Second Division K.O. Cup winners, 1974.
Most points: 59 out of 76, 1975.
Promoters and managers include: Fred Mockford, Geoff Bennett, Joe Thurley.
Leading appearances: George Major, 165 (1971–75); Arthur Browning, 147 (1972–76).
Leading points scorers: George Major, 1245 (1971–75); Arthur Browning, 1137 (1972–76).
Other leading riders include: Wally Lloyd, Sören Sjösten, Ray Wilson.

BIRMINGHAM (HALL GREEN)
Hall Green Greyhound Stadium, Edgbaston, Birmingham.
Years of operation: 1928 (Open Licence); 1929 (resigned); 1930 (Southern League); 1931 (Open Licence); 1934 (National League); 1937 (Provincial League); 1938 (National League, Second Division).
Nickname: (as Hall Green, 1928–31) The Blues and (as Birmingham, 1934–38) Bulldogs.
Highest league position: 5th in Southern League, 1930.
Most points: 27 out of 48, 1930.
Promoters and managers include: A. J. Hunting, Stanley Glanfield, Tom Bradbury-Pratt, Fred Evans, Arthur Westwood.
Leading riders include: Bill Dallison, Wally Lloyd, Les Wotton, Jack Chapman, Dickie Wise, Alec Statham, Malcolm Craven, Phil Hart, Tommy Price.

BOSTON
New Hammond Beck Road, Boston, Lincolnshire.
Years of operation: 1970*–74 (British League, Second Division); 1975 to date ((New) National League).
Track length: 380 yards.
Nickname: Barracudas.
Honours: Second Division champions, 1973; Second Division K.O. Cup winners, 1973.
Most points: 58 out of 68, 1973.
Promoters and managers include: Cyril Crane, Gordon Parkins, Ted Holding.
Leading appearances: Robert Hollingworth, 144 (1974–77); Carl Glover, 143 (1971–77); Russell Osborne, 139 (1970–74); Jim Ryman, 110 (1971–74); Arthur Price, 105 (1970–73); David Gagen, 101 (1973–75).
Leading points scorers: Carl Glover, 1203 (1970–77); Robert Hollingworth, 1176½ (1974–77); Arthur Price, 951 (1970–73).
Other leading riders include: Ray Bales, Michael Lee.

* Boston took over from King's Lynn II during 1970.

Note – appearances and points prior to the transfer are not included.

BRADFORD
Odsal Stadium, Bradford, Yorkshire.
Years of operation: 1945 (Open Licence); 1946–57* (National League); 1959 (Open Licence); 1960 (Provincial League); 1970**–74 (British League, Second Division); 1975 (New National League).
Track length: 370 yards (1945–60); 385 yards (1970–75).
Nicknames: Boomerangs, Tudors, Northern.
Highest league position: 2nd in Second Division, 1971.
Most points: 45 out of 88, 1949.
Promoters and managers include: Johnnie Hoskins, Mike Parker, Les Whaley, Alan Knapkin, Jim Streets.
Leading appearances: Ron Clarke, 259 (1946–57); Eddie Rigg, 227 (1947–57); Oliver Hart, 167 (1947–52).
Leading points scorers: Eddie Rigg, 1631 (1947–57); Ron Clarke, 1448 (1946–57); Arthur Forrest, 1229 (1952–57); Oliver Hart, 1147½ (1947–52); Dave Baugh, 1070½ (1971–75); Alan Knapkin, 1025 (1971–75).
World Final qualifiers: Ron Clarke, 1949, 1950; Jackie Biggs, 1950; Eddie Rigg, 1951, 1954; Arthur Forrest, 1952, 1953, 1954, 1955, 1956; Arthur Wright, 1955.
Other leading riders include: Max Grosskreutz, Joe Abbott, Ernie Price, Dent Oliver, Lloyd Goffe, Nigel Boocock.
* Took over from Birmingham, 1957.
** Took over from Nelson, 1970.
Note – appearances and points include those before transfers.

BRADFORD (GREENFIELDS)
Greenfields Greyhound Stadium, Bradford, Yorkshire.
Years of operation: 1928 (Open Licence); 1961 (Open Licence); 1962 (Provincial League).
Track length: 335 yards.
Nickname: Panthers.
Highest League position: 13th in Provincial League, 1962.
Most points: 16 out of 48, 1962.
Promoters include: Jess Halliday.
Leading appearances: Geoff Pymar, 22 (1962); Wal Morton, 21 (1962).
Leading points scorers: Reg Duval, 125 (1962); Wal Morton, 114 (1962).

BRAFIELD
Brafield Stadium, Brafield on the Green, Northamptonshire.
Years of operation: 1954–55 (Southern Area League); 1966–67 (Open Licence).
Track length: 335 yards.
Nicknames: Flying Foxes, Badgers.
Highest league position: 3rd in Southern Area League, 1955.
Most points: 12 out of 24, 1955.
Promoters and managers include: Paddy Mills, John La Trobe.

BRISTOL
(1) Knowle Greyhound Stadium, Bristol.
Years of operation: 1928–35 (Open Licence); 1936–37 (Provincial League); 1938 (National League, First Division); 1939 (National League, Second Division); 1946 (Open Licence); 1947–49 (National League, Second Division); 1950–53 (First Division); 1954–55 (Second Division, resigned); 1959 (Open Licence); 1960 (Provincial League).
Track length: 290 yards.
Nickname: Bulldogs.
Honours: Provincial League champions, 1937. National League Second Division champions, 1948, 1949, 1954 (highest First Division position, 6th in 1951). South Shield winners, 1954. Provincial League K.O. Cup winners, 1960.
Most points: 69 out of 88, 1949.
Promoters and managers include: Ronnie Greene, Fred Mockford, Cecil Smith, George Allan, Trevor Redmond.
Leading appearances: Billy Hole, 232 (1947–55); Johnny Hole, 208 (1948–60); Eric Salmon, 204 (1947–53); Jack Mountford, 201 (1947–52).
Leading points scorers: Billy Hole, 1718 (1947–55); Dick Bradley, 1345 (1948–55); Jack Mountford, 1269½ (1947–52); Eric Salmon, 1158½ (1947–55).
World Final qualifiers: Cordy Milne 1938, 1939*; Dick Bradley, 1952, 1953; Olle Nygren, 1953.
Other leading riders include: Morian Hansen, Vic Duggan, Wal Morton, Bert Spencer, Roger Wise, Geoff Pymar.
Record victory: 70–14 v Glasgow, 1949 (a 5–1 in every race).
(2) Eastville Stadium, Bristol.
Years of operation: 1977 to date (British League).
Track length: 414 yards.
Nickname: Bulldogs.
League position: 12th in British League, 1977.
Most points: 34 out of 72, 1977.
Promoters and managers include: Wally Mawdsley and John Richards.
Leading appearances: Phil Herne, 34 (1977); Tormod Langli, 34 (1977).
Leading points scorers: Phil Herne, 324 (1977); Phil Crump, 260 (1977).
Other leading riders include: Nigel Boocock.
* Final not staged.

CALIFORNIA
California Stadium, California in England, near Wokingham, Berkshire.
Years of operation: from 1934 as Longmoor training track. 1954–56 (Southern Area League); 1957 (Open Licence).
Track length: 334 yards.
Nickname: Poppies.
Highest league position: 2nd in Southern Area League, 1954 and 1955.
Most points: 18 out of 32, 1955.
Promoters and managers include: N. E. Cartlidge, Freddie Millward.
Leading riders include: George Bason, Bob Andrews.

CANTERBURY
Kingsmead Stadium, Kingsmead Road, Canterbury, Kent.
Years of operation: 1968–74 (British League, Second Division); 1975 to date ((New) National League).
Track length: 390 yards.
Nickname: Crusaders.
Honours: Second Division champions, 1970; Second Division K.O. Cup winners, 1968.
Most points: 47 out of 64, 1970.
Promoters and managers include: Johnnie Hoskins, Wally Mawdsley.
Leading appearances: Brian Kennett, 219 (1971–77); Graham Banks, 183 (1969–77); Les Rumsey, 157 (1972–77); Ted Hubbard, 131 (1970–74).
Leading points scorers: Graham Banks, 1285 (1969–77); Brian Kennett, 1238 (1971–77); Les Rumsey, 1030 (1972–77).
Other leading riders include: Barry Thomas, Reg Luckhurst.

CARDIFF
(1) White City Stadium, Sloper Road, Cardiff.
(2) Penarth Road R.F.C., Cardiff.
Years of operation: (1) 1928–30 (Open Licence); 1936 (Provincial League, resigned). (2) 1951 (National League, Third Division); 1952–53 (Southern League, resigned).
Track length: 400 yards.
Nickname: Dragons.
Highest League position: 2nd in Southern League, 1952.
Most points: 46 out of 72, 1952.
Promoters and managers include: L. Maidment, Bill Dutton.
Leading appearances: Gerald Pugh, 82 (1951–53); Mick Holland, 80 (1951–53); Kevin Hayden, 79 (1951–53).
Leading points scorers: Mick Holland, 583 (1951–53); Gerald Pugh, 522 (1951–53); Charlie May, 519 (1951–53).
Other leading riders include: Chum Taylor, Les Moore.

COATBRIDGE
Cliftonhill Stadium, Coatbridge, Lanarkshire.
Years of operation: 1968–69 (British League, First Division); 1973 (British League, First Division); 1974 (British League, Second Division); 1975–77* ((New) National League).
Track length: 380 yards.
Nicknames: Monarchs, Tigers.
Honours: Scottish Cup winners, 1969.
Highest league position: 7th in National League, 1976; 8th in First Division, 1969.
Most points: 37 out of 72, 1969.
Promoters and managers include: Ian Hoskins, Tommy Hughson, Jim Beaton, John Docherty, Neil MacFarlane.
Leading appearances: Brian Collins, 178 (1968–76); Jimmy Gallacher, 109 (1973–76); Grahame Dawson, 102 (1974–76).

Leading points scorers: Brian Collins, 1336 (1968–76); Grahame Dawson, 634 (1974–76); Reidar Eide, 593 (1968–69).
World Final qualifiers: Reidar Eide, 1968; Bernt Persson, 1968.
Other leading riders include: Bert Harkins, George Hunter, Jimmy McMillan, Doug Templeton, Bobby Beaton, Dave Gifford, Mitch Shirra.

* Transferred to Glasgow (Blantyre) in 1977.

Note – appearances and points do not include 1977.

COVENTRY

(1) Foleshill Stadium, Coventry.
(2) Brandon Stadium, Rugby Road, Brandon, Coventry.
Years of operation: (1) 1928 (Open Licence). (2) 1928 (Open Licence); 1929–31 (Southern League); 1932–33 (National League); 1948 (National League, Third Division); 1949–56 (National League, Second Division) 1957–64 (National League); 1965 to date (British League).
Track length: 380 yards.
Nickname: Bees.
Honours: British League champions, 1968. Second Division champions, 1953; Speedway Star K.O. Cup winners, 1967; Midland Cup winners, 1952, 1960, 1966, 1969, 1971, 1976, 1977.
Most points: 55 out of 88, 1952.
Promoters and managers include: Stanley Glanfield, Charles Ochiltree, Mick Blackburn.
Leading appearances: Nigel Boocock, 502 (1959–76); Les Owen, 334 (1957–73); Ron Mountford, 279 (1957–72); Jim Lightfoot, 256 (1953–66); Rick France, 235 (1960–72); Roger Hill, 235 (1965–75); Col Cottrell, 222 (1962–71).
Leading points scorers: Nigel Boocock, 5068 (1959–76); Ron Mountford, 1855 (1957–73); Jim Lightfoot, 1740 (1953–66); Les Owen, 1481 (1957–73); Rick France, 1478 (1960–72); Charlie New, 1309 (1951–57); Col Cottrell, 1182 (1962–71); Les Hewitt, 1151 (1949–53); Vic Emms, 1028 (1948–55); Johnny Reason, 1003 (1949–55).
World Final qualifiers: PeO Söderman, 1956; Jack Young, 1960; Henryk Zyto, 1960; Ron Mountford, 1962; Ken McKinlay, 1962, 1964; Jim Lightfoot, 1963; Nigel Boocock, 1963, 1964, 1965, 1966, 1968, 1969, 1971, 1972; Rick France, 1967, 1972; Jiri Stancl, 1976; Ole Olsen, 1977; Tommy Nilsson, 1977.
Other leading riders include: Arthur Forrest, Lionel Levy, Tony Lomas.

CRAYFORD

Ladbroke Stadium, London Road, Crayford, Kent.
Years of operation: 1968–70 (British League, Second Division); 1975 to date ((New) National League).
Track length: 300 yards (1968–69); 265 yards (1970 to date).
Nicknames: Highwaymen, Kestrels.
Highest league position: 4th in Second Division, 1969.
Most points: 42 out of 76, 1975.
Promoters and managers include: Mike Parker, Bill Bridgett, Peter Thorogood.
Leading appearances: Alan Sage, 108 (1975–77); Laurie Etheridge, 106 (1975–77).
Leading points scorers: Laurie Etheridge, 1083 (1975–77); Alan Sage, 1005 (1975–77); Anthony Childs, 650 (1968–70).
Other leading riders include: Mike Broadbanks, Colin Gooddy.

CRADLEY HEATH

Dudley Wood, Dudley, Worcestershire.
Years of operation: 1947–48 (National League, Third Division); 1949–52 (National League, Second Division); 1959 (Open Licence); 1960–64 (Provincial League); 1965 to date (British League).
Track length: 367 yards.
Nicknames: Heathens, United.
Honours: Provincial League K.O. Cup winners, 1961, 1963; South Shield winners, 1950; Midland Shield winners, 1951.
Highest league position: 2nd in Third Division, 1947, 1948; highest British League, 7th in 1969.
Most points: 60 out of 88, 1948.
Promoters and managers include: Dudley Marchant, Dickie Wise, Les Marshall, Eli Sumner, Phil Malpass, Roy Moreton, Ted Flanaghan, Harry Bastable, Vic White, Dan McCormick.
Leading appearances: Phil Malpass, 193 (1947–52); Ivor Brown, 188 (1961–68); Harry Bastable, 187 (1950–65); Bernt Persson, 184 (1969–77); Roy Trigg, 174 (1968–72); John Hart, 170 (1961–72); Bruce Cribb, 150 (1973–77).
Leading points scorers: Bernt Persson, 1941½ (1969–77); Ivor Brown, 1726 (1961–68); Roy Trigg, 1550 (1968–72); Harry Bastable, 1246 (1950–65); Alan Hunt, 1064 (1947–50).
World Final qualifiers: Bernt Persson, 1971, 1972, 1973, 1975; Anders Michanek, 1970.
Other leading riders include: Gil Craven, Les Tolley, Eric Boothroyd, Leo McAuliffe, Brian Brett, Colin Pratt, Howard Cole, John Boulger.

CREWE

L.M.R. Sports Ground, Earle Street, Crewe, Cheshire.
Years of operation: 1969–74 (British League, Second Division); 1975 ((New) National League).
Track length: 470 yards (1969–70); 430 yards (1971–75).
Nickname: Kings.
Honours: Second Division champions, 1972; Second Division K.O. Cup winners, 1972.
Promoters and managers include: Maurice Littlechild, Ken Adams, Len Silver, Dave Parry.
Leading appearances: John Jackson, 154 (1970–74); Dave Parry, 109 (1969–73).
Leading points scorers: John Jackson, 1451 (1970–74); Phil Crump, 658 (1971–72); Dave Morton, 626½ (1971–74).
Other leading riders include: Geoff Curtis, Les Collins.

CRYSTAL PALACE

Crystal Palace Grounds, Sydenham, London S.E.
Years of operation: 1928 (Open Licence); 1929–31 (Southern League); 1932–33 (National League); 1934–38 (Open Licence); 1939 (National League, Second Division, resigned); 1940 (Open Licence).
Track length: 440 yards.
Nickname: Glaziers.
Highest League position: 2nd in N.P.A. Trophy, 1932; 3rd in National League, 1932.
Most points: 24 out of 36, 1932.
Promoters and managers include: Fred Mockford, Cecil Smith.
Leading riders include: Triss Sharp, Jack Barnett, Ron Johnson, Wally Key, Tom Farndon, Clem Mitchell, George Newton.

DONCASTER

Greyhound Stadium, York Road, Doncaster, Yorkshire.
Years of operation: 1969–70 (British League, Second Division).
Track length: 350 yards.
Nicknames: Stallions, Dragons.
Highest league position: 12th in Second Division, 1969.
Most points: 24 out of 60, 1969.
Promoters include: Mike Parker, Joe Thurley.
Leading appearances: Alan Bridgett, 30 (1969); Hec Haslinger, 30 (1970).
Leading points scorers: Gordon McGregor, 257 (1970); George Major, 226 (1970).
Other leading riders include: Reg Wilson, Doug Wyer.

EASTBOURNE

Arlington Stadium, Hailsham, Sussex.
Years of operation: 1928–38 (Open Licence); 1946 (Open Licence); 1947 (National League, Third Division); 1950–53 (Open Licence); 1954–57 (Southern Area League); 1958 (Open Licence); 1959 (Southern Area League); 1960–64 (Open Licence); 1969–74 (British League, Second Division); 1975 to date ((New National League).
Track length: 342 yards.
Nickname: Eagles.
Honours: Second Division champions, 1971; National League champions, 1977; Third Division champions, 1947; Southern Area League champions, 1959.
Most points: 58 out of 72, 1977.
Promoters and managers include: Charlie Dugard, Dave Lanning, Bobby Dugard, Arthur Nutley.
Leading appearances: Mike Sampson, 121 (1974–77); Paul Gachet, 119 (1972–75); Pete Jarman, 118 (1974–77); Bobby McNeil, 110 (1971–74); Trevor Geer, 103 (1971–74); Colin Richardson, 103 (1975–77).
Leading points scorers: Mike Sampson, 903 (1974–77); Paul Gachet, 894 (1972–75); Bobby McNeil, 853 (1971–74); Gordon Kennett, 697 (1970–72).
Other leading riders include: Harry Saunders, Wally Green, Basil Harris, Leo McAuliffe, Ivan Mauger, Reg Trott, Dave Jessup, Steve Weatherley.

EDINBURGH

(1) Marine Gardens, Portobello, Edinburgh.
Years of operation: 1928–29 (Open Licence); 1930 (Northern League); 1931–39 (Open Licence).
Track length: 440 yards.
Nickname: Thistles.
League position: 8th in Northern League, 1930.
Most points: 8 out of 22, 1930.
Promoters and managers include: Bob Sinclair, Jimmy Fraser.
Leading riders include: George Greenwood, Oliver Hart, Jack Chapman (Union Cup, 1939).

(2) Old Meadowbank Stadium, Clockmill Road, Edinburgh.
Years of operation: 1948–54 (National League, Second Division, resigned); 1960–64 (Provincial League); 1965–67 (British League).
Track length: 363 yards.
Nickname: Monarchs.
Highest league position: 3rd in Second Division, 1951.
Most points: 48 out of 88, 1949.
Honours: Border Cup winners, 1950; Scottish Cup winners, 1951, 1964, 1967; North Shield winners, 1951; Queen's Cup winners, 1953; Provincial League K.O. Cup winners, 1961.
Promoters and managers include: Johnnie Hoskins, Frank Varey, Alice Hart, Clem Mitchell, Bob Rae, Bobby Baxter, Ian Hoskins.
Leading appearances: Dick Campbell, 266 (1948–62); Doug Templeton, 199 (1960–67); George Hunter, 199 (1960–67); Eddie Lack, 198 (1948–54).
Leading points scorers: Dick Campbell, 1805 (1948–62); George Hunter, 1638 (1960–67); Doug Templeton, 1621 (1960–67); Don Cuppleditch, 1171½ (1948–54); Eddie Lack, 1013 (1948–54).
World Champion: Jack Young, 1951.
World Final qualifiers: Jack Young, 1950, 1951; Bernie Persson, 1967.
Other leading riders include: Bengt Jansson, Reidar Eide.

(3) Powderhall Stadium, Warriston Road, Edinburgh.
Years of operation: 1977 to date (National League).
Track length: 335 yards.
Nickname: Monarchs.
League position: 15th in National League, 1977.
Most points: 30 out of 72, 1977.
Promoters and managers include: Mike Parker, Bill Bridgett, Neil Macfarlane.
Leading appearances: Bert Harkins, 36 (1977); Alan Bridgett, 35 (1977); Jack Millen, 35 (1977).
Leading points scorers: Bert Harkins, 296 (1977); Jack Millen, 240 (1977); Charlie Monk, 222 (1977).

ELLESMERE PORT

Thornton Road, Ellesmere Port, Cheshire.
Years of operation: 1972–74 (British League, Second Division); 1975 to date ((New) National League).
Highest League position: 2nd in National League, 1976.
Most points: 49 out of 68, 1976.
Track length: 423 yards.
Nickname: Gunners.
Promoters and managers include: Ian Thomas, Joe Shaw, Ernie Park.
Leading appearances: Colin Goad, 132 (1972–75); Duncan Meredith, 109 (1974–77); John Jackson, 105 (1975–77).

Leading points scorers: John Jackson, 1178 (1975–77); Colin Goad, 873 (1972–75); Graham Drury, 799 (1972–74).
Other leading riders include: Chris Morton.

EXETER

County Ground, Church Road, St Thomas, Exeter, Devon.
Years of operation: 1929–30 (Open Licence); 1947–51 (National League, Third Division); 1952–53 (Southern League); 1954–55 (National League, Second Division); 1960 (Open Licence); 1961–64 (Provincial League); 1965 to date (British League).
Track length: 443 yards.
Nickname: Falcons.
Honours: National League Third Division champions, 1948; Southern League champions, 1953; British League champions, 1974; Provincial League K.O. Cup winners, 1962.

Most points: 65 out of 88, 1948.
Promoters and managers include: L. G. Glanfield, F. W. Buckland, W. J. T. Eastmond, Pete Lansdale, Wally Mawdsley.
Leading appearances: Don Hardy, 258 (1947–55); Neil Street, 242 (1952–70); Jimmy Squibb, 205 (1963–72); Jack Geran, 200 (1952–67); Goog Hoskin, 188 (1949–63); Vic Gent, 171 (1949–53); Scott Autrey, 162 (1973–77); Chris Julian, 158 (1970–74).
Leading points scorers: Don Hardy, 1799 (1947–55); Ivan Mauger, 1626 (1973–77); Neil Street, 1580½ (1952–70); Jack Geran, 1544 (1952–67); Jimmy Squibb, 1470½ (1963–72); Scott Autrey, 1354½ (1973–77); Goog Hoskin, 1286 (1949–63); Martin Ashby, 1034 (1968–70).
World Champion: Ivan Mauger, 1977.
World Final qualifiers: Martin Ashby, 1968; Ivan Mauger, 1973, 1974, 1975, 1976, 1977; Scott Autrey, 1976.
Other leading riders include: Charlie May, Bob Roger, Bert Roger, Cyril Roger, Hugh Geddes, Len Silver.

FLEETWOOD
The Stadium, Highbury Avenue, Fleetwood, Lancashire.
Years of operation: 1948–51 (National League, Second Division).
Track length: 336 yards.
Nickname: Flyers.
Highest league position: 8th in Second Division, 1948.
Most points: 21 out of 64, 1948.
Promoters and managers include: Joseph Waxman, James Wolfenden.
Leading appearances: Norman Hargreaves, 133 (1948–51); Don Potter, 87 (1949–51).
Leading points scorers: Norman Hargreaves, 962 (1948–51); Wilf Plant, 591 (1948–50).
Other leading riders include: Wilf Jay, George Newton, Dick Geary.

GLASGOW
(1) White City Stadium, Glasgow S.W.2.
(2) Hampden Park, Mount Florida, Glasgow, S.4.
Years of operation: (1) 1929 (Open Licence); 1939 (Open Licence); 1945 (Open Licence); 1946 (Northern League); 1947–54 (National League, Second Division, resigned); 1964 (Provincial League); 1965–68 (British League). (2) 1969–72 (British League).
Track length: (1) 420 yards; (2) 430 yards.
Nickname: Tigers.
Honours: Scottish Cup winners, 1952, 1953, 1965, 1966.
Highest league position: 2nd in Second Division, 1950.
Most points: 47 out of 88, 1952.
Promoters and managers include: Johnnie Hoskins, Ian Hoskins, Trevor Redmond, Danny Taylor, Les Whaley, Jimmy Beaton.
Leading appearances: Charlie Monk, 264 (1964–72); Willie Templeton, 243 (1965–72); Jimmy McMillan, 215 (1966–72); Junior Bainbridge, 190 (1947–53); Bill McMillan, 163 (1964–71).
Leading points scorers: Charlie Monk, 2458 (1964–72); Jimmy McMillan, 1794 (1966–72); Tommy Miller, 1366 (1950–53); Junior Bainbridge, 1357 (1947–53); Willie Templeton, 1154 (1965–72).
Other leading riders include: Joe Crowther, Ken McKinlay, Gordon McGregor.

GLASGOW
(3) Blantyre Sports Stadium, Blantyre, Lanarkshire.
Years of operation: 1977* to date (National League).
Track length: 340 yards.
Nickname: Tigers.
League position: 11th in National League, 1977.
Promoters and managers include: Jim Beaton, David Thomson.
Leading appearances: Brian Collins, 36 (1977); Mick McKeon, 36 (1977).
Leading points scorers: Brian Collins, 336 (1977); Mick McKeon, 295 (1977).

* Took over from Coatbridge during 1977.

Note – appearances and points include those recorded for Coatbridge before transfer.

HACKNEY (WICK)
Hackney Stadium, Waterden Road, London E.15.
Years of operation: 1935–37 (National League); 1938–39 (National League, Second Division); 1963–64 (Provincial League); 1965 to date (British League).
Track length: 345 yards.
Nicknames: Wolves, Hawks.
Honours: Second Division champions, 1938; (best in First Division, 2nd in 1968); Speedway Star K.O. Cup winners, 1971; London Cup winners, 1936, 1971, 1973; Metropolitan Gold Cup winners, 1971.
Most points: 44 out of 72, 1968.
Promoters and managers include: Fred Evans, Mike Parker, Len Silver, Alec Ford, Maurice Morley, Dave Erskine.
Leading appearances: Barry Thomas, 247 (1970–77); Les McGillivray, 236 (1964–70); Laurie Etheridge, 222 (1968–77); Colin Pratt, 191 (1964–69); David Kennett, 177 (1971–77); Bengt Jansson, 173 (1967–73).
Leading points scorers: Barry Thomas, 1797 (1970–77); Colin Pratt, 1720 (1964–69); Bengt Jansson, 1682½ (1967–73); Les McGillivray, 1152 (1964–70).
World Final qualifiers: Cordy Milne, 1936, 1937; Morian Hansen, 1936, 1937; Dickie Case, 1936; Bengt Jansson, 1967, 1971; Colin Pratt, 1967; Dag Lovaas, 1974; Zenon Plech, 1976.
Other leading riders include: Phil Hart, Squib Burton, Dusty Haigh, Vic Duggan, Jimmy Gooch, Jackie Biggs, Garry Middleton, Dave Morton.

HALIFAX
(1) Thrum Hall Cricket Ground, Halifax, Yorkshire.
(2) The Shay, Halifax, Yorkshire.
Years of operation: (1) 1929 (Open Licence); 1929 (English League). (2) 1949 (National League, Third Division); 1950–51 (National League, Second Division); 1965 to date (British League).
Track length: 402 yards (1949–51); 378 yards (1965–70); 410 yards (1971 to date).
Nickname: Dukes.
Honours: British League champions, 1966; Speedway Star K.O. Cup winners, 1966; North Shield winners, 1950; North Cup winners, 1966.
Most points: 58 out of 96, 1949.
Promoters and managers include: Bruce Booth, Eric Langton, Reg Fearman, Eric Boothroyd, Dennis Gavros.
Leading appearances: Eric Boocock, 312 (1965–74); Dave Younghusband, 229 (1965–72); Greg Kentwell, 207 (1966–72); Alan Jay, 152 (1968–72); Dennis Gavros, 150 (1965–72).
Leading points scorers: Eric Boocock, 3352 (1965–74); Dave Younghusband, 1966 (1965–72); Eric Boothroyd, 1101 (1965–68); Greg Kentwell, 1013 (1966–72).
World Final qualifier: Eric Boocock, 1967, 1971, 1972.
Other leading riders include: Arthur Forrest, Vic Emms, John Titman, Henny Kroeze, Chris Pusey.

HARRINGAY
Harringay Stadium, Green Lanes, London N.22.
Years of operation: 1928 (Open Licence); 1929–31 (Southern League, resigned); 1934–39 (National League); 1946 (Open Licence); 1947–54 (National League).
Track length: 333 yards.
Nicknames: Canaries, Tigers, Racers.
Honours: National Trophy winners, 1952; London Cup winners, 1935, 1952, 1953; First Division Anniversary Cup winners, 1948; Coronation Cup winners, 1953.
Highest league position: 2nd in National League, 1935, 1948, 1953.
Most points: 45 out of 72, 1952.
Promoters and managers include: A. J. Hunting, Charles Knott, Tom Bradbury-Pratt, Fred Whitehead, George Kay, Sid Singleton.
Leading appearances: Danny Dunton, 160 (1949–54); Nobby Stock, 149 (1947–52); Jackie Biggs, 132 (1947–54).
Leading points scorers: Vic Duggan, 1099 (1947–50); Split Waterman, 999 (1950–54); Jackie Biggs, 904 (1947–54).
World Final qualifiers: Jack Ormston, 1936; Bill Pitcher, 1936; Jack Parker, 1937, 1938, 1939*; Alec Statham, 1938, 1939*; Lloyd Goffe, 1949; Vic Duggan, 1950; Split Waterman, 1950, 1951, 1952, 1953, 1954; Danny Dunton, 1950; Jeff Lloyd, 1951, 1952, 1953; Jackie Biggs, 1951, 1953, 1954; Ron How, 1952.
Other leading riders include: Frank Arthur, Phil Bishop, Norman Parker, Ray Duggan, Geoff Pymar, Olle Nygren, Cliff Watson.

* Final not staged.

HASTINGS
Pilot Field, Elphinstone Road, Hastings, Sussex.
Years of operation: 1948–49 (National League, Third Division).
Track length: 388 yards.
Nickname: Saxons.
Highest league position: 6th in Third Division, 1948.
Most points: 44 out of 88, 1948.
Promoter: Charlie Dugard.
Leading appearances: Ken Middleditch, 85 (1948–49).
Leading points scorers: Jock Grierson, 766 (1948–49).
Other leading riders include: Ron Clarke, Wally Green, Buddy Fuller.

HIGH BEECH
King's Oak, High Beech, near Loughton, Essex.
Years of operation: 1928–29 (Open Licence); 1930–31 (Southern League); 1932 (Open Licence); and as a training track, 1935–48.
Track length: 394 yards.
Nicknames: Foresters, Rabbits.
Promoters and managers include: Jack Hill-Bailey, W. J. Cearns.
Leading riders include: Phil Bishop, Jack Barnett, Syd Edmonds, Frank Pearce, Bill Dallison.

HULL
(1) Hedon Stadium, Hedon, near Kingston Upon Hull, Yorkshire.
Years of operation: 1948–49 (National League, Third Division, resigned*).
Track length: 442 yards.
Nickname: Angels.
Highest league position: 9th in Second Division, 1948.
Most league points: 38 out of 88, 1948.
Leading appearances: Mick Mitchell, 77 (1948–49); George Craig, 77 (1948–49).
Leading points scorers: Mick Mitchell, 627 (1948–49); George Craig, 456 (1948–49).

* Replaced by Swindon.

HULL
(2) The Boulevard, Airlie Street, Kingston-upon-Hull, Humberside.
Years of operation: 1971–73 (British League, Second Division); 1974 to date (British League).
Honours: Inter-Divisional K.O. Cup winners, 1976.
Highest league position: 6th in First Division, 1976.
Promoters and managers include: Ian Thomas, Brian Larner, Colin Tucker, Derek Tattersall.
Track length: 423 yards.
Nickname: Vikings.
Leading appearances: Bobby Beaton, 132 (1974–77); Mitch Graham, 126 (1974–77); Tony Childs, 89 (1971–74).
Leading points scorers: Bobby Beaton, 1026½ (1974–77); Tony Childs, 863 (1971–74).
World Final qualifier: Egon Müller, 1976.
Other leading riders include: Barry Briggs, Jimmy McMillan.

IPSWICH
Foxhall Heath Stadium, Ipswich, Suffolk.
Years of operation: 1951 (Open Licence); 1952–53 (Southern League); 1954–56 (National League, Second Division); 1957–58 (National League); 1959 (Southern Area League); 1960–62 (National League, resigned); 1964–65 (Open Licence); 1969–71 (British League, Second Division); 1972 to date (British League).
Track length: 410 yards (1951–65); 328 yards (1969 to date).
Nickname: Witches.
Honours: British League champions, 1975, 1976; Speedway Star K.O. Cup winners, 1976; Inter-Divisional K.O. Cup winners, 1977; Second Division K.O. Cup winners, 1970, 1971; Spring Gold Cup winners, 1976.
Most league points: 55 out of 72, 1976.
Promoters and managers include: D. F. Bostock, Arthur Franklyn, Maurice Littlechild, Vic Gooden, Aub Lawson, John Berry, Joe Thurley, Howdy Byford, Ron Bagley.
Leading appearances: John Louis, 255 (1970–77); Tony Davey, 225 (1970–77); Billy Sanders, 203 (1972–77); Ted Howgego, 149 (1971–77); Tich Read, 128 (1952–62); Mike

Lanham, 126 (1972–77); Bob Sharp, 112 (1954–58).
Leading points scorers: John Louis, 2684 (1970–77); Tony Davey, 1737 (1970–77); Billy Sanders, 1590 (1972–77); Peter Moore, 1049½ (1957–62).
World Final qualifiers: Peter Moore, 1958, 1960; Ray Cresp, 1961; John Louis, 1972, 1974, 1975, 1976; Billy Sanders, 1977.
Other leading riders include: Junior Bainbridge, Nigel Boocock, Les McGillivray, Cyril Roger, Split Waterman, Jackie Biggs, Olle Nygren.

KING'S LYNN
Saddlebow Road, King's Lynn, Norfolk.
Years of operation: 1965 (Open Licence); 1966 to date (British League).
Track length: 400 yards (1965–75); 375 yards (1975 to date).
Nickname: Stars.
Honours: Spring Gold Cup winners, 1973; Speedway Star K.O. Cup winners, 1977.
Highest league position: 3rd in British League, 1972, 1973.
Most points: 51 out of 68, 1972.
Promoters and managers include: Maurice Littlechild, Cyril Crane, Violet Littlechild, Alan Littlechild, Martin Rogers.
Leading appearances: Terry Betts, 395 (1966–77); Ian Turner, 227 (1970–77); Malcolm Simmons, 223 (1968–74); Clive Featherby, 168 (1967–72); Howard Cole, 164 (1967–72).
Leading points scorers: Terry Betts, 4120 (1966–77); Malcolm Simmons, 2112½ (1968–74); Ian Turner, 1278½ (1970–77); Howard Cole, 1105, (1967–72).
World Final qualifiers: Howard Cole, 1969; Terry Betts, 1974; Michael Lee, 1977.
Other leading riders include: Peter Moore, Garry Middleton, Phil Crump, Olle Nygren, Trevor Hedge.

KING'S LYNN II
Years of operation: 1969–70 (British League, Second Division, resigned*).
Nickname: Starlets.
Leading appearances: Tony Featherstone, 49 (1969–70); Ian Turner, 48 (1969–70); Arthur Price, 48 (1969–70).
Leading points scorers: Ian Turner, 418 (1969–70); Arthur Price 332½ (1969–70).
Highest league position: 16th in Second Division, 1969.
Most league points: 17 out of 60, 1969.
* Boston took over King's Lynn II fixtures, 1970.

LEA BRIDGE (CLAPTON)
Lea Bridge Stadium, Lea Bridge Road, London E.17
Years of operation: 1928 (Open Licence); 1929–31 (Southern League); 1934 (National League, resigned*); 1938 (National League, Second Division).
(As Clapton) 1932–33 (National League).
Track length: 440 yards.
Nickname: Saints.
Highest league position: 5th in National League, 1933; 5th in Second Division, 1938.
Most points: 41 out of 72, 1933.
Promoters and managers include: Charles Knott, Tom Bradbury-Pratt.
Leading riders include: Roy Dook, Alf Foulds, Squib Burton, Tommy Croombs, Max Grosskreutz, Jack Parker, Norman Parker, Wally Lloyd, Phil Bishop.
* Team transferred en bloc to Walthamstow.

LEEDS
Fullerton Park, Leeds, Yorkshire.
Years of operation: 1928 (Open Licence); 1929 (English League); 1930 (Open Licence); 1931 (Northern League); 1938* (National League, Second Division).
Track length: 402 yards.
League honours: English League champions, 1929.
Most points: 35 out of 46, 1929.
Promoter: Capt. J. McNaughton.
Leading riders include: Arthur Atkinson, George Greenwood, Eva Askquith.
* Took over from Nottingham.

LEICESTER
Blackbird Road, Leicester.
Years of operation: (as Leicester Stadium); 1928 (Open Licence); 1929 (English League); 1930–31 (Southern League, resigned); 1932 (Open Licence).
(As Leicester) 1937 (Provincial League, resigned); 1948 (Open Licence); 1949–50 (National League, Third Division); 1951–56 (National League, Second Division); 1957–61 (National League); 1962 (Provincial League); 1963 (Open Licence); 1968 to date (British League).
Track length: 380 yards.
Nicknames: Hunters, Lions.
Honours: Midland Cup winners, 1951.
Highest league position: 2nd in Second Division, 1951; 2nd in National League, 1959; 2nd in British League, 1971.
Most points: 52 out of 88, 1952.
Promoters and managers include: Alan Sanderson, Squib Burton, Mike Parker, Ron Wilson, Reg Fearman, Vic White.
Leading appearances: Ray Wilson, 270 (1968–76); Norman Storer, 265 (1968–75); John Boulger, 235 (1968–77); Charlie Barsby, 213 (1952–61); Malcolm Brown, 202 (1969–74); Len Williams, 161 (1951–56); Ken McKinlay, 157 (1954–61).
Leading points scorers: Ray Wilson, 2887, (1968–76); John Boulger, 2028 (1968–77); Ken McKinlay, 1982 (1954–61); Len Williams, 1238 (1951–56); Norman Storer, 1035 (1968–75).
World Final qualifiers: Ken McKinlay, 1956, 1957, 1958, 1960, 1961; Jack Geran, 1957, 1958; Stefan Kwoczala, 1960; Bryan Elliott, 1960; Anders Michanek, 1968; Ray Wilson, 1971, 1973, 1975; Dave Jessup, 1974; John Boulger, 1973, 1977.
Other leading riders include: Syd Jackson, Wilf Plant, Paddy Mills, Lloyd Goffe, Gerry Hussey, Marian Kaiser, Pawel Waloszek, Ila Teromaa.

LEICESTER SUPER
Super Stadium, Melton Road, Leicester.
Years of operation: 1929 (Open Licence); 1930–31 (Northern League); 1932 (Open Licence).
Track length: 587 yards.
Nickname: Super.
Promoters include: Fred Mockford.
Leading riders include: Squib Burton, Bert Spencer.

LIVERPOOL
Stanley Stadium, Prescot Road, Liverpool.
Years of operation: 1928 (Open Licence); 1929 (English League); 1930 (Northern League); 1936–37 (Provincial League, resigned*); 1949–52 (National League, Second Division); 1953 (Open Licence); 1957 (Open Licence); 1959 (Open Licence); 1960 (Provincial League).
Track length: 446 yards.
Nicknames: Chads, Pirates.
Promoters and managers include: Ossie Wade, Jimmy Baxter, Gordon Parkins, Mike Parker.
Leading appearances: Harry Welch, 165 (1949–53); Reg Duval, 120 (1949–52); Bill Griffiths, 106 (1950–53).
Leading points scorers: Harry Welch, 1025 (1949–53); Reg Duval, 737 (1949–52); Peter Robinson, 724 (1951–53).
Other leading riders include: Ginger Lees, Ernie Price, Oliver Hart, Les Wotton, George Newton, Tommy Allott, Wal Morton, Peter Craven.
* Belle Vue 'Merseysiders' took over Liverpool fixtures, 1937.

LONG EATON
Long Eaton Stadium, Station Road, Long Eaton, Nottinghamshire.
Years of operation: 1929 (English League, did not ride); 1950 (Open Licence); 1951 (National League, Third Division); 1952 (Southern League, resigned); 1953 (Open Licence); 1963–64 (Provincial League); 1965–67 (British League); 1969–74 (British League, Second Division).
Track length: 367 yards.
Nicknames: Archers, Rangers.
Highest league position: 9th in Second Division, 1951; 9th in Second Division, 1973.
Most points: 35 out of 68, 1973.
Promoters and managers include: Stan Lish, Ken Lish, Reg Fearman, Ron Wilson, Ivor Brown, Vic White.
Leading appearances: Geoff Bouchard, 168 (1970–74); Norman Storer, 133 (1963–67); Ray Wilson, 113 (1963–67).
Leading points scorers: Geoff Bouchard, 1315½ (1970–74); Ray Wilson, 1002 (1963–67).
World Final qualifiers: Leif Enecrona, 1966; Ray Wilson, 1967; Anders Michanek, 1967.
Other leading riders include: Peter Moore, Wilf Plant, Ray Cresp, Howard Cole, Ove Fundin, John Boulger.

MILDENHALL
West Row, Mildenhall, Suffolk.
Years of operation: 1975 to date ((New) National League).
Track length: 307 yards.
Nickname: Fen Tigers.
Highest league position: 8th in National League, 1977.
Most points: 36 out of 72, 1977.
Promoters and managers include: Colin Barber, Terry Waters, Barry Klatt.
Leading appearances: Bob Coles, 103 (1975–77); Fred Mills, 95 (1975–77).
Leading points scorers: Bob Coles 1020½ (1975–77); Kevin Jolly, 390 (1975–76); Robert Henry, 377 (1975–77).

MOTHERWELL
Milton Street, Motherwell, Lanarkshire.
Years of operation: 1950 (Open Licence); 1951–54 (National League, Second Division), 1958 (Open Licence); 1972 (Open Licence).
Track length: 430 yards.
Nickname: Eagles.
Honours: North Shield winners, 1954.
Highest league position: 6th in Second Division, 1953.
Most points: 40 out of 88, 1952.
Promoters and managers include: Ian Hoskins.
Leading appearances: Gordon McGregor, 124 (1951–54); Noel Watson, 100 (1951–53); Bluey Scott, 99 (1951–54).
Leading points scorers: Gordon McGregor, 908 (1951–54); Derek Close, 882½ (1951–54); Noel Watson, 661 (1951–53).
World Final qualifier: Derek Close, 1952.
Other leading riders include: Keith Gurtner, Tommy Miller.

NEATH
Abbey Stadium, Neath, Glamorgan.
Year of operation: 1962 (Provincial League).
Track length: 375 yards.
Nickname: Dragons.
League position: 2nd in Provincial League, 1962.
Most points: 29 out of 48, 1962.
Promoter: Trevor Redmond.
Leading appearances: Charlie Monk, 24 (1962); Glyn Chandler, 24 (1962); George Major, 24 (1962).
Leading points scorers: Trevor Redmond, 190 (1962); Charlie Monk, 169 (1962).

NELSON
Seedhill Stadium, Carr Road, Nelson, Lancashire.
Years of operation: 1967 (Open Licence); 1968–70* (British League, Second Division).
Track length: 300 yards.
Nickname: Admirals.
Highest league position: 2nd in Second Division, 1968.
Most points: 24 out of 60, 1969.
Promoters and managers include: Mike Parker, Bill Bridgett, Derek Tattersall.
Leading appearances: Dave Schofield, 41 (1968–69); Alan Knapkin, 34 (1968–69).
Leading points scorers: Dave Schofield, 352 (1968–69); Alan Knapkin. 217½ (1968–69).
Other leading riders include: Gary Peterson.
* Transferred to Bradford in 1970.
Note – Statistics do not include matches prior to switch.

NEWCASTLE
Brough Park, Byker, Newcastle-upon-Tyne.
Years of operation: 1929 (English League); 1938–39 (National League, Second Division); 1945 (Open Licence); 1946 (Northern League); 1947–51 (National League, Second Division); 1961–64 (Provincial League); 1965–70 (British League); 1975 to date ((New National League).
Track length: 361 yards.
Nicknames: Magpies, Diamonds.
Honours: Provincial League champions, 1964; National League champions, 1976; North Cup winners, 1938; English Cup winners, 1939; National League K.O. Cup winners, 1976.
Most points: 61 out of 68, 1976.
Promoters and managers include: Harry Whitfield, Johnnie Hoskins, Stan Greatrex, Arthur Atkinson, Mike Parker, Ian Hoskins, Ian Thomas, Brian Larner, Dave Younghusband.
Leading appearances: Mike Watkin, 273 (1962–75); Dave Gifford, 168 (1965–70); Ivan Mauger, 164 (1963–68); Russ Dent, 153 (1961–70).
Leading points scorers: Ivan Mauger, 1735 (1963–68); Mike Watkin, 1215 (1962–75); Tom Owen, 1205 (1975–77).
World Champion: Ivan Mauger, 1968.
World Final qualifiers: Ivan Mauger, 1966, 1967, 1968; Anders Michanek, 1970.
Other leading riders: Derek Close, Wilf Jay, Jeff Lloyd, Wal Morton, Ken Le Breton, Brian Brett, Ole Olsen, Dag Lovaas.

NEW CROSS
Hornshay Street, London S.E.14.
Years of operation: 1934–39 (National League); 1945 (Open Licence); 1946–53 (National League, resigned); 1959 (Open Licence); 1960–61 (National League); 1963 (Provincial League, resigned).
Track length: 262 yards.
Nicknames: Lambs, Tammers, Rangers.
Honours: National League champions, 1938, 1948; London Cup winners, 1934, 1937, 1947; Spring Cup winners, 1950.
Promoters and managers include: Fred Mockford, Cecil Smith, Johnnie Hoskins.
Leading appearances: Eric French, 204 (1946–53); Frank Lawrence, 195 (1946–53); Bill Longley, 186 (1947–53).
Leading points scorers: Eric French, 1383 (1946–53); Bill Longley, 1088 (1947–53); Cyril Roger, 1071 (1948–53).
World Champion: Jack Milne, 1937.
World Final qualifiers: Jack Milne, 1936, 1937, 1938, 1939*; George Newton, 1936, 1937, 1938; Ron Johnson, 1939*; Bill Longley, 1949; Cyril Roger, 1949, 1952; Barry Briggs, 1960.
Other leading riders include: Tom Farndon, Stan Greatrex, Lionel Van Praag, Ken Le Breton, Eric Williams, Split Waterman, Doug Davies.

* Final not staged.

NEWPORT
Somerton Park, Newport, Gwent.
Years of operation: 1964 (Provincial League); 1965–76 (British League); 1977 to date (National League).
Track length: 380 yards.
Nicknames: Wasps, Dragons.
Highest league position: 3rd in First Division, 1975.
Honours: Provincial League K.O. Cup winners, 1964; Spring Gold Cup winners, 1974, 1975.
Most points: 49 out of 68, 1975.
Promoters and managers include: Charles Foot, Ken Sharples, Eddie Glennon, Maurice Morley, Bob Radford, Pat Tapson.
Leading appearances: Bob Hughes, 231 (1964–71); Jon Erskine, 200 (1964–70); Alby Golden, 167 (1964–69); Neil Street, 143 (1972–76); Sandor Levai, 106 (1969–71).
Leading points scorers: Phil Crump, 1184 (1974–76); Jon Erskine, 1095 (1964–70); Sandor Levai, 996 (1969–71).
World Final qualifiers: Göte Nordin, 1966; Torbjörn Harrysson, 1968, Phil Crump, 1975, 1976.
Other leading riders include: Jimmy Gooch, Dick Bradley, Jackie Biggs, Reidar Eide.

NORWICH
The Firs, Holt Road, Norwich, Norfolk.
Years of operation: 1937 (Provincial League); 1938–39 (National League, Second Division); 1946 (Northern League); 1947–51 (National League, Second Division); 1952–64 (National League).
Track length: 425 yards.
Nickname: Stars.
Honours: Second Division champions, 1950, 1951; (highest First Division position, 2nd in 1958, 1963); National Trophy winners, 1955, 1963; A.C.U. Cup winners, 1946; Northern Trophy winners, 1946; Provincial Trophy winners, 1938.
Most points: 48 out of 60, 1951.
Promoters and managers include: Max Grosskreutz, Fred Evans, Jack Thompson, Gordon Parkins.
Leading appearances: Phil Clarke, 309 (1947–59); Billy Bales, 245 (1952–64); Jack Freeman, 190 (1947–53); Paddy Mills, 181 (1946–52); Fred Rogers, 176 (1948–54).
Leading points scorers: Phil Clarke, 2162 (1947–59); Ove Fundin, 1826 (1955–64); Billy Bales, 1580 (1952–64); Aub Lawson, 1347 (1953–60); Paddy Mills, 1306½ (1946–52).
World Champion: Ove Fundin, 1956, 1960, 1961, 1963.
World Final qualifiers: Bob Leverenz, 1951; Aub Lawson, 1953, 1954, 1957, 1958, 1959, 1960; Fred Brand, 1954; Ove Fundin, 1955; 1956, 1957, 1958, 1959, 1960, 1961, 1962, 1963, 1964; Billy Bales, 1955; Phil Clarke, 1955; Cyril Roger, 1955, 1956; Gerry Hussey, 1956, 1958; Peter Moore, 1959.
Other leading riders include: Wilf Jay, Bert Spencer, Wal Morton, Geoff Pymar, Johnnie Chamberlain, Terry Betts, Olle Nygren, Trevor Hedge.

NOTTINGHAM
White City Stadium, Trent Lane, Nottingham.
Years of operation: 1929 (Open Licence); 1930–31 (Southern League, resigned); 1933 (National League); 1936–37 (Provincial League); 1938 (National League, Second Division, resigned*).
Track length: 412 yards.
Honours: Provincial Trophy winners, 1937; Coronation Cup winners, 1937.
Highest league position: 3rd in Provincial League, 1936, 1937.
Most points: 22 out of 40, 1937.
Promoters and managers include: Arthur Westwood.
Leading riders include: George Greenwood, Jack Chapman, Les Wotton, Cliff Parkinson.

* Leeds took over Nottingham fixtures, 1938.

OXFORD
Cowley Stadium, Cowley Road, Oxford.
Years of operation: 1949–50 (National League, Third Division); 1951–52 (National League, Second Division); 1953 (Southern League); 1954–56 (National League, Second Division); 1957–64 (National League); 1965–75 (British League); 1976 to date (National League).
Track length: 354 yards.
Nicknames: Cheetahs, Rebels.
Honours: National League champions, 1964; Third Division champions, 1950; South Shield winners, 1951; National League K.O. Cup winners, 1964.
Most points: 54 out of 72, 1950.
Promoters and managers include: John Deeley, Dickie Worth, Ted Flanaghan, Danny Dunton, Harry Bastable.
Leading appearances: Ronnie Genz, 283 (1954–71); Colin Gooddy, 255 (1958–72); Rick Timmo, 236 (1967–74); Eddie Reeves, 222 (1964–73); John Bishop, 166 (1962–69); Arne Pander, 160 (1959–68).
Leading points scorers: Ronnie Genz, 2256½ (1954–71); Arne Pander, 1522 (1959–68); Colin Gooddy, 1493½ (1958–72); Eddie Reeves, 1238 (1964–73); Rick Timmo, 1149½ (1967–74).
World Final qualifiers: Ron How, 1964; Jimmy Gooch, 1965.
Other leading riders include: Gordon McGregor, Eric Boothroyd, Hasse Holmqvist, Jackie Biggs, Jack Geran, Ken McKinlay, Gordon Kennett.

PAISLEY
St Mirren F.C., Love Street, Paisley, Lanarkshire.
Years of operation: 1975–76 ((New) National League).
Track length: 428 yards.
Nickname: Lions.
Highest league position: 15th in New National League, 1975.
Most points: 28 out of 76, 1975.
Promoters and managers include: Neil MacFarlane, Joe Thurley.
Leading appearances: Stuart Mountford, 58 (1975–76); Mike Fullerton, 55 (1975–76); Alan Bridgett, 52 (1975–76).
Leading points scorers: Mike Fullerton, 356 (1975–76); Sid Sheldrick, 342 (1975–76); Stuart Mountford, 308 (1975–76).

PETERBOROUGH
East of England Showground, Alwalton, Peterborough.
Years of operation: 1970–74 (British League, Second Division); 1975 to date ((New) National League).
Track length: 380 yards.
Nickname: Panthers.
Highest league position: 3rd in Second Division, 1972.
Most points: 44 out of 72, 1977.
1977.
Promoters and managers include: Danny Dunton, Alec Ford, Ron Orchard.
Leading appearances: Brian Clark, 226 (1970–77); Roy Carter, 176 (1971–77); Ken Matthews, 133 (1973–77); Richard Greer, 124 (1970–73).
Leading points scorers: Brian Clark, 1565 (1970–77); Richard Greer, 1069 (1970–73); Roy Carter, 1047½ (1971–77).
Other leading riders include: John Davis, Andy Ross.

PLYMOUTH
Pennycross Stadium, Plymouth, Devon.
Years of operation: 1932–34 (National League); 1936 (Provincial League); 1947–49 (National League, Third Division); 1950 (National League, Second Division); 1951 (National League, Third Division); 1952–53 (Southern League); 1954 (National League, Second Division); 1959–60 (Open Licence); 1961–62 (Provincial League); 1968–69 (British League, Second Division); 1970 (Open Licence).
Track length: 400 yards.
Nickname: Devils.
Highest league position: 2nd in Provincial League, 1961.
Most points: 58 out of 96, 1949.
Promoters and managers include: Jimmy Baxter, Gordon Parkins, Trevor Redmond, Bernard Curtiss, Pete Lansdale.
Leading appearances: Pete Lansdale, 170 (1948–54); George Wall, 167 (1949–54); Alan Smith, 164 (1949–54); Len Read, 153 (1947–53).
Leading points scorers: Pete Lansdale, 1549 (1948–54); Len Read, 1152 (1947–53); Peter Robinson, 957 (1948–50); Alan Smith, 947 (1949–54); George Wall, 881 (1949–54).
Other leading riders include: Jack Scott, Jimmy Squibb.

POOLE
Wimborne Road, Poole, Dorset
Years of operation: 1948–51 (National League, Third Division); 1952–55 (National League, Second Division); 1956 (National League, First Division); 1958–59 (National League); 1960–64 (Provincial League); 1965 to date (British League).
Track length: 420 yards (1948–57); 380 yards (1958 to date).
Nickname: Pirates.
Honours: British League champions, 1969; Second Division champions, 1952, 1955; Third Division champions, 1957; Provincial League champions, 1961, 1962; Festival Trophy winners, 1951; Southern League winners, 1962.
Most points: 63 out of 88, 1952.
Promoters and managers include: Herby Hayden, Len Matcham, Charles Knott, Charles Foot, Ron Hart, Ken Middleditch, Tony Lewis.
Leading appearances: Pete Smith, 464 (1963–77); Geoff Mudge, 314 (1960–70); Tony Lewis, 290 (1950–68); Norman Strachan, 268 (1953–73); Ken Middleditch, 255 (1950–62); Terry Small, 250 (1949–59); Alan Kidd, 233 (1950–61); Odd Fossengen, 208 (1968–74).
Leading points scorers: Pete Smith, 2758½ (1963–77); Geoff Mudge, 2488½ (1960–70); Ken Middleditch, 2422½ (1950–62); Tony Lewis, 1828 (1950–68); Terry Small, 1542 (1949–59); Odd Fossengen, 1417 (1968–74); Bill Holden, 1229 (1951–58); Norman Strachan, 1153½ (1953–73); Ross Gilbertson, 1077 (1960–69); Alan Kidd, 1023½ (1950–61).
World Final qualifiers: Brian Crutcher, 1952; Christer Löfqvist, 1972; Malcolm Simmons, 1975, 1976.
Other leading riders include: Göte Nordin, Ronnie Genz, Reidar Eide, Antoni Woryna, Eric Broadbelt.

RAYLEIGH
Weir Stadium, Arterial Road, Rayleigh, Essex.
Years of operation: 1948 (Open Licence); 1949–51 (National League, Third Division); 1952–53 (Southern League); 1954–56 (National League, Second Division); 1957 (Southern Area League); 1959 (Open Licence); 1960–61 (Provincial League); 1963 (Provincial League); 1964–65 (Open Licence); 1968–74 (British League, Second Division).
Track length: 365 yards.
Nicknames: Rovers, Rockets.
Honours: Southern League champions, 1952; Southern Area League champions, 1957; Provincial League champions, 1960.
Most points: 56 out of 72, 1952.
Promoters and managers include: Frank Arnold, Arthur Atkinson, Wally Mawdsley, Len Silver.
Leading appearances: Les McGillivray, 216 (1949–63); Gerald Jackson, 209 (1950–56); Jack Unstead, 204 (1949–57); Maury McDermott, 166 (1952–63); Ron Howes, 163 (1949–54).
Leading points scorers: Gerald Jackson, 1720 (1950–56); Jack Unstead, 1614 (1949–57); Les McGillivray, 1603 (1949–63); Maury McDermott, 1040 (1952–63).
Other leading riders include: Ken Adams, Alan Smith, Reg Reeves.

READING
(1) Greyhound Stadium, Oxford Road, Tilehurst, Reading, Berkshire.
(2) Smallmead Stadium, Bennet Road, Reading, Berkshire.
Years of operation: (1) 1968–70 (British League, Second Division); 1971–73 (British League, First Division).
(2) 1975 to date (British League).
Track length: (1) 360 yards; (2) 336 yards.
Nickname: Racers.
Honours: British League champions, 1973; Spring Gold Cup winners, 1972, 1977.

Promoters and managers include: Reg Fearman, Dick Bailey, Bob Radford, Frank Higley.
Leading appearances: Bernie Leigh, 247 (1968–77); Mick Bell, 200 (1969–76); Richard May, 185 (1969–75).
Leading points scorers: Anders Michanek, 1161 (1971–75); Richard May, 1077 (1969–75); Bernie Leigh, 1058½ (1968–77).
World Final qualifiers: Anders Michanek, 1971, 1972, 1973, 1975; Bengt Jansson, 1977.
Other leading riders: Geoff Curtis, Dag Lovaas, Dave Jessup, John Davis.

RINGWOOD
Matchams Park, Ringwood, Hampshire.
Years of operation: Training track from 1951; 1954–55 (Southern Area League, resigned).
Track length: 375 yards.
Nickname: Turfs.
Highest league position: 3rd in Southern Area League, 1954.
Most points: 18 out of 32, 1954.
Promoter: Len Matcham.
Leading riders include: Ernie Lessiter, Tony Lewis.

ROCHDALE
The Athletic Grounds, Rochdale, Lancashire.
Years of operation: 1928 (Open Licence); 1929 (English League); 1930 (Northern League); 1970–71 (British League, Second Division).
Track length: 418 yards.
Nickname: Hornets.
Highest league position: 3rd in Second Division, 1970.
Most points: 44 out of 64, 1970.
Promoters and managers include: Dent Oliver, Alan Middleton.
Leading appearances: Ken Moss, 58 (1970–71); Paul Tyrer, 56 (1970–71).
Leading points scorers: Paul Tyrer, 398 (1970–71); Alan Wilkinson, 331 (1970–71); Eric Broadbelt, 321 (1970).
Other leading riders: Peter Collins, Graham Drury.

ROMFORD
Brooklands Stadium, Brooklands Road, Romford, Essex.
Years of operation: 1969–71 (British League, Second Division).
Track length: 375 yards.
Nickname: Bombers.
Highest league position: 3rd in Second Division, 1969.
Most points: 39 out of 60, 1969.
Promoters and managers include: Pete Lansdale, Wally Mawdsley, Maurice Morley.
Leading appearances: Charlie Benham, 77 (1969–71); Brian Foote, 75 (1969–71).
Leading points scorers: Ross Gilbertson, 582 (1969–70); Phil Woodcock, 541½ (1969–71).
Other leading riders include: Kevin Holden.

RYE HOUSE
Rye House Stadium, Rye Road, Hoddesdon, Hertfordshire.
Years of operation: 1935–41 (Open Licence); 1946–53 (Open Licence); 1954–57 (Southern Area League); 1958 (Open Licence); 1959 (Southern Area League); 1960–66 (Open Licence); 1969–73 (Open Licence); 1974 (British League, Second Division); 1975 to date ((New) National League).
Track length: 440 yards (now go-kart circuit); 284 yards (since 1965).
Nicknames: Roosters, Red Devils, Rockets.
Honours: Southern Area League champions, 1954, 1955, 1956.
Highest league position: 2nd in National League, 1977.
Most points: 51 out of 72, 1977.
Promoters and managers include: George Kay, Sid Singleton, Dickie Case, Freddie Millward, Len Silver, Colin Pratt.
Leading appearances: Kelvin Mullarkey, 99 (1975–77); Hugh Saunders, 92 (1975–77); Karl Fiala, 88 (1975–77).
Leading points scorers: Kelvin Mullarkey, 730 (1975–77); Brian Foote, 689 (1974–76); Hugh Saunders, 587 (1975–77).
Other leading riders include: Mike Broadbanks, Brian Brett, Colin Pratt, Peter Moore.

ST. AUSTELL
Cornish Stadium, St. Austell, Cornwall.
Years of operation: 1949 (Open Licence); 1950–51 (National League, Third Division); 1952–53 (Southern League); 1957–62 (Open Licence); 1963 (Provincial League).
Track length: 360 yards.
Nickname: Gulls.
Highest league position: 5th in Provincial League, 1963.
Most points: 28 out of 48, 1963.
Promoters and managers include: Trevor Redmond, George Newton.
Leading appearances: Harold Bull, 124 (1950–53); Norman Street, 122 (1950–53).
Leading points scorers: Norman Street, 766½ (1950–53); Harold Bull, 744 (1950–53).
Other leading riders include: Allan Quinn, George Newton, Lloyd Goffe, Cyril Maidment, Ray Cresp, Trevor Redmond.

SCUNTHORPE
Quibell Park, Scunthorpe, Lincolnshire.
Years of operation: 1971–74 (British League, Second Division); 1975 to date ((New) National League).
Track length: 440 yards.
Nickname: Saints.
Promoters and managers include: Ivor Brown, Vic White, Brian Osborn.
Highest league position: 13th in New National League, 1975.
Most points: 35 out of 76, 1975.
Leading appearances: Keith Evans, 93 (1974–76); Ken McKinlay, 85 (1973–75).
Leading points scorers: Keith Evans, 711½ (1974–76); Ken McKinlay, 588 (1973–75).

SHEFFIELD
Owlerton Sports Stadium, Penistone Road, Sheffield, Yorkshire.
Years of operation: 1929 (English League); 1930–31 (Northern League); 1932 (National League N.P.A. Trophy); 1933 (National League); 1938–39 (National League, Second Division); 1945 (Open Licence); 1946 (Northern League); 1947–51 (National League, Second Division, resigned); 1960–64 (Provincial League); 1965 to date (British League).
Track length: 395 yards.
Nicknames: Tigers, Tars.
Honours: British Speedway Cup winners, 1947; Northern League winners, 1962, 1963, 1964; Speedway Star K.O. Cup winners, 1974.
Highest league position: 2nd in Northern League, 1946; 2nd in Second Division, 1949; 2nd in First Division, 1973.
Most points: 59 out of 88, 1949.
Promoters and managers include: Arthur Westwood, Bluey Wilkinson, Frank Varey, Alice Hart, Terry Thornhill, John Dews.
Leading appearances: Arnold Haley, 360 (1965–77); Bob Paulson, 284 (1965–74); John Dews 254 (1962–70); Doug Wyer, 193 (1969–77); Bengt Larsson, 179 (1967–75); Billy Bales, 166 (1965–69); Reg Wilson, 159 (1969–77); Alan Jay, 155 (1961–67).
Leading points scorers: Arnold Haley, 2397½ (1965–77); Doug Wyer, 1638 (1969–77); Bob Paulson, 1480 (1965–74); John Dews, 1363½ (1962–70); Reg Wilson, 1279 (1969–77); Jim Airey, 1163½ (1969–71); Bengt Larsson, 1125 (1967–75); Clive Featherby, 1021 (1961–65).
World Final qualifiers: Jim Airey, 1971; Doug Wyer, 1976.
Other leading riders include: Squib Burton, Cliff Watson, Ernie Evans, Paddy Mills, Tommy Allott, Henry Long, Charlie Monk, Bob Valentine.

SOUTHAMPTON
Bannister Court, Southampton, Hampshire.
Years of operation: 1928 (Open Licence); 1929–31 (Southern League); 1932 (National League, resigned*); 1936–37 (Provincial League); 1938 (National League, Second Division); 1939 (National League, First Division); 1947–48 (National League, Third Division); 1949–51 (National League, Second Division, resigned); 1952–53 (Southern League); 1954–56 (National League, Second Division); 1957–63 (National League).
Track length: 378 yards (1928–39); 333 yards (1947–63).
Nickname: Saints.
Honours: National League champions, 1962; Provincial League champions, 1936; North-South Cup, 1948; National League K.O. Cup, 1961 and 1963; National Trophy, 1961.
Promoters and managers include: Jimmy Baxter, Frank Goulden, Charles Knott, Bert Croucher.
Leading appearances: Jimmy Squibb, 192 (1947–59); Alby Golden, 185 (1955–63); Dick Bradley, 164 (1955–63); Brian Hanham, 161 (1952–62).
Leading points scorers: Jimmy Squibb, 1371 (1947–59); Dick Bradley, 1342 (1955–63); Björn Knutsson, 971 (1959–63).
World Final qualifiers: Cordy Milne, 1939*, Benny Kaufman, 1939*, Brian Crutcher, 1959; Geoff Mardon, 1959; Chum Taylor, 1960; Björn Knutsson, 1961, 1962, 1963; Barry Briggs, 1961, 1962, 1963.
Other leading riders include: Gus Kuhn, Wally Kilmister, Bob Oakley, Cyril Roger.

* Moved to Lea Bridge, 1932.
* Final not staged.

STAMFORD BRIDGE
Stamford Bridge Stadium, Fulham Road, London S.W.6.
Years of operation: 1928 (Open Licence); 1929–31 (Southern League); 1932 (National League).
Track length. 440 yards.
Nickname: Pensioners.
Honours: Southern League champions, 1929; National League N.P.A. Trophy champions, 1932.
Most points: 54 out of 76, 1931.
Promoters and managers include: Claude Langdon, A. C. Brake, Arthur Warwick.
Leading riders include: Les Blakeborough, Gus Kuhn, Wal Phillips, Fred Ralph.

STOKE
(1) Hanley Stadium, Sun Street, Hanley, Staffordshire.
Years of operation: (As Hanley) 1929 (English League, resigned); 1947–49 (National League, Third Division); 1950–51 (National League, Second Division).
(As Stoke) 1939 (National League, Second Division, resigned*); 1952–53 (National League, Second Division); 1960–63 (Provincial League).
Track length: 347 yards.
Nickname: Potters.
Honours: Third Division champions, 1949; Northern League champions, 1961.
Most points: 71 out of 96, 1949.
Promoters and managers include: Tiger Stevenson, Les Gregory, Mike Parker, Reg Fearman, Peter Morrish.
Leading appearances: Ray Harris, 285 (1947–63); Ken Adams, 282 (1948–63); Les Jenkins, 252 (1947–60); Gil Blake, 209 (1947–52).
Leading points scorers: Ken Adams, 2037 (1948–63); Les Jenkins, 1581 (1947–60); Ray Harris, 1403 (1947–63); Gil Blake, 1268 (1947–52).
Other leading riders include: Reg Fearman, Pete Jarman, Colin Pratt, Kid Bodie (Howard Cole).

* Replaced by Belle Vue II.

STOKE
(2) Newcastle Under Lyne Stadium, Loomer Road, Chesterton, Stoke, Staffordshire.
Years of operation: (as Chesterton) 1973 (British League, Second Division); (as Stoke) 1974 (British League, Second Division); 1975 to date ((New) National League).
Track length: 395 yards.
Nickname: Potters.
Highest league position: 3rd in New National League, 1975.
Most points: 52 out of 76, 1975.
Promoters and managers include: Russ Bragg, Chris Van Straaten, Harry Bastable, Chris Harrison.
Leading appearances: Alan Bridgett, 74 (1973–75); Geoff Pusey, 68 (1973–74); Steve Bastable, 67 (1974–75).
Leading points scorers: Mike Broadbanks, 620 (1973–74); Geoff Pusey, 476 (1973–74); Steve Bastable, 444½ (1974–75).
Other leading riders include: Brian Woodward, Les Collins, Jack Millen.

SUNDERLAND
Greyhound Stadium, Newcastle Road, Cleadon, County Durham.
Years of operation: 1964 (Provincial League, resigned); 1971–74 (British League, Second Division).
Track length: 310 yards.
Nicknames: Saints, Stars, Gladiators.
Highest league position: 11th in Second Division, 1973.
Most points: 32 out of 68, 1973.
Promoters and managers include: Mike Parker, Alan Middleton, Len Silver.
Leading appearances: Russ Dent, 129 (1971–74); George Barclay, 110 (1971–74); Jim Wells, 96 (1972–74).
Leading points scorers: Russ Dent, 875 (1971–74); George Barclay, 683 (1971–74); Jim Wells, 569 (1972–74).
Other leading riders include: Jim Airey, Gordon Guasco, Jack Millen, Graeme Smith.

SWINDON
(1) Swindon Autodrome, Gorse Hill, Swindon
(2) Abbey Stadium, Blunsdon, Near Swindon, Wiltshire.
Years of operation: (1) 1928 (Open Licence); (2) 1949*–51 (National League, Third Division); 1952–53 (Southern League); 1954–56 (National League, Second Division); 1957–64 (National League); 1965 to date (British League).
Track length: 410 yards (1949–59); 395 yards (1960 to date).
Nickname: Robins.
Honours: National League champions, 1957; British League champions, 1967; Second Division champions, 1956; Midland Cup winners, 1967, 1968.
Most points: 48 out of 72, 1967.
Promoters and managers include: Reg Witcomb, Bill Dutton, Bert Hearse, Ted Nelson, Roger Wise, Bob Jones, Norman Parker, Dick Bradley.
Leading appearances: Martin Ashby, 390 (1962–77); Mike Broadbanks, 374 (1957–72); Mike Keen, 314 (1965–75); Bob Kilby, 311 (1964–77); Ian Williams, 264 (1952–63); Barry Briggs, 246 (1964–72); Clive Hitch, 225 (1966–73).
Leading points scorers: Martin Ashby, 3586½ (1962–77); Barry Briggs, 2874 (1964–72); Mike Broadbanks, 2827 (1957–72); Bob Kilby, 2323 (1964–77); Ian Williams, 1983 (1952–63); Mike Keen, 1242 (1965–75); George White, 1147½ (1954–61); Bob Roger, 1016 (1954–61); Danny Malone, 1014 (1950–56).
World Champion: Barry Briggs, 1964, 1966.
World Final qualifiers: Bob Roger, 1957; George White, 1957, 1959; Ian Williams, 1957; Mike Broadbanks, 1958, 1961, 1962, 1964, 1966; Arne Carlsson, 1962; Peter Moore, 1963; Barry Briggs, 1964, 1965, 1966, 1967, 1968, 1969, 1970, 1972; Brian Brett, 1965.
Other leading riders include: Neil Street, Teo Teodorowicz.

* Swindon took over Hull's fixtures, 1949.

TAMWORTH
Fazeley Stadium, Tamworth, Staffordshire.
Years of operation: 1947–50 (National League, Third Division).
Track length: 352 yards.
Nicknames: Greyhounds, Tammies.
Highest league position: 3rd in Third Division, 1949.
Most points: 66 out of 96, 1949.
Promoters and managers include: Les Marshall, Phil Hart.
Leading appearances: Steve Langton, 111 (1947–49); Bill Dalton, 99 (1947–49).
Leading points scorers: Steve Langton, 713 (1947–49); Bill Dalton, 659 (1947–49).
Other leading riders include: Cyril Page, Eric Boothroyd.

TEESSIDE
Cleveland Park, Stockton Road, Middlesbrough.
Years of operation: (as Middlesbrough) 1929 (Open Licence); 1929 (English League); 1938 (Open Licence); 1939 (National League, Second Division, resigned); 1945 (Open Licence); 1946 (Northern League); 1947–48 (National League, Second Division); 1961–64 (Provincial League); 1965–66 (Open Licence); (as Teesside) 1968–74 (British League, Second Division); 1975 to date ((New) National League).
Track length: 335 yards.
Nicknames: Bears, Teessiders, Tigers.
Honours: Northern League champions, 1946; Second Division champions, 1947.
Most points: 40 out of 56, 1947.
Promoters and managers include: Harry Whitfield, Mike Parker, Reg Fearman, Eric Boothroyd, Ron Wilson, Tony Coupland.
Leading appearances: Pete Reading, 335 (1968–77); Dave Durham, 197 (1968–75); Bruce Forrester, 154 (1969–75); Tim Swales, 142 (1969–74); Alan Emerson, 132 (1973–77); Tom Leadbitter, 131 (1968–76).
Leading points scorers: Peter Reading, 1589½ (1968–77); Tom Leadbitter, 1183 (1968–76); Dave Durham, 1167 (1968–75); Bruce Forrester, 1161 (1969–75).
Other leading riders include: Wilf Plant, Derek Close, Geoff Pymar, Wal Morton, Eric Boocock, Eric Boothroyd, Graham Plant.

WALTHAMSTOW
Walthamstow Stadium, Chingford Road, London E.4.
Years of operation: 1934* (National League); 1949–51 (National League, Second Division).
Track length: 282 yards.
Nickname: Wolves.
Highest league position: 5th in Second Division, 1950, 1951.
Most points: 34 out of 60, 1951.
Promoters and managers include: Dicky Maybrook, Wally Lloyd, John Deeley, Charles Chandler.
Leading appearances: Harry Edwards, 101 (1949–51); Reg Reeves, 101 (1949–51).
Leading points scorers: Jim Boyd, 666 (1949–51); Harry Edwards, 592 (1949–51); Reg Reeves, 585 (1949–51).
Other leading riders include: Benny King, Wilf Jay, Dick Geary, Charlie May, George Newton.

* Took over Lea Bridge fixtures.

WEMBLEY
Empire Stadium, Wembley, Middlesex.
Years of operation: 1929–31 (Southern League); 1932–39 (National League); 1946–56 (National League).
Track length: 378 yards.
Nickname: Lions.
Honours: Southern League champions, 1930, 1931; National League champions, 1932, 1946, 1947, 1949, 1950, 1951, 1952, 1953; National Trophy winners, 1931, 1932, 1948, 1954; London Cup winners, 1930, 1932, 1933, 1946, 1948, 1949, 1950, 1951, 1954; British Speedway Cup winners, 1947.
Most points: 59 out of 76, 1931.
Promoters and managers include: Sir Arthur Elvin, Johnnie Hoskins, Alec Jackson, Trevor Redmond, Bernard Cottrell, Freddie Williams.
Leading appearances: Tommy Price, 287 (1946–56); Freddie Williams, 237 (1947–56); Bill Kitchen, 203 (1946–54); George Wilks, 166 (1946–54); Eric Williams, 162 (1950–55); Jimmy Gooch, 136 (1950–56); Bill Gilbert, 134 (1946–50).
Leading points scorers: Tommy Price, 2403 (1946–56); Freddie Williams, 1854 (1947–56); Bill Kitchen, 1289½ (1946–54); Eric Williams, 1180 (1950–55); George Wilks, 1160 (1946–54); Brian Crutcher, 902 (1953–56).
World Champions: Lionel Van Praag, 1936; Tommy Price, 1949; Freddie Williams, 1950, 1953.
World Final qualifiers: Lionel Van Praag, 1936, 1937 1938, 1939*; Frank Charles, 1936, 1937; Ginger Lees, 1936, 1937; Tommy Price, 1938, 1949, 1950, 1954; Aub Lawson, 1939*; Bill Kitchen, 1949; Bill Gilbert, 1949; Freddie Williams, 1950, 1951, 1952, 1953; Eric Williams, 1951, 1953, 1955; Bob Oakley, 1952; Brian Crutcher, 1953, 1954, 1955, 1956; Trevor Redmond, 1954.
Other leading riders include: Billy Lamont, Cliff Parkinson, Gus Kuhn, Colin Watson, Dickie Case, George Greenwood, Wally Kilmister, Eric French, Bruce Abernethy, Split Waterman, Reidar Eide, Ove Fundin, Göte Nordin, Sverre Harrfeldt, Dave Jessup.

* Final not staged.

WEST HAM
Custom House Stadium, Prince Regent Lane, London E.16.
Years of operation: 1928 (Open Licence); 1929–31 (Southern League); 1932–39 (National League); 1946–55 (National League); 1964 (National League); 1965–71 (British League); 1972* (British League, Second Division).
Track length: 440 yards (1928–53); 415 yards (1954–72).
Nickname: Hammers.
Honours: National League champions, 1937; British League champions, 1965; A.C.U. Cup winners, 1938; Speedway Star K.O. Cup winners, 1965; London Cup winners, 1965, 1966, 1967.
Most points: 47 out of 68, 1965.
Promoters and managers include: Jimmy Baxter, Johnnie Hoskins, Alec Jackson, Arthur Atkinson, Stan Greatrex, Tommy Price, Dave Lanning, Phil Bishop, Gordon Parkins.
Leading appearances: Malcolm Craven, 251 (1946–54); Howdy Byford, 201 (1947–55); Wally Green, 199 (1946–55); Fred Curtis, 176 (1948–53); Ken McKinlay, 161 (1965–69).
Leading scorers: Malcolm Craven, 1817 (1946–54); Ken McKinlay, 1449½ (1965–69); Norman Hunter, 1277½ (1964–68); Sverre Harrfeldt, 1255½ (1965–70); Wally Green, 1244½ (1946–55).
World Champions: Bluey Wilkinson, 1938; Jack Young, 1952.
World Final qualifiers: Bluey Wilkinson, 1936, 1938; Arthur Atkinson, 1936, 1937, 1938, 1939*; Tommy Croombs, 1937, 1938; Eric Chitty, 1937, 1939*; Aub Lawson, 1949, 1950, 1951; Cliff Watson, 1949; Wally Green, 1950; Jack Young, 1952, 1953, 1954, 1955; Björn Knutsson, 1964; Ken McKinlay, 1965, 1969; Sverre Harrfeldt, 1966.
Other leading riders include: Tiger Stevenson, Phil Bishop, Colin Watson, Malcolm Simmons, Olle Nygren, Tony Clarke, Christer Löfqvist.

* Barrow took over from West Ham Fixtures, 1972.
* Final not staged.

WEST HAM II
Years of operation: 1934 (National League, Second Division); 1938 (National League, Second Division).
Honours: Second Division winners, 1934.
Most points: 23 out of 24, 1934.

WEYMOUTH
Radipole Lane, Weymouth, Dorset.
Years of operation: 1954 (Open Licence); 1955 (National League, Second Division, resigned); 1962–65 (Open Licence); 1968 (British League, Second Division); 1974 (British League, Second Division); 1975 to date ((New) National League).
Track length: 379 yards.
Nicknames: Scorchers, Royals, Eagles, Wizards.
Highest league position: 9th in Second Division, 1968.
Most points: 25 out of 72, 1977.
Promoters and managers include: Bill Dutton, Wally Mawdsley, Harry Davis, Ted Holding.
Leading appearances: Vic Harding, 84 (1975–77); Geoff Swindells, 78 (1974–75); Chris Robins, 74 (1975–77).
Leading points scorers: Vic Harding, 582 (1975–77); Martin Yeates, 566 (1975–76).
Other leading riders include: Danny Dunton, Tony Lomas.

WHITE CITY (LONDON)
White City Stadium, Wood Lane, London W.12.
Years of operation: 1928 (Open Licence); 1929 (Southern League); 1976 to date (British League).
Track length: 352 yards (1928–29); 418 yards (1976 to date).
Nickname: Rebels.
Honours: British League champions, 1977.
Most points: 55 out of 72, 1977.
Promoters and managers include: A. J. Hunting, Danny Dunton, Bobby Dugard, Lee Dunton.
Leading appearances: Trevor Geer, 71 (1976–77); Gordon Kennett, 71 (1976–77).
Leading points scorers: Gordon Kennett, 908 (1976–77); Trevor Geer, 417 (1976–77).
Other leading riders include: Colin Watson, Hilary Buchanan, Dag Lovaas, Marek Cieslak.

WHITE CITY (MANCHESTER)
White City Greyhound Stadium, Old Trafford, Manchester.
Years of operation: 1928 (Open Licence); 1929 (English League, resigned); 1930 (Northern League).
Track length: 446 yards.
Highest league position: 2nd in Northern League, 1930.
Most points: 36 out of 42, 1929.
Promoter: Charles Pashley.

WIGAN
(1) Poolstock Stadium, Wigan, Lancashire.
(2) Woodhouse Lane, Wigan, Lancashire.
Years of operation: (1) 1947 (National League, Second Division); 1960 (Open Licence); (2) 1952 (Open Licence).
Track length: (1) 321 yards (1947); 294 yards (1960). (2) 360 yards.
Nicknames: Warriors, Panthers.
League position: 7th in Second Division, 1947.
Most points: 20 out of 56, 1947.
Leading appearances: Dick Geary, 28 (1947); Percy Brine, 28 (1947); Cyril Cooper, 28 (1947).
Leading points scorers: Dick Geary, 299 (1947); Jack Gordon, 163 (1947).
Promoters and managers include: Joe Waxman, James Wolfenden, Don Potter.
Other leading riders include: Norman Hargreaves, Harry Welch.

WIMBLEDON
Plough Lane, London S.W.17.
Years of operation: 1928 (Open Licence); 1929–31 (Southern League); 1932–39 (National League); 1946–64 (National League); 1965 to date (British League).
Track length: 343 yards (1928–55); 355 yards (1956–67); 327 yards (1968 to date).
Nickname: Dons.
Honours: National League champions, 1954, 1955, 1956, 1958, 1959, 1960, 1961; National Trophy winners, 1938, 1950, 1951, 1953, 1959, 1960, 1962; London Cup winners, 1938, 1939, 1961, 1964, 1968, 1969, 1970, 1972, 1974, 1975, 1976; National League K.O. Cup winners, 1962; R.A.C. Cup winners, 1954; Britannia Trophy winners, 1959; Speedway Star K.O. Cup winners, 1968, 1969, 1970.
Promoters and managers include: A. J. Hunting, Dicky Maybrook, Norman Pritchard, Ronnie Greene, Cyril Maidment.
Leading appearances: Cyril Brine, 391 (1946–62); Ronnie Moore, 374 (1950–72); Jim Tebby, 349 (1959–72); Trevor Hedge, 336 (1965–74); Cyril Maidment, 301 (1951–71); Reg Luckhurst, 289 (1965–75); Barry Briggs, 207 (1952–75); Norman Parker, 167 (1946–53); Ron How, 166 (1955–63); Bob Andrews, 158 (1956–64); Bobby Dugard, 153 (1965–70).
Leading points scorers: Ronnie Moore, 3847 (1950–72); Trevor Hedge, 2944 (1965–74); Cyril Brine, 2312 (1946–62); Barry Briggs, 1984 (1952–75); Reg Luckhurst, 1853 (1965–75); Ron How, 1604½ (1955–63); Norman Parker, 1511½ (1946–53); Cyril Maidment, 1481 (1951–71); Olle Nygren, 1477 (1954–68); Jim Tebby, 1298 (1959–72).
World Champions: Ronnie Moore, 1954, 1959; Barry Briggs, 1957, 1958.
World Final qualifiers: Vic Huxley, 1936; Wal Phillips, 1936; Wilbur Lamoreaux, 1937, 1938, 1939*; Benny Kaufman, 1938; Geoff Pymar, 1938; Vic Duggan, 1939*; Eric Collins, 1939*; Norman Parker, 1949, 1951; Cyril Brine, 1950, 1951; Ronnie Moore, 1950, 1951, 1952, 1953, 1954, 1955, 1956, 1958, 1959, 1960, 1961, 1962, 1969, 1971; Ernie Roccio, 1951; Geoff Mardon, 1953, 1954; Barry Briggs, 1954, 1955, 1956, 1957, 1958, 1959; Peter Moore, 1956; Ron How, 1957, 1958, 1959, 1961, 1962, 1963; Cyril Maidment, 1961; Bob Andrews, 1961, 1962, 1964; Sverre Harrfeldt, 1963; Leo McAuliffe, 1963; Reg Luckhurst, 1965; Trevor Hedge, 1970; Tommy Jansson, 1975; Edward Jancarz, 1977.
Other leading riders include: Jim Kempster, Claude Rye, Gus Kuhn, Billy Lamont, Ray Tauser, Dickie Case, Geoff Pymar, Lloyd Goffe, Oliver Hart, Alec Statham, Göte Nordin.

* Final not staged.

WOMBWELL
Station Road, Wombwell, Nottinghamshire.
Years of operation: 1928–29 (Open Licence); 1930 (Northern League); 1947–48 (National League, Third Division).
Track length: 443 yards.
Nicknames: Hares, Colliers.
Highest league position: 7th in Third Division, 1947.
Most points: 24 out of 56, 1947.
Leading appearances: Harwood Pike, 66 (1947–48); Jeff Bishop, 64 (1947–48).
Leading points scorers: Harwood Pike, 458 (1947–48); Len Tupling, 316 (1947–48).

WOLVERHAMPTON
Monmore Green Stadium, Bilston Road, Wolverhampton, Staffs.
Years of operation: 1928 (Open Licence); 1949–50 (Open Licence); 1951 (National League, Third Division); 1952 (Southern League); 1953–54 (National League, Second Division, resigned); 1961–64 (Provincial League); 1965 to date (British League).
Track length: 329 yards.
Nicknames: Wasps, Wolves.
Honours: Provincial League champions, 1963; Midland League champions, 1962.
Most points: 41 out of 72, 1952.
Promoters and managers include: Arthur Simcock, John Deeley, Mike Parker, Bill Bridgett, Bob Wasley, Dave Parry.
Leading appearances: James Bond, 218 (1963–71); Peter Vandenberg, 173 (1966–70); Ole Olsen, 166 (1970–75); George Hunter, 159 (1972–77).
Leading points scorers: Ole Olsen, 2057 (1970–75); Peter Vandenberg, 1384 (1966–70); George Hunter, 1065 (1972–77).
World Champion: Ole Olsen, 1971, 1975.
World Final qualifiers: Hasse Holmqvist, 1968; Ole Olsen, 1970, 1971, 1972, 1973, 1974, 1975; Finn Thomsen, 1977.
Other leading riders include: Graham Warren, Howard Cole, Terry Betts, Jim Airey, Tommy Sweetman, Jimmy McMillan, Norman Hunter.

WORKINGTON
(1) Lonsdale Park, Workington, Cumberland.
(2) Derwent Park, Workington, Cumberland.
Years of operation: (1) 1937–38 (Open Licence); (2) 1970–74 (British League, Second Division); 1975 to date ((New) National League).
Track length: (1) 359 yards; (2) 398 yards.
Nickname: Comets.
Highest league position: 2nd in Second Division, 1973.
Most points: 48 out of 76, 1975.
Promoters and managers include: Ian Thomas, George Graham, Alan Middleton, Geoff Penniket.
Leading appearances: Lou Sansom, 182 (1970–76); Taffy Owen, 171 (1970–76); Malcolm Mackay, 153 (1970–75); Steve Watson, 129 (1971–75).
Leading points scorers: Lou Sansom, 1654 (1970–76); Taffy Owen, 1376 (1970–76); Malcolm Mackay, 1335 (1970–75).
Other leading riders include: Mitch Graham, Bob Valentine, Reg Wilson, Steve Lawson.

YARMOUTH
Caister Road, Great Yarmouth, Norfolk.
Years of operation: 1948–49 (National League, Third Division); 1950–53 (National League, Second Division); 1957–58 (Open Licence); 1959 (Southern Area League); 1960 (Provincial League); 1961 (Open Licence).
Track length: 325 yards.
Nickname: Bloaters.
Promoters and managers include: Dickie Wise, Percy Leighton, Ted Courtnell, Alf Weedon.
Leading appearances: Reg Morgan, 189 (1948–53); Fred Brand, 158 (1949–53); Bob Baker, 104 (1951–53); Bill Carruthers, 104 (1948–50).
Leading points scorers: Fred Brand, 1308 (1949–53); Reg Morgan, 1086½ (1948–53); Bob Baker, 889 (1951–53); Billy Bales, 752½ (1948–50).
Other leading riders include: Johnny Chamberlain, Ronnie Genz, Danny Dunton, Ivor Brown, Geoff Pymar.

OTHER LEAGUE TRACKS

BARNSLEY
Competed in the English League (1929) and Northern League (1930). Boasted two tracks – at Queen's Park and Lundwood. Leading rider: Tommy Allott.

BOLTON
Opened, August 1928. Entered the English League, 1929, but resigned during the season.

BURNLEY
Their record in the 1929 English League was deleted when they resigned in mid-season. Leading rider, Joe Abbott, moved to Preston.

GOSFORTH (NEWCASTLE)
Rode just nine matches in Northern League, 1930. First club involved in a cash transfer when they signed Buzz Hibberd from White City, Manchester.

PRESTON
English League 1929, runners-up. Beat Halifax 87–39 on aggregate in English League Cup Final. Competed in the Northern League, 1930, 1931.

SALFORD
Opened, August 1928. Competed in the English League, 1929. Johnnie Hoskins was manager at one time.

WARRINGTON
Expelled from the English League, 1929, although their record was not deleted. Rode in Northern League, 1930.

Non-League Tracks

ASHINGTON
Staged open meetings, 1972.

BIRMINGHAM (GREET)
The Autodrone track ran during 1928; later used by B.S.A. works for testing.

BRIGHTON
Operated in 1928, with Johnnie Hoskins as manager.

COWDENBEATH
Featured open meetings in 1965.

GLASGOW (CELTIC PARK)
Staged first meeting in Scotland, April 28, 1928. Promoter: Jimmy Baxter.

GLASGOW (CARNTYNE)
Short-lived 1928 promotion.

HUDDERSFIELD
Years of operation, 1928–29.

NEWTONGRANGE
Scottish training track, Open Licence, 1970.

PORTSMOUTH
Meetings at Copnor Gardens, 1929.

PONTYPRIDD
Opened for business, 1929.

ROCHESTER
Staged pre-war meetings; entered Second Division 1969 but planning permission refused and team transferred to Romford.

Irish Tracks
Chapelizod, Dublin
Dunmore Stadium, Belfast
Harold's Cross, Dublin
Santry Stadium
Shelbourne Park, Dublin

Other Tracks
Aycliffe, Co. Durham
Caerphilly (1931)
Catford
Earls Barton
Mansfield
New Brighton
Northampton
Tredegar
Seaforth (near Liverpool)
Trentham (Staffordshire)
White City (Hull)
Whitley Bay
York

Trotting Tracks where speedway has been staged
Audenshaw
Blackpool
Droylesden
Glasgow (Nelson Athletic Ground)
Greenford

Training Tracks who have not achieved League status
Alphington (Exeter)
Bothwell (Lanarkshire)
Calderbank
Chiswick
Corstorphine
Dagenham
Iwade
Newton Heath
Luton
Smallford (St. Albans)

Grass Speedway Tracks
Barnet
Calmore
Cannfield
Crown (Tolldown, Bristol)
Farleigh Castle
Holbeach (Bell End)
March
Newmarket
Norwich (Horsford)
Peterborough (Fengate)
Salisbury
St. Ives
Shaftesbury
Shepperton
Swainswick (Bath)
Taunton
Wisbech

LEAGUE TABLES

1929

Southern League

	P	W	D	L	Pts
Stamford Bridge	20	17	0	3	34
Southampton	20	16	0	4	32
Coventry	20	14	0	6	28
Crystal Palace	20	11	0	9	22
Wembley	20	11	0	9	22
West Ham	20	8	0	12	16
White City (London)	20	8	0	12	16
Harringay	20	7	0	13	14
Birmingham	20	7	0	13	14
Lea Bridge	20	6	0	14	12
Wimbledon	20	5	0	15	10

English Dirt Track League

	P	W	D	L	Pts
Leeds	23	17	1	5	35
Preston	24	16	0	8	32
Halifax	22	14	1	7	29
Rochdale	24	12	1	11	25
Leicester Stadium	23	10	1	12	21
Salford	21	10	0	11	20
Liverpool	21	10	0	11	20
Sheffield	21	8	1	12	17
Newcastle	18	8	0	10	16
Barnsley	21	8	0	13	16
Middlesbrough	21	6	0	15	12

(Note – The English Dirt-Track League, also known at the Northern League, included White City (Manchester) who resigned after scoring 36 points from 18 matches. Warrington were expelled in September after scoring 11 points from 18 matches. Belle Vue and Burnley also participated, but both resigned in mid-season.)

1930

Southern League

	P	W	D	L	Pts
Wembley	24	20	1	3	41
Southampton	24	17	1	6	35
Stamford Bridge	24	16	1	7	33
Wimbledon	24	16	1	7	33
Birmingham	24	13	1	10	27
Coventry	24	13	1	10	27
Crystal Palace	24	11	1	12	23
Lea Bridge	24	10	1	13	21
West Ham	24	10	0	14	20
Leicester Stadium	24	8	1	15	17
High Beach	24	8	0	16	16
Harringay	24	7	0	17	14
Nottingham	24	2	1	21	5

Northern League

	P	W	D	L	Pts
Belle Vue	21	19	1	1	39
White City (M/cr)	15	13	0	2	26
Liverpool	18	13	0	5	26
Preston	15	8	0	7	16
Warrington	17	8	0	9	16
Sheffield	13	6	0	7	12
Leicester Super	13	4	1	8	9
Edinburgh	11	4	0	7	8
Barnsley	12	4	0	8	8
Newcastle	9	2	0	7	4
Wombwell	10	2	0	8	4
Rochdale	10	2	0	8	4
Glasgow	11	2	0	9	4

1931

Southern League

	P	W	D	L	Pts
Wembley	38	29	1	8	59
Stamford Bridge	38	27	0	9	54
West Ham	38	23	0	15	46
Crystal Palace	38	22	0	16	44
Wimbledon	38	19	1	18	39
High Beech	38	19	1	18	39
Southampton	38	18	0	20	36
Belle Vue	38	14	0	24	28
Lea Bridge	38	11	0	27	22
Coventry	38	8	1	29	17

(Note – Belle Vue took over from Harringay and Coventry from Leicester.)

Northern League

	P	W	D	L	Pts
Belle Vue	18	12	0	6	24
Leeds	18	10	1	7	21
Sheffield	17	10	0	7	20
Leicester Super	15	8	0	7	16
Preston	16	5	1	10	11
Glasgow	12	2	0	10	4

(Note – Nottingham resigned from the Southern League. All other teams were credited with four points.)

1932

N.P.A. Trophy Competition

	P	W	D	L	Pts
Stamford Bridge	18	16	0	2	32
Wembley	18	14	0	4	28
Crystal Palace	18	12	0	6	24
Belle Vue	18	11	0	7	22
West Ham	18	11	0	7	22
Wimbledon	18	11	0	7	22
Clapton	18	5	0	13	10
Coventry	18	5	0	13	10
Sheffield	18	3	0	15	6
Plymouth	18	2	0	16	4

(Note – This competition ended in July. Clapton took over from Southampton.)

National League
League Championship

	P	W	D	L	Pts
Wembley	16	13	0	3	26
Crystal Palace	16	11	1	4	23
Belle Vue	16	9	1	6	19
Stamford Bridge	16	8	1	7	17
Wimbledon	16	8	1	7	17
West Ham	16	7	0	9	14
Coventry	16	6	0	10	12
Clapton	16	4	0	12	8
Plymouth	16	4	0	12	8

1933

National League

	P	W	D	L	Pts
Belle Vue	36	31	0	5	62
Wimbledon	36	23	0	13	46
West Ham	36	21	3	12	45
Crystal Palace	36	21	0	15	42
Clapton	36	19	3	14	41
Wembley	36	19	1	16	39
Coventry	36	10	2	24	22
Sheffield	36	11	0	25	22
Plymouth	36	11	0	25	22
Nottingham	36	9	1	26	19

1934

National League

	P	W	D	L	Pts
Belle Vue	32	27	0	5	54
Wembley	32	26	0	6	52
New Cross	32	21	0	11	42
West Ham	32	16	1	15	33
Wimbledon	32	16	0	16	32
Harringay	32	14	1	17	29
Birmingham	32	9	0	23	18
Plymouth	32	8	2	18	18
Walthamstow	32	5	0	27	10

(Note – Walthamstow replaced Lea Bridge during the season.)

Second Division

	P	W	D	L	Pts
West Ham	12	11	0	0	22
Wembley	12	7	2	3	16
Harringay	12	6	1	5	13
Wimbledon	12	6	1	5	13
Birmingham	12	4	0	8	8
Belle Vue	12	3	0	9	6
New Cross	12	2	1	9	5

(Note – Essentially a reserve competition featuring existing tracks.)

1935

National League

	P	W	D	L	Pts
Belle Vue	24	18	2	4	38
Harringay	24	13	0	11	26
West Ham	24	12	1	11	25
Wembley	24	11	0	13	22
Hackney Wick	24	10	1	13	21
New Cross	24	10	0	14	20
Wimbledon	24	8	0	16	16

1936

National League

	P	W	D	L	Pts
Belle Vue	24	18	1	5	37
Wembley	24	15	0	9	30
Harringay	24	12	0	12	24
Hackney Wick	24	11	0	13	22
Wimbledon	24	11	0	13	22
New Cross	24	9	0	15	18
West Ham	24	7	1	16	15

Provincial League

	P	W	D	L	Pts
Southampton	16	10	0	6	20
Bristol	16	10	0	6	20
Nottingham	16	9	0	19	18
Liverpool	16	9	0	9	18
Plymouth	16	2	0	14	4

(Note – Cardiff withdrew; results deleted.)

1937

National League

	P	W	D	L	Pts
West Ham	24	18	0	6	36
Wembley	24	16	0	8	32
New Cross	24	16	0	8	32
Belle Vue	24	13	0	11	26
Hackney Wick	24	10	0	14	20
Harringay	24	9	0	15	18
Wimbledon	24	2	0	22	4

Provincial League

	P	W	D	L	Pts
Bristol	20	15	0	5	30
Southampton	20	13	0	7	26
Nottingham	20	11	0	9	22
Liverpool	20	8	0	12	16
Norwich	20	8	0	12	16
Birmingham	20	5	0	15	10

(Note – Leicester withdrew; results deleted.)

1938
National League

First Division

	P	W	D	L	Pts
New Cross	24	15	1	8	32
West Ham	24	13	1	10	27
Wembley	24	13	1	10	27
Wimbledon	24	12	3	9	27
Belle Vue	24	11	0	13	22
Harringay	24	10	1	13	21
Bristol	24	6	1	17	13

Second Division

	P	W	D	L	Pts
Hackney Wick	16	12	0	4	24
Norwich	16	12	0	4	24
Southampton	16	9	0	7	18
West Ham II	16	8	2	6	18
Lea Bridge	16	8	0	8	16
Newcastle	16	7	1	8	15
Sheffield	16	6	1	9	13
Birmingham	16	6	0	10	12
Leeds	16	2	0	14	4

(Note – Leeds took over Nottingham fixtures during season.)

1939
National League
(Positions at the outbreak of war)

First Division

	P	W	D	L	Pts
Belle Vue	16	12	1	3	25
Wimbledon	18	12	0	6	24
Wembley	19	11	1	7	23
West Ham	19	9	0	10	18
Harringay	15	6	1	8	13
Southampton	17	5	0	12	10
New Cross	18	4	1	13	9

Second Division

	P	W	D	L	Pts
Newcastle	15	10	0	5	20
Sheffield	9	8	0	1	16
Harringay	15	6	1	8	13
Norwich	12	6	0	6	12
Bristol	13	4	0	9	8
Belle Vue II	14	4	0	10	8

(Note – Belle Vue II replaced Stoke; Middlesbrough and Crystal Palace resigned during season.)

1946
National League

	P	W	D	L	Pts
Wembley	20	18	0	2	36
Belle Vue	20	12	1	7	25
Bradford	20	9	1	10	19
Wimbledon	20	8	1	11	17
New Cross	20	6	1	13	13
West Ham	20	4	2	14	10

Northern League

	P	W	D	L	Pts
Middlesbrough	20	12	4	4	28
Sheffield	20	11	1	8	23
Norwich	20	10	1	9	21
Birmingham	20	9	1	10	19
Newcastle	20	8	1	11	17
Glasgow	20	6	0	14	12

1947
National League

First Division

	P	W	D	L	Pts
Wembley	24	19	0	5	38
Belle Vue	24	15	1	8	31
Wimbledon	24	13	1	10	27
Bradford	24	10	1	13	21
New Cross	24	10	0	14	20
West Ham	24	8	0	16	16
Harringay	24	7	1	16	15

Second Division

	P	W	D	L	Pts
Middlesbrough	28	20	0	8	40
Sheffield	28	17	2	9	36
Norwich	28	16	0	12	32
Birmingham	28	14	0	14	28
Newcastle	28	12	2	14	26
Bristol	28	11	0	17	22
Wigan	28	9	2	17	20
Glasgow	28	10	0	18	20

Third Division

	P	W	D	L	Pts
Eastbourne	28	18	0	10	36
Cradley Heath	28	18	0	10	36
Southampton	28	17	1	10	35
Exeter	28	15	0	13	30
Tamworth	28	12	0	16	24
Hanley	28	12	0	16	24
Wombwell	28	12	0	16	24
Plymouth	28	7	1	20	15

1948
National League

First Division

	P	W	D	L	Pts
New Cross	24	17	0	7	34
Harringay	24	16	0	8	32
West Ham	24	14	1	9	29
Wembley	24	12	1	11	25
Belle Vue	24	12	1	11	25
Wimbledon	24	5	2	17	12
Bradford	24	5	1	18	11

Second Division

	P	W	D	L	Pts
Bristol	32	23	0	9	46
Birmingham	32	20	1	11	41
Middlesbrough	32	18	2	12	38
Sheffield	32	17	1	14	35
Norwich	32	17	0	15	34
Glasgow	32	14	3	15	31
Newcastle	32	11	0	21	22
Fleetwood	32	10	1	21	21
Edinburgh	32	10	0	22	20

Third Division

	P	W	D	L	Pts
Exeter	44	32	1	11	65
Cradley Heath	44	29	2	13	60
Southampton	44	29	0	15	58
Tamworth	44	23	4	17	50
Hanley	44	24	1	19	49
Hastings	44	22	0	22	44
Plymouth	44	21	1	22	43
Coventry	44	19	1	24	39
Hull	44	19	0	25	38
Poole	44	17	0	27	34
Yarmouth	44	13	1	30	27
Wombwell	44	10	1	33	21

1949
National League

First Division

	P	W	D	L	Pts
Wembley	42	28	1	13	57
Belle Vue	42	24	0	18	48
New Cross	42	24	0	18	48
West Ham	42	23	0	19	46
Bradford	42	22	1	19	45
Harringay	42	18	0	24	36
Birmingham	42	16	1	25	33
Wimbledon	42	11	1	30	23

Second Division

	P	W	D	L	Pts
Bristol	44	34	1	9	69
Sheffield	44	29	1	14	59
Norwich	44	27	0	17	54
Cradley Heath	44	25	0	19	50
Edinburgh	44	24	0	20	48
Walthamstow	44	21	3	20	45
Southampton	44	21	3	20	45
Glasgow	44	20	0	24	40
Fleetwood	44	18	1	25	37
Newcastle	44	17	1	26	35
Ashfield	44	12	1	31	25
Coventry	44	10	1	33	21

Third Division

	P	W	D	L	Pts
Hanley	48	35	1	12	71
Yarmouth	48	35	1	12	71
Tamworth	48	33	0	15	66
Halifax	48	28	2	18	58
Plymouth	48	28	2	18	58
Poole	48	27	0	21	54
Exeter	48	24	0	24	48
Hastings	48	21	1	26	43
Liverpool	48	19	0	29	38
Leicester	48	17	1	30	35
Swindon	48	15	1	32	31
Rayleigh	48	14	0	34	28
Oxford	48	11	1	36	23

(Note – Swindon took over Hull fixtures during season.)

1950
National League

First Division

	P	W	D	L	Pts
Wembley	32	24	0	8	48
Belle Vue	32	19	0	13	38
Wimbledon	32	17	1	14	35
New Cross	32	16	1	15	33
West Ham	32	16	0	16	32
Bradford	32	16	0	16	32
Bristol	32	15	0	17	30
Birmingham	32	12	0	20	24
Harringay	32	8	0	24	16

Second Division

	P	W	D	L	Pts
Norwich	28	18	1	9	37
Glasgow	28	18	0	10	36
Cradley Heath	28	18	0	10	36
Coventry	28	16	0	12	32
Walthamstow	28	16	0	12	32
Halifax	28	16	0	12	32
Southampton	28	14	1	13	29
Edinburgh	28	14	1	13	29
Plymouth	28	13	0	15	26
Sheffield	28	13	0	15	26
Ashfield	28	12	0	16	24
Yarmouth	28	12	0	16	24
Newcastle	28	10	0	18	20
Hanley	28	9	2	17	20
Fleetwood	28	8	1	19	17

Third Division

	P	W	D	L	Pts
Oxford	36	26	2	8	54
Poole	36	23	3	10	49
Leicester	36	21	0	15	42
Swindon	36	19	1	16	39
Aldershot	36	18	1	17	37
Tamworth	36	17	0	19	34
Exeter	36	16	1	19	33
Liverpool	36	14	1	21	29
Rayleigh	36	12	0	24	24
St. Austell	36	9	1	26	19

1951
National League

First Division

	P	W	D	L	Pts
Wembley	32	25	0	7	50
Belle Vue	32	19	1	12	39
Wimbledon	32	17	1	14	35
West Ham	32	16	1	15	33
Birmingham	32	16	0	16	32
Bristol	32	15	1	16	31
Harringay	32	15	1	16	31
New Cross	32	9	1	22	19
Bradford	32	9	0	23	18

Second Division

	P	W	D	L	Pts
Norwich	30	24	0	6	48
Leicester	30	19	0	11	38
Edinburgh	30	18	0	12	36
Coventry	30	16	3	11	35
Walthamstow	30	17	0	13	34
Halifax	30	17	0	13	34
Motherwell	30	16	1	13	33
Ashfield	30	16	0	14	32
Hanley	30	15	0	15	30
Glasgow	30	14	1	15	29
Yarmouth	30	13	1	16	27
Oxford	30	12	2	16	26
Liverpool	30	12	1	17	25
Fleetwood	30	9	2	19	20
Cradley Heath	30	9	0	21	18
Newcastle	30	7	1	22	15

(Note – Sheffield and Southampton withdrew; results deleted.)

Third Division

	P	W	D	L	Pts
Poole	36	30	0	6	60
Exeter	36	28	0	8	56
Aldershot	36	21	1	14	43
Rayleigh	36	21	0	15	42
Swindon	36	16	2	18	34
Plymouth	36	16	1	19	33
Cardiff	36	13	3	20	29
St. Austell	36	13	0	23	26
Long Eaton	36	13	0	23	26
Wolverhampton	36	5	1	30	11

1952
National League

First Division

	P	W	D	L	Pts
Wembley	36	28	1	7	57
Birmingham	36	23	0	13	46
Harringay	36	21	3	12	45
West Ham	36	18	2	16	38
Wimbledon	36	17	2	17	36
Belle Vue	36	18	0	18	36
New Cross	36	15	1	20	31
Bristol	36	13	0	23	26
Bradford	36	11	1	24	23
Norwich	36	10	2	24	22

Second Division

	P	W	D	L	Pts
Poole	44	31	1	12	63
Coventry	44	25	5	14	55
Leicester	44	25	2	17	52
Cradley Heath	44	24	0	20	48
Glasgow	44	23	1	20	47
Edinburgh	44	21	4	19	46
Ashfield	44	19	3	22	41
Motherwell	44	19	2	23	40
Yarmouth	44	20	0	24	40
Stoke	44	18	1	25	37
Liverpool	44	16	3	25	35
Oxford	44	11	2	31	24

Southern League

	P	W	D	L	Pts
Rayleigh	36	28	0	8	56
Cardiff	36	23	0	13	46
Plymouth	36	20	1	15	41
Wolverhampton	36	20	1	15	41
Exeter	36	20	1	15	41
Swindon	36	18	0	18	36
Aldershot	36	15	1	20	31
Ipswich	36	12	0	24	24
Southampton	36	11	0	25	22
St. Austell	36	11	0	25	22

(Note – Long Eaton withdrew; results deleted.)

1953

National League

First Division

	P	W	D	L	Pts
Wembley	16	11	1	4	23
Harringay	16	11	0	5	22
Birmingham	16	9	1	6	19
Bradford	16	8	1	7	17
Wimbledon	16	8	0	8	16
West Ham	16	7	0	9	14
Norwich	16	6	0	10	12
Belle Vue	16	5	1	10	11
Bristol	16	5	0	11	10

(Note – New Cross withdrew; results deleted.)

Second Division

	P	W	D	L	Pts
Coventry	32	19	1	12	39
Poole	32	18	2	12	38
Great Yarmouth	32	18	0	14	36
Glasgow	32	16	2	14	34
Edinburgh	32	15	1	16	31
Motherwell	32	15	0	17	30
Wolverhampton	32	13	1	18	27
Leicester	32	13	1	18	27
Stoke	32	12	2	18	26

Southern League

	P	W	D	L	Pts
Exeter	27	21	1	5	43
Rayleigh	27	21	1	5	43
Ipswich	28	13	2	13	28
Swindon	28	13	2	13	28
Southampton	28	12	2	14	26
Oxford	28	9	1	18	19
St. Austell	28	9	0	19	18
Plymouth	28	8	1	19	17

(Note – Cardiff withdrew; results deleted. After a protest Rayleigh v Exeter result deleted.)

1954

National League

First Division

	P	W	D	L	Pts
Wimbledon	28	21	2	5	44
Wembley	28	20	0	8	40
Bradford	28	15	0	13	30
Norwich	27	14	0	13	28
West Ham	28	11	1	16	23
Harringay	28	10	1	17	21
Belle Vue	27	9	0	18	18
Birmingham	28	9	0	19	18

Second Division

	P	W	D	L	Pts
Bristol	20	14	0	6	28
Poole	20	12	0	8	24
Swindon	20	11	0	9	22
Leicester	20	11	0	9	22
Ipswich	20	10	0	10	20
Exeter	20	10	0	10	20
Oxford	20	10	0	10	20
Coventry	20	10	0	10	20
Southampton	20	9	0	11	18
Motherwell	20	9	0	11	18
Rayleigh	20	4	0	16	8

(Note – Wolverhampton, Edinburgh, Glasgow (White City) and Plymouth withdrew; results deleted.

1955

National League

First Division

	P	W	D	L	Pts
Wimbledon	24	16	2	6	34
Belle Vue	24	15	0	9	30
Wembley	24	11	1	12	23
Bradford	24	11	0	13	22
Birmingham	24	9	2	13	20
Norwich	24	9	1	14	19
West Ham	24	8	2	14	18

Second Division

	P	W	D	L	Pts
Poole	32	23	0	9	46
Coventry	32	19	0	13	38
Rayleigh	32	16	0	16	32
Oxford	32	15	1	16	31
Southampton	32	15	0	17	30
Ipswich	32	13	3	16	29
Leicester	32	14	0	18	28
Swindon	32	14	0	18	28
Exeter	32	13	0	19	26

1956

National League

First Division

	P	W	D	L	Pts
Wimbledon	24	17	1	6	35
Wembley	24	14	1	9	29
Birmingham	24	12	1	11	25
Norwich	24	10	4	10	24
Belle Vue	24	11	1	12	23
Poole	24	9	2	13	20
Bradford	24	6	0	18	12

Second Division

	P	W	D	L	Pts
Swindon	24	16	0	8	32
Southampton	24	15	1	8	31
Rayleigh	24	14	1	9	29
Ipswich	24	13	0	11	26
Coventry	24	12	0	12	24
Oxford	24	6	1	17	13
Leicester	24	6	1	17	13

1957

National League

	P	W	D	L	Pts
Swindon	20	15	1	4	31
Belle Vue	20	15	0	5	30
Wimbledon	20	12	0	8	24
Norwich	20	11	0	9	22
Leicester	20	10	1	9	21
Southampton	20	9	0	11	18
Bradford	20	9	0	11	18
Coventry	20	9	0	11	18
Oxford	20	7	1	12	15
Ipswich	20	6	0	14	12
Rayleigh	20	5	1	14	11

1958

National League

	P	W	D	L	Pts
Wimbledon	18	12	2	4	26
Norwich	18	12	0	6	24
Southampton	18	11	0	7	22
Leicester	18	11	0	7	22
Belle Vue	18	10	0	8	20
Swindon	18	10	0	8	20
Coventry	18	9	1	8	19
Oxford	18	5	2	11	12
Poole	18	6	0	12	12
Ipswich	18	1	1	16	3

1959

National League

	P	W	D	L	Pts
Wimbledon	16	13	0	3	26
Leicester	16	8	1	7	17
Coventry	16	8	1	7	17
Norwich	16	8	0	8	16
Southampton	16	8	0	8	16
Poole	16	8	0	8	16
Oxford	16	7	0	9	14
Swindon	16	6	0	10	12
Belle Vue	16	5	0	11	10

1960

National League

	P	W	D	L	Pts
Wimbledon	17	13	0	4	26
Belle Vue	18	11	1	6	23
Oxford	18	11	0	7	22
Ipswich	18	10	0	8	20
Norwich	17	8	1	8	17
Leicester	18	7	2	9	16
Southampton	18	7	1	10	15
New Cross	18	7	1	10	15
Coventry	18	7	0	11	14
Swindon	18	5	0	13	10

Provincial League

	P	W	D	L	Pts
Rayleigh	18	16	0	2	32
Poole	18	16	0	2	32
Bristol	18	15	0	3	30
Sheffield	18	9	0	9	18
Stoke	18	8	1	9	17
Cradley Heath	18	8	0	10	16
Yarmouth	18	7	0	11	14
Edinburgh	18	5	1	12	11
Liverpool	18	4	0	14	8
Bradford	18	1	0	17	2

1961

National League

	P	W	D	L	Pts
Wimbledon	18	15	0	3	30
Southampton	18	13	2	3	28
Coventry	18	10	1	7	21
Belle Vue	18	10	0	8	20
Swindon	18	8	0	10	16
Ipswich	18	7	1	10	15
Norwich	18	7	0	11	14
New Cross	18	7	0	11	14
Oxford	18	6	1	11	13
Leicester	18	4	1	13	9

Provincial League

	P	W	S	L	Pts
Poole	20	15	1	4	31
Plymouth	20	12	0	8	24
Stoke	20	12	0	8	24
Cradley Heath	20	11	1	8	23
Rayleigh	20	11	0	9	22
Edinburgh	20	10	1	9	21
Sheffield	20	10	0	10	20
Exeter	20	9	0	11	18
Wolverhampton	20	7	0	13	14
Middlesbrough	20	6	1	13	13
Newcastle	20	5	0	15	10

1962

National League

	P	W	D	L	Pts
Southampton	24	18	0	6	36
Wimbledon	24	14	1	9	29
Coventry	24	13	0	11	26
Belle Vue	24	12	0	12	24
Norwich	24	12	0	12	24
Swindon	24	9	2	13	20
Oxford	24	4	0	20	8

Provincial League

	P	W	D	L	Pts
Poole	24	17	0	7	34
Neath	24	14	1	9	29
Exeter	24	14	0	10	28
Stoke	24	14	0	10	28
Edinburgh	24	12	2	10	26
Plymouth	24	12	2	10	26
Sheffield	24	12	1	11	25
Cradley Heath	24	12	0	12	24
Newcastle	24	12	0	12	24
Wolverhampton	24	11	1	12	23
Middlesbrough	24	11	0	13	22
Leicester	24	6	0	18	12
Bradford	24	5	1	18	11

1963

National League

	P	W	D	L	Pts
Belle Vue	24	17	0	7	34
Norwich	24	13	2	9	28
Wimbledon	24	12	1	11	25
Coventry	24	11	2	11	24
Swindon	24	10	2	12	22
Southampton	24	11	0	13	22
Oxford	24	6	1	17	13

Provincial League

	P	W	D	L	Pts
Wolverhampton	24	15	1	8	31
Stoke	24	14	1	9	29
Poole	24	14	0	10	28
Sheffield	24	14	0	10	28
St. Austell	24	13	2	9	28
Newcastle	24	13	1	10	27
Exeter	24	12	1	11	25
Edinburgh	24	12	1	11	25
Cradley Heath	24	11	1	12	23
Hackney	24	10	1	13	23
Middlesbrough	24	9	2	13	20
Long Eaton	24	7	2	15	16
Rayleigh	24	5	1	18	11

1964

National League

	P	W	D	L	Pts
Oxford	12	9	0	3	18
Coventry	12	8	1	3	17
Norwich	12	6	0	6	12
Belle Vue	12	5	1	6	11
Swindon	12	4	1	7	9
Wimbledon	12	4	1	7	9
West Ham	12	4	0	8	8

Provincial League

	P	W	D	L	Pts
Newcastle	22	17	0	5	34
Hackney	22	15	1	6	31
Wolverhampton	22	12	1	9	25
Newport	22	11	1	10	23
Edinburgh	22	10	2	10	22
Exeter	22	10	1	11	21
Poole	22	10	1	11	21
Sheffield	22	9	2	11	20
Middlesbrough	22	9	2	11	20
Cradley Heath	22	8	1	13	17
Long Eaton	22	8	0	14	16
Glasgow	22	6	2	14	14

1965

British League

	P	W	D	L	Pts
West Ham	34	23	1	10	47
Wimbledon	34	22	2	10	46
Coventry	34	20	0	14	40
Oxford	34	19	2	13	40
Halifax	33	18	3	13	39
Newport	34	19	0	15	38
Wolverhampton	34	18	1	15	37
Hackney	34	18	1	15	37
Exeter	34	18	0	16	36
Poole	34	17	1	16	35
Sheffield	34	16	2	16	34
Newcastle	34	16	1	17	33
Glasgow	34	15	1	18	31
Belle Vue	34	15	0	19	30
Swindon	34	13	2	19	28
Cradley Heath	33	11	1	22	23
Edinburgh	34	11	0	23	22
Long Eaton	34	7	0	17	14

1966

British League

	P	W	D	L	Pts
Halifax	36	27	0	9	54
Coventry	36	25	1	10	51
Swindon	36	23	0	13	46
Wimbledon	36	22	0	14	44
Newcastle	36	20	0	16	40
Poole	36	19	2	15	40
West Ham	36	19	1	16	39
Glasgow	36	18	0	18	36
Wolverhampton	36	17	2	17	36
Exeter	36	17	1	18	35
Sheffield	36	17	0	19	34
Edinburgh	35	16	0	19	32
Belle Vue	36	16	0	20	32
Hackney	36	15	1	20	31
Oxford	36	14	2	20	30
King's Lynn	36	15	0	21	30
Newport	36	12	1	23	25
Long Eaton	36	12	1	23	25
Cradley Heath	35	10	0	25	20

1967

British League

	P	W	D	L	Pts
Swindon	36	24	0	12	48
Coventry	36	22	2	12	46
West Ham	36	21	3	12	45
Edinburgh	36	20	2	14	42
Hackney	36	20	1	15	41
Poole	36	17	3	16	37
Halifax	36	18	1	17	37
Wolverhampton	36	18	1	17	37
Sheffield	36	18	1	17	37
Newcastle	36	18	0	18	36
Wimbledon	36	16	3	17	35
Newport	36	17	1	18	35
Glasgow	36	16	2	18	34
Oxford	36	16	1	19	33
Exeter	36	16	0	20	32
Belle Vue	36	16	0	20	32
Long Eaton	36	14	3	19	31
Cradley Heath	36	12	0	24	24
King's Lynn	36	11	0	25	22

1968
British League

First Division

	P	W	D	L	Pts
Coventry	36	22	0	14	44
Hackney	36	22	2	12	44
Exeter	36	20	1	15	41
Sheffield	36	20	1	15	41
Newcastle	36	20	0	16	40
West Ham	36	19	1	16	39
Halifax	36	19	1	16	39
Coatbridge	36	18	1	17	37
Wimbledon	36	18	0	18	36
Belle Vue	36	18	0	18	36
Swindon	36	17	1	18	35
Leicester	36	17	1	18	35
Newport	36	17	1	18	35
Cradley Heath	36	15	4	17	34
Oxford	36	17	0	19	34
Wolverhampton	36	16	0	20	32
Poole	36	13	2	21	28
King's Lynn	36	13	1	22	27
Glasgow	36	13	1	22	27

Second Division

	P	W	D	L	Pts
Belle Vue II	18	14	0	4	28
Nelson	18	11	0	7	22
Middlesbrough	18	10	1	7	21
Plymouth	18	10	0	8	20
Rayleigh	18	9	1	8	19
Crayford	18	8	1	9	17
Canterbury	18	8	1	9	17
Reading	18	6	2	10	14
Weymouth	18	5	2	11	12
Berwick	18	5	0	13	10

1969
British League

First Division

	P	W	D	L	Pts
Poole	36	26	1	9	53
Belle Vue	36	23	1	12	47
Wimbledon	36	22	2	12	46
Halifax	36	22	2	12	46
Leicester	36	21	2	13	44
Sheffield	36	19	1	16	39
Cradley Heath	36	18	2	16	38
Glasgow	36	17	3	16	37
King's Lynn	36	18	0	18	36
Swindon	36	18	0	18	36
Coatbridge	36	17	1	18	35
Exeter	36	16	0	20	32
Newcastle	36	15	2	19	32
Coventry	36	14	3	19	31
Oxford	36	15	1	20	31
Wolverhampton	36	13	1	22	27
Newport	36	13	1	22	27
West Ham	36	11	3	22	25
Hackney	36	10	2	24	22

Second Division

	P	W	D	L	Pts
Belle Vue II	30	23	1	6	47
Reading	30	19	1	10	39
Romford	30	19	1	10	39
Crayford	30	19	0	11	38
Rayleigh	30	16	2	12	34
Canterbury	30	15	2	13	32
Crewe	30	15	0	15	30
Eastbourne	30	14	2	14	30
Middlesbrough	30	14	1	15	29
Long Eaton	30	14	1	15	29
Ipswich	30	13	1	16	27
Doncaster	30	12	0	18	24
Nelson	30	11	2	17	24
Berwick	30	11	1	18	23
Plymouth	30	9	0	21	18
King's Lynn II	30	8	1	21	17

1970
British League

First Division

	P	W	D	L	Pts
Belle Vue	36	27	3	6	57
Coventry	36	23	0	13	46
Wimbledon	36	22	0	12	46
Leicester	36	21	0	15	42
Poole	36	20	0	16	40
Halifax	36	19	0	17	38
Sheffield	36	17	4	15	38
Glasgow	36	18	1	17	37
Wolverhampton	36	16	2	18	34
Exeter	36	16	2	18	34
Hackney	36	16	1	19	33
King's Lynn	36	16	0	20	32
Oxford	36	16	2	18	32
Wembley	36	15	2	19	32
Cradley Heath	36	15	1	20	31
Swindon	36	14	2	20	30
Newcastle	36	15	0	21	30
West Ham	36	14	2	20	30
Newport	36	12	0	24	24

Second Division

	P	W	D	L	Pts
Canterbury	32	23	1	8	47
Eastbourne	32	22	1	9	45
Rochdale	32	21	2	9	44
Bradford	32	18	1	13	37
Teesside	32	18	0	14	36
Ipswich	32	17	2	13	36
Crewe	32	17	1	14	35
Romford	32	17	1	14	35
Reading	32	17	0	15	34
Peterborough	32	14	2	16	30
Workington	32	13	1	18	27
Rayleigh	32	13	1	18	27
Boston	32	12	2	18	26
Doncaster	32	11	1	20	23
Crayford	32	11	1	20	23
Berwick	32	10	0	22	20
Long Eaton	32	8	3	21	19

(Note – Boston took over from King's Lynn II during the season and Bradford took over from Nelson.)

1971
British League

First Division

	P	W	D	L	Pts
Belle Vue	36	25	1	10	51
Leicester	36	22	3	11	47
Coventry	36	23	0	13	46
Sheffield	36	21	1	14	43
Swindon	36	19	3	14	41
Reading	36	18	4	14	40
Hackney	36	17	4	15	38
Newport	36	19	0	17	38
Wembley	36	17	3	16	37
Wimbledon	36	18	1	17	37
Poole	36	17	2	17	36
Wolverhampton	36	17	1	18	35
King's Lynn	36	16	2	18	34
Halifax	36	16	2	28	34
Exeter	36	16	0	20	32
Glasgow	36	15	1	20	31
Oxford	36	12	1	23	25
Cradley Heath	36	8	4	24	20
West Ham	36	9	1	27	19

Second Division

	P	W	D	L	Pts
Eastbourne	32	22	3	7	47
Bradford	32	21	1	10	43
Ipswich	32	20	3	9	43
Boston	32	18	3	14	39
Rayleigh	32	18	2	12	38
Hull	32	16	2	14	34
Crewe	32	16	1	15	33
Berwick	32	16	0	16	32
Rochdale	32	16	0	16	32
Long Eaton	32	13	3	16	29
Birmingham	32	13	3	16	29
Romford	32	13	0	19	26
Teesside	32	13	0	19	26
Canterbury	32	12	2	18	26
Workington	32	12	1	19	25
Peterborough	32	11	1	20	23
Sunderland	32	9	1	22	19

1972
British League
First Division

	P	W	D	L	Pts
Belle Vue	34	31	1	2	63
Reading	34	27	1	8	51
King's Lynn	34	24	3	7	51
Sheffield	34	23	3	8	49
Leicester	34	17	5	12	39
Ipswich	34	17	1	16	35
Poole	34	15	2	17	32
Hackney	34	16	0	18	32
Wolverhampton	34	16	0	18	32
Coventry	34	14	2	18	30
Exeter	34	13	2	19	28
Halifax	34	13	2	19	28
Wimbledon	34	14	0	20	28
Glasgow	34	12	2	20	26
Swindon	34	12	1	21	25
Cradley Heath	34	11	3	20	25
Oxford	34	10	0	24	20
Newport	34	9	0	25	18

Second Division

	P	W	D	L	Pts
Crewe	32	22	1	9	45
Boston	32	21	1	10	43
Peterborough	32	21	0	11	42
Rayleigh	32	17	4	11	38
Eastbourne	32	18	2	12	38
Birmingham	32	18	1	13	37
Workington	32	18	0	14	36
Hull	32	16	0	16	32
Barrow	32	14	3	15	31
Teesside	32	14	3	15	31
Bradford	32	15	0	17	30
Sunderland	32	13	2	17	28
Canterbury	32	13	1	18	27
Berwick	32	12	3	17	27
Ellesmere Port	32	12	0	20	24
Long Eaton	32	11	2	19	24
Scunthorpe	32	5	1	26	11

(Note – Barrow took over from West Ham during the season.)

1973
British League
First Division

	P	W	D	L	Pts
Reading	34	25	1	8	51
Sheffield	34	22	3	9	47
King's Lynn	34	20	3	11	43
Leicester	34	21	0	13	42
Ipswich	34	19	3	12	41
Belle Vue	34	19	1	14	39
Wolverhampton	34	18	1	15	37
Exeter	34	16	3	15	35
Halifax	34	16	2	16	34
Newport	34	16	0	18	32
Oxford	34	14	2	18	30
Wimbledon	34	14	1	19	29
Swindon	34	13	3	18	29
Poole	34	13	2	19	28
Coventry	34	13	0	21	26
Hackney	34	11	4	19	26
Coatbridge	34	12	1	21	25
Cradley United	34	7	4	23	18

Second Division

	P	W	D	L	Pts
Boston	34	29	0	5	58
Workington	34	21	2	11	44
Eastbourne	34	19	2	13	40
Peterborough	34	19	1	14	39
Birmingham	34	19	0	15	38
Teesside	34	19	0	15	38
Bradford	34	18	0	16	36
Crewe	34	17	1	16	35
Long Eaton	34	17	1	16	35
Barrow	34	15	2	17	32
Sunderland	34	15	2	17	32
Hull	34	13	5	16	31
Chesterton	34	14	1	19	29
Ellesmere Port	34	14	0	20	28
Canterbury	34	13	2	19	28
Scunthorpe	34	12	1	21	25
Berwick	34	11	1	22	23
Rayleigh	34	9	3	22	21

1974
British League
First Division

	P	W	D	L	Pts
Exeter	32	25	1	6	51
Belle Vue	32	23	0	9	46
Ipswich	32	22	1	9	43
Sheffield	32	21	0	11	42
King's Lynn	32	20	1	11	41
Newport	32	17	3	12	37
Halifax	32	14	3	15	31
Wimbledon	32	14	1	17	29
Hackney	32	13	2	17	28
Leicester	32	13	1	18	27
Wolverhampton	32	13	1	18	27
Swindon	32	12	2	18	26
Cradley United	32	12	1	19	25
Poole	32	12	1	19	25
Coventry	32	12	0	20	24
Oxford	32	11	0	21	22
Hull	32	9	0	23	18

Second Division

	P	W	D	L	Pts
Birmingham	35	26	3	6	55
Eastbourne	36	24	3	9	51
Boston	36	23	2	11	48
Workington	36	22	3	22	47
Crewe	36	22	0	14	44
Bradford	36	19	1	16	39
Teesside	36	19	1	16	39
Peterborough	34	18	1	15	37
Coatbridge	36	18	0	18	36
Canterbury	36	18	0	18	36
Barrow	36	16	2	18	34
Berwick	36	16	1	19	33
Stoke	36	16	0	20	32
Ellesmere Port	35	14	3	18	31
Long Eaton	36	14	2	20	30
Rye House	36	13	0	23	26
Sunderland	36	11	0	25	22
Scunthorpe	36	9	2	25	20
Weymouth	36	10	0	26	20

1975
Gulf British League

	P	W	D	L	Pts
Ipswich	34	26	1	7	53
Belle Vue	34	25	2	7	52
Newport	34	24	1	9	49
Exeter	34	21	3	10	45
Sheffield	34	21	0	13	42
Reading	34	21	0	13	42
Leicester	34	16	4	14	34
Oxford	34	17	0	17	34
Wimbledon	34	16	2	16	34
Halifax	34	15	3	16	33
Cradley United	34	15	2	17	32
King's Lynn	34	14	3	17	31
Wolverhampton	34	13	1	20	27
Hull	34	10	4	20	24
Poole	34	10	3	21	23
Coventry	34	9	2	23	20
Hackney	34	9	1	24	19
Swindon	34	8	0	26	16

New National League

	P	W	D	L	Pts
Birmingham	38	29	1	8	59
Newcastle	38	27	0	11	54
Stoke	38	26	0	12	52
Eastbourne	38	25	0	13	50
Boston	38	24	2	12	50
Workington	38	23	2	13	48
Berwick	38	21	3	14	45
Crayford	38	20	2	16	42
Ellesmere Port	38	19	1	18	39
Canterbury	38	19	0	19	38
Bradford	38	17	2	19	36
Coatbridge	38	17	1	20	35
Scunthorpe	38	17	0	21	35
Rye House	38	13	2	23	28
Paisley	38	14	0	24	28
Crewe	37	13	1	23	27
Teesside	38	13	0	25	26
Peterborough	37	13	0	24	26
Mildenhall	38	11	1	26	23
Weymouth	38	8	2	28	18

1976
Gulf British League

	P	W	D	L	Pts
Ipswich	36	27	1	8	55
Belle Vue	36	23	2	11	48
Exeter	36	23	2	11	48
Coventry	36	21	2	13	44
Swindon	36	19	4	13	42
Reading	36	19	3	14	41
Hackney	36	20	0	16	40
Newport	36	19	1	16	39
Cradley United	36	19	1	16	39
Poole	36	18	1	17	37
Wolverhampton	36	18	1	17	37
Hull	36	18	0	18	36
White City	36	16	3	17	35
King's Lynn	36	16	3	17	35
Halifax	36	14	1	21	29
Wimbledon	36	12	3	21	27
Sheffield	36	13	1	22	27
Birmingham	36	7	0	29	14
Leicester	36	5	1	30	12

Gulf British League

	P	W	D	L	Pts
Newcastle	34	30	1	3	61
Ellesmere Port	34	24	1	9	49
Workington	34	20	1	13	41
Canterbury	34	20	0	14	40
Rye House	34	17	2	15	36
Crayford	34	17	1	16	35
Coatbridge	34	17	1	16	35
Eastbourne	34	17	0	17	34
Peterborough	34	16	2	16	34
Berwick	34	17	0	17	34
Stoke	34	15	1	18	31
Boston	34	15	1	18	31
Mildenhall	34	15	1	18	31
Oxford	34	14	1	19	29
Weymouth	34	11	2	21	24
Paisley	34	12	0	22	24
Scunthorpe	34	11	1	22	23
Teesside	34	10	0	24	20

1977
Gulf British League

	P	W	D	L	Pts
White City	36	27	1	8	55
Exeter	36	25	3	8	53
Reading	36	25	3	8	53
Ipswich	36	25	1	10	51
Belle Vue	36	19	3	14	41
King's Lynn	36	19	2	15	40
Cradley Heath	36	20	0	16	40
Coventry	36	19	1	16	39
Wimbledon	36	17	2	17	36
Poole	36	17	2	17	36
Swindon	36	17	1	18	35
Bristol	36	17	0	19	34
Sheffield	36	16	2	18	34
Hull	36	15	0	21	30
Wolverhampton	36	14	0	22	28
Hackney	36	13	1	22	27
Halifax	36	12	0	24	24
Birmingham	36	8	0	28	16
Leicester	36	6	0	30	12

National League

	P	W	D	L	Pts
Eastbourne	36	29	0	7	58
Rye House	36	24	3	9	51
Ellesmere Port	36	22	2	12	46
Canterbury	36	23	0	13	46
Peterborough	36	22	0	14	44
Newcastle	36	21	1	14	43
Boston	36	20	0	16	40
Mildenhall	36	16	4	16	36
Teesside	36	17	1	18	35
Crayford	36	17	0	19	34
Glasgow	36	16	0	20	32
Newport	36	16	0	20	32
Oxford	36	15	1	20	31
Scunthorpe	36	15	1	20	31
Edinburgh	36	15	0	21	30
Workington	36	14	1	21	29
Weymouth	36	11	3	22	25
Berwick	36	11	1	24	23
Stoke	36	9	0	27	18

(Note – Glasgow moved from Coatbridge to Blantyre during the season.)

MAJOR TITLE WINNERS

WORLD BEST PAIRS
Champions

1968 (Kempten): **Sweden**
Ove Fundin (14) and Törbjorn Harrysson (10).
1969 (Stockholm): **New Zealand**
Ivan Mauger (18) and Bob Andrews (10).
1970 (Malmo): **New Zealand**
Ronnie Moore (16) and Ivan Mauger (12).
1971 (Wroclaw): **Poland**
Jerzy Szczakiel (16) and Andrzej Wyglenda (14).
1972 (Boras): **England**
Ray Wilson (15) and Terry Betts (9).
1973 (Boras): **Sweden**
Anders Michanek (15) and Tommy Jansson (9).
1974 (Belle Vue): **Sweden**
Anders Michanek (14) and Soren Sjösten (14).
1975 (Wroclaw): **Sweden.**
Anders Michanek (17) and Tommy Jansson (7).
1976 (Eskilstuna): **England**
John Louis (17) and Malcolm Simmons (10).
1977 (Belle Vue): **England**
Peter Collins (15) and Malcolm Simmons (13).

STAR RIDERS CHAMPIONSHIP
Winners

1929 (British section) Roger Frogley (Overseas section) Frank Arthur (Australia)
1930 Vic Huxley (Australia)
1931 Ray Tauser (USA)
1932 Eric Langton (England)
1933 Tom Farndon (England)
1934 Jack Parker (England)
1935 Frank Charles (England)

BRITISH INDIVIDUAL CHAMPIONSHIP
(Held at Belle Vue in war years)

1940 Eric Chitty (Canada)
1941 Eric Chitty (Canada)
1942 Eric Chitty (Canada)
1943 Ron Clarke (England)
1944 Frank Varey (England)
1945 Bill Kitchen (England)

BRITISH RIDERS' CHAMPIONSHIP
Winners

1946 Tommy Price (England)
1947 Jack Parker (England)
1948 Vic Duggan (Australia)

INTERNATIONALE
Winners

1961 Ove Fundin (Sweden)
1962 Ove Fundin (Sweden)
1963 Ove Fundin (Sweden)
1964 Barry Briggs (New Zealand)
1965 Charlie Monk (Australia)
1966 Göte Nordin (Sweden)
1967 Göte Nordin (Sweden)
1968 Nigel Boocock (England)
1969 Trevor Hedge (England)
1970 Ivan Mauger (New Zealand)
1971 Ivan Mauger (New Zealand)
1972 Ivan Mauger (New Zealand)
1973 Ole Olsen (Denmark)
1974 Peter Collins (England)
1975 Ole Olsen (Denmark)
1976 Malcolm Simmons (England)
1977 Edward Jancarz (Poland)

BRITISH LEAGUE RIDERS' CHAMPIONSHIP
Winners

1965 Barry Briggs
1966 Barry Briggs
1967 Barry Briggs
1968 Barry Briggs
1969 Barry Briggs
1970 Barry Briggs
1971 Ivan Mauger
1972 Ole Olsen
1973 Ivan Mauger
1974 Peter Collins
1975 Peter Collins
1976 Ole Olsen
1977 Ole Olsen

SECOND DIVISION/NATIONAL LEAGUE RIDERS' CHAMPIONSHIP
Winners

1968 Graham Plant
1969 Geoff Ambrose
1970 Dave Jessup
1971 John Louis
1972 Phil Crump
1973 Arthur Price
1974 Carl Glover
1975 Laurie Etheridge
1976 Joe Owen
1977 Colin Richardson

NATIONAL TROPHY

	Winners	**Runners-up**
1931	Wembley	Stamford bridge
1932	Wembley	Belle Vue
1933	Belle Vue	Wembley
1934	Belle Vue	Wembley
1935	Belle Vue	Harringay
1936	Belle Vue	Hackney Wick
1937	Belle Vue	New Cross
1938	Wimbledon	Wembley
1946	Belle Vue	Wimbledon
1947	Belle Vue	Wembley
1948	Wembley	New Cross
1949	Belle Vue	West Ham
1950	Wimbledon	Bradford
1951	Wimbledon	Wembley
1952	Harringay	Birmingham
1953	Wimbledon	Wembley
1954	Wembley	Norwich
1955	Norwich	Wembley
1956	Wimbledon	BelleVue
1958	Belle Vue	Norwich
1959	Wimbledon	Southampton
1960	Wimbledon	Norwich
1961	Southampton	Swindon
1962	Wimbledon	Swindon
1963	Norwich	Belle Vue
1964	Oxford	West Ham

SPEEDWAY STAR K.O. CUP FINAL

	Winners	**Runners-up**
1965	West Ham	Exeter
1966	Halifax	Wimbledon
1967	Coventry	West Ham
1968	Wimbledon	Wolverhampton
1969	Wimbledon	Sheffield
1970	Wimbledon	Belle Vue
1971	Hackney	Cradley Heath
1972	Belle Vue	Hackney
1973	Belle Vue	Reading
1974	Sheffield	Ipswich
1975	Belle Vue	Leicester
1976	Ipswich	King's Lynn
1977	King's Lynn	Reading

TEST MATCH RECORD

To chart every international match ridden goes beyond the scope of this book. Thus the following section concentrates upon listing in chronological order, test matches involving Great Britain and/or England at home and abroad, and other full internationals staged in England. British Lions tours comprising riders from the United Kingdom have been included under the classification of England v Australia. In general, series in which England met Scotland, Overseas, and South Africa, are discounted, as are internationals classified with 'B' or 'C' status or otherwise unrepresentative of full Test match strength. There are one or two exceptions if historical interest dictates.

1930
ENGLAND v AUSTRALIA
First Test at Wimbledon:
ENGLAND 17 (R. Frogley 6).
AUSTRALIA 35 (V. Huxley 9).
Second Test at Belle Vue:
ENGLAND 56 (J. Kempster 10).
AUSTRALIA 39 (M. Grosskreutz 12).
Third Test at Stamford Bridge:
ENGLAND 49 (W. Phillips 12).
AUSTRALIA 46 (V. Huxley 11).
Fourth Test at Belle Vue:
ENGLAND 51 (F. Varey 9, J. Parker 9).
AUSTRALIA 45 (V. Huxley 12).
Fifth Test at Wembley:
ENGLAND 49 (J. Ormston 8, C. Watson 8).
AUSTRALIA 45 (V. Huxley 12, B. Lamont 10).

1931
ENGLAND v AUSTRALIA
First Test at Crystal Palace:
ENGLAND 55 (E. Langton 12, S. Burton 10, W. Phillips 10).
AUSTRALIA 37: (F. Arthur 9).
Second Test at Leicester Super:
ENGLAND 46 (A. Jervis 9).
AUSTRALIA 47 (L. Van Praag 9).
Third Test at Wembley:
ENGLAND 53 (J. Parker 11, R. Bounds 10).
AUSTRALIA 43 (F. Arthur 11).
Fourth Test at Belle Vue:
ENGLAND 53 (J. Parker 12, G. Lees 11).
AUSTRALIA 41 (V. Huxley 10).
Fifth Test at Stamford Bridge:
ENGLAND 48 (J. Parker 12).
AUSTRALIA 46 (V. Huxley 10).

1932
ENGLAND v AUSTRALIA
First Test at Stamford Bridge:
ENGLAND 50 (T. Farndon 11, W. Phillips 10).
AUSTRALIA 41 (M. Grosskreutz 7).
Second Test at Wembley:
ENGLAND 35 (G. Greenwood 8).
AUSTRALIA 59 (D. Case 12).
Third Test at Belle Vue:
ENGLAND 53 (G. Lees 11, T. Farndon 11, F. Varey 11).
AUSTRALIA 43 (D. Case 10).
Fourth Test at Crystal Palace:
ENGLAND 45 (E. Langton 10).
AUSTRALIA 49 (D. Case 10).
Fifth Test at Wembley:
ENGLAND 51 (E. Langton 10, G. Lees 10).
AUSTRALIA 42 (V. Huxley 12).

1933
ENGLAND v AUSTRALIA*
First Test at Wembley
ENGLAND 76 (G. Lees 20, E. Langton 16, S. Jackson 15, T. Stevenson 13).
AUSTRALIA 47 (V. Huxley 12).
Second Test at Belle Vue:
ENGLAND 61 (G. Lees 22, S. Jackson 12).
AUSTRALIA 65 (V. Huxley 16, B. Wilkinson 16, D. Case 12).
Third Test at Crystal Palace:
ENGLAND 63½ (J. Parker 17, G. Lees 13, T. Stevenson 12, T. Farndon 11).
AUSTRALIA 62½ (D. Case 15, B. Wilkinson 14, M. Grosskreutz 13).
Fourth Test at Wimbledon:
ENGLAND 62 (G. Lees 17, T. Stevenson 13, T. Farndon 11).

AUSTRALIA 64 (M. Grosskreutz 18, B. Wilkinson 14, V. Huxley 12, D. Case 10).
Fifth Test at West Ham:
ENGLAND 74 (F. Varey 18, T. Stevenson 15, S. Burton 12, T. Farndon 10).
AUSTRALIA 52 (B. Wilkinson 16, V. Huxley 13, D. Case 12).
* Scoring was 4–2–1 in this series.

1934
ENGLAND v AUSTRALIA
First Test at Wembley:
ENGLAND 38 (G. Lees 15).
AUSTRALIA 69 (M. Grosskeutz 15, D. Case 13, V. Huxley 12½, B. Wilkinson 12, R. Johnson 10).
Second Test at New Cross:
ENGLAND 58 (E. Langton 14, G. Lees 13, J. Abbott 13).
AUSTRALIA 48 (D. Case 13, R. Johnson 10).
Third Test at Wimbledon:
ENGLAND 51 (E. Langton 14, G. Lees 13, J. Abbott 11).
AUSTRALIA 54 (M. Grosskeutz 15, J. Sharp 13).
Fourth Test at Belle Vue:
ENGLAND 60½ (E. Langton 15, G. Lees 14, F. Charles 13, J. Abbott 10).
AUSTRALIA 45½ (R. Johnson 15, M. Grosskeutz 11).
Fifth Test at West Ham:
ENGLAND 50 (E. Langton 13, G. Lees 11).
AUSTRALIA 57 (B. Wilkinson 16, M. Grosskeutz 15, R. Johnson 10).

1934–35
AUSTRALIA v ENGLAND
First Test at Sydney:
AUSTRALIA 35 (M. Grosskreutz 8, L. Van Praag 8).
ENGLAND 19 (T. Stevenson 8).
Second Test at Melbourne:
AUSTRALIA 30 (M. Grosskreutz 9, D. Case 7).
ENGLAND 24 (E. Langton 7).
Third Test at Sydney:
AUSTRALIA 26 (M. Grosskeutz 7).
ENGLAND 27 (T. Stevenson 9).
Fourth Test at Sydney:
AUSTRALIA 29 (W. Little 7).
ENGLAND 24 (J. Abbott 9).
Fifth Test at Sydney:
AUSTRALIA 26½ (B. Wilkinson 9, M. Grosskreutz 8).
ENGLAND 27½ (J. Abbott 8, E. Langton 7).

1935
ENGLAND v AUSTRALIA
First Test at Wembley:
ENGLAND 56 (E. Langton 15, B. Kitchen 12, F. Charles 11, J. Parker 10).
AUSTRALIA 52 (M. Grosskreutz 15, B. Wilkinson 10).
Second Test at New Cross:
ENGLAND 59 (T. Farndon 14, E. Langton 13, B. Kitchen 10).
AUSTRALIA 46 (D. Case 12, M. Grosskreutz 11).
Third Test at Belle Vue:
ENGLAND 59 (E. Langton 17, J. Abbott 13, T. Farndon 11, B. Kitchen 10).
AUSTRALIA 48 (B. Wilkinson 13, R. Johnson 11).
Fourth Test at West Ham:
ENGLAND 40 (T. Croombs 9).
AUSTRALIA 66 (M. Grosskreutz 17, R. Johnson 13, L. Van Praag 12).
Fifth Test at Harringay:
ENGLAND 63 (E. Langton 14, J. Ormston 14, F. Charles 12, T. Farndon 10).
AUSTRALIA 44 (M. Grosskreutz 12, V. Huxley 10).

1935–36
AUSTRALIA v ENGLAND
First Test at Sydney:
AUSTRALIA 47 (M. Grosskreutz 12, V. Huxley 9, C. Mitchell 9).
ENGLAND 25 (T. Stevenson 8, D. Haigh 7).
Second Test at Sydney:
AUSTRALIA 44 (M. Grosskreutz 12, V. Huxley 11, B. Wilkinson 10).
ENGLAND 28 (W. Phillips 7).
Third Test at Sydney:
AUSTRALIA 44 (M. Grosskreutz 12, V. Huxley 11, B. Wilkinson 11).
ENGLAND 28 (N. Key 7).
Fourth Test at Sydney:
AUSTRALIA 39 (M. Grosskreutz 12, F. Pearce 8).
ENGLAND 33 (W. Phillips 10).
Fifth Test at Sydney:
AUSTRALIA 32 (V. Huxley 11, M. Grosskreutz 9).
ENGLAND 39 (W. Phillips 10, N. Key 8).

1936
ENGLAND v AUSTRALIA
First Test at Wembley:
ENGLAND 65 (G. Newton 16, F. Charles 13, J. Parker 12, E. Langton 12).
AUSTRALIA 43 (M. Grosskreutz 13, B. Wilkinson 11).
Second Test at New Cross:
ENGLAND 49 (F. Charles 18).
AUSTRALIA 56 (D. Case 16, M. Grosskreutz 13, L. Van Praag 12).
Third Test at Belle Vue:
ENGLAND 70 (B. Kitchen 16, F. Charles 16, J. Abbott 13, E. Langton 13).
AUSTRALIA 38 (L. Van Praag 11).
Fourth Test at Wimbledon:
ENGLAND 58 (E. Langton 15, F. Charles 13, B. Kitchen 11).
AUSTRALIA 47 (L. Van Praag 15, V. Huxley 12).
Fifth Test at West Ham:
ENGLAND 35 (F. Charles 9).
AUSTRALIA 73 (B. Wilkinson 16, L. Van Praag 15, V. Huxley 11, D. Case 11, M. Grosskreutz 10).

1936–37
AUSTRALIA v ENGLAND
First Test at Sydney:
AUSTRALIA 29 (W. Little 9, C. Mitchell 8).
ENGLAND 25 (T. Croombs 5, J. Parker 5).
Second Test at Melbourne:
AUSTRALIA 33 (W. Little 9, C. Mitchell 9).
ENGLAND 21 (J. Parker 7).
Third Test at Sydney:
AUSTRALIA 25 (B. Wilkinson 9).
ENGLAND 28 (T. Croombs 7, J. Parker 7).
Fourth Test at Sydney:
AUSTRALIA 26 (B. Wilkinson 9).
ENGLAND 28 (N. Parker 8).
Fifth Test at Sydney:
AUSTRALIA 31 (W. Little 8, V. Huxley 8).
ENGLAND 22 (J. Parker 7).

1937
ENGLAND v AUSTRALIA
First Test at Wembley:
ENGLAND 66 (J. Parker 13, E. Langton 12, A. Atkinson 12, J. Ormston 11, B. Kitchen 10).
AUSTRALIA 41 (B. Wilkinson 17, L. Van Praag 12).
(Series abandoned.)
ENGLAND v USA
International Challenge at Wimbledon:
ENGLAND 51 (B. Kitchen 13, J. Abbott 11, J. Parker 10).
USA 57 (J. Milne 18, W. Lamoreaux 15, C. Milne 11).

1937–38
AUSTRALIA v ENGLAND
First Test at Sydney:
AUSTRALIA 26 (B. Wilkinson 9, C. Mitchell 8).
ENGLAND 28 (J. Abbott 6, L. Wotton 6).
Second Test at Sydney:
AUSTRALIA 31 (B. Wilkinson 9).
ENGLAND 23 (B. Kitchen 6).
Third Test at Sydney:
AUSTRALIA 27 (B. Wilkinson 9, C. Mitchell 9).
ENGLAND 26 (J. Abbott 7, L. Wotton 7, J. Parker 7).
Fourth Test at Sydney:
AUSTRALIA 30 (B. Wilkinson 9, C. Mitchell 9).
ENGLAND 24 (J. Abbott 6).
Fifth Test at Sydney:
AUSTRALIA 29 (B. Wilkinson 9, C. Mitchell 8).
ENGLAND 25 (B. Kitchen 7).

1938
ENGLAND v AUSTRALIA
First Test at Belle Vue:
ENGLAND 52 (B. Kitchen 13, F. Varey 12, G. Newton 11).
AUSTRALIA 56 (M. Grosskreutz 15, B. Wilkinson 15).
Second Test at Wembley:
ENGLAND 63 (F. Charles 13, F. Varey 13, B. Kitchen 11, G. Newton 11, A. Atkinson 10).
AUSTRALIA 44 (B. Wilkinson 15, L. Van Praag 15).
Third Test at New Cross:
ENGLAND 47 (B. Kitchen 12, A. Atkinson 12, S. Greatrex 10).
AUSTRALIA 61 (L. Van Praag 18, B. Wilkinson 18, R. Johnson 11).
Fourth Test at West Ham:
ENGLAND 55 (A. Atkinson 13, B. Kitchen 11, T. Croombs 10).
AUSTRALIA 51 (B. Wilkinson 14, M. Grosskreutz 10).
Fifth Test at Wimbledon:
ENGLAND 58 (G. Pymar 13, G. Newton 12).
AUSTRALIA 49 (B. Wilkinson 18, L. Van Praag 10).

1938–39
AUSTRALIA v ENGLAND
First Test at Sydney:
AUSTRALIA 22 (B. Wilkinson 9).
ENGLAND 32 (A. Statham 7, G. Pymar 7).
Second Test at Sydney:
AUSTRALIA 32 (B. Wilkinson 8, L. Van Praag 8).
ENGLAND 22 (A. Statham 7).
Third Test at Sydney:
AUSTRALIA 23 (B. Wilkinson 9).
ENGLAND 31 (A. Statham 8).
Fourth Test at Sydney:
AUSTRALIA 28 (B. Wilkinson 9).
ENGLAND 24 (J. Parker 8).
Fifth Test at Sydney:
AUSTRALIA 35 (B. Wilkinson 9, L. Van Praag 8, B. Longley 8).
ENGLAND 19 (J. Parker 7, A. Atkinson 7).

1939
ENGLAND v AUSTRALIA
First Test at New Cross:
ENGLAND 62 (A. Atkinson 18, B. Kitchen 15, J. Parker 11).
AUSTRALIA 46 (V. Duggan 15, R. Johnson 12).
Second Test at Wimbledon:
ENGLAND 55 (B. Kitchen 14, E. Langton 10, J. Parker 10).
AUSTRALIA 53 (L. Van Praag 17, V. Duggan 16).
Third Test at Harringay:
ENGLAND 48 (A. Atkinson 12, B. Kitchen 10).
AUSTRALIA 58 (R. Johnson 16, L. Van Praag 14, V. Duggan 12).
Fourth Test at Belle Vue:
ENGLAND 65 (B. Kitchen 16, J. Parker 15, A. Atkinson 10).
AUSTRALIA 42 (V. Duggan 12).
Fifth Test at Wembley:
ENGLAND 71 (B. Kitchen 16, E. Langton 15, M. Craven 11, J. Parker 11, A. Atkinson 11).
AUSTRALIA 36 (L. Van Praag 11, V. Duggan 11).

1947
ENGLAND v AUSTRALIA
First Test at Bradford:
ENGLAND 65 (B. Kitchen 16, A. Statham 16, N. Parker 13).
AUSTRALIA 43 (V. Duggan 16, M. Grosskreutz 10).
Second Test at West Ham:
ENGLAND 58 (J. Parker 18, G. Wilks 10).
AUSTRALIA 50 (V. Duggan 13, M. Grosskreutz 10, L. Van Praag 10).
Third Test at Wembley:
ENGLAND 49 (J. Parker 10).
AUSTRALIA 57 (V. Duggan 17, L. Van Praag 14, M. Grosskreutz 10).

1947–48
AUSTRALIA v ENGLAND
First Test at Brisbane:
AUSTRALIA 57 (B. Rogers 15, B. Longley 13, C. Smythe 12).
ENGLAND 47 (N. Parker 12, B. Pitcher 12).
Second Test at Sydney:
AUSTRALIA 57 (J. Biggs 13, B. Rogers 12, B. Longley 10).
ENGLAND 51 (J. Parker 13, N. Parker 10, B. Pitcher 10).
Third Test at Melbourne:
AUSTRALIA 61 (V. Duggan 18, B. Rogers 16, B. Longley 13).
ENGLAND 47 (J. Parker 13, B. Pitcher 10).
Fourth Test at Newcastle:
AUSTRALIA 79 (A. Lawson 16, V. Duggan 15, M. Grosskreutz 14, B. Rogers 11, B. Longley 11).
ENGLAND 29 (D. Oliver 10).
Fifth Test at Sydney:
AUSTRALIA 62 (V. Duggan 14, A. Lawson 14, M. Grosskreutz 12, J. Biggs 10).
ENGLAND 46 (J. Parker 15, O. Hart 13).

1948
ENGLAND v AUSTRALIA
First Test at Wimbledon:
ENGLAND 61 (A. Statham 17, N. Parker 14, G. Wilks 11).
AUSTRALIA 45 (V. Duggan 12).
Second Test at Belle Vue:
ENGLAND 69 (D. Oliver 18,

J. Parker 16, J. Lloyd 13).
AUSTRALIA 39 (V. Duggan 14).
Third Test at New Cross:
ENGLAND 57 (J. Parker 14, S. Waterman 12, A. Statham 11).
AUSTRALIA 51 (V. Duggan 15, R. Johnson 14, B. Longley 10).
Fourth Test at Harringay:
ENGLAND 58 (J. Parker 15, B. Gilbert 13).
AUSTRALIA 50 (V. Duggan 15, R. Johnson 10).

Fifth Test at West Ham:
ENGLAND 45 (N. Parker 11).
AUSTRALIA 63 (V. Duggan 18, A. Lawson 15, B. Longley 12).
ENGLAND v OVERSEAS
International Challenge at Bradford:
ENGLAND 54 (A. Statham 13, N. Parker 10, O. Hart 10).
OVERSEAS 53 (V. Duggan 13, E. Chitty 12, B. Longley 12).

1949
ENGLAND v AUSTRALIA
First Test at Wembley
ENGLAND 41 (F. Williams 9, B. Gilbert 9, J. Parker 9).
AUSTRALIA 67 (V. Duggan 18, G. Warren 18, R. Johnson 12).
Second Test at Birmingham:
ENGLAND 53 (L. Lawson 12, D. Oliver 11).
AUSTRALIA 55 (V. Duggan 18, A. Payne 13, B. Longley 10).
Third Test at New Cross:
ENGLAND 62 (J. Parker 17, D. Oliver 14, B. Gilbert 11, T. Price 11).
AUSTRALIA 46 (R. Johnson 12, G. Warren 10).
Fourth Test at Harringay:
ENGLAND 53 (J. Parker 16, B. Gilbert 12).
AUSTRALIA 55 (J. Biggs 15, G. Warren 14, C. Watson 10).
Fifth Test at Bradford:
ENGLAND 72 (D. Oliver 18, J. Parker 15, R. Clarke 14, T. Price 10).
AUSTRALIA 36 (A. Lawson 13, G. Warren 11).

1949–50
AUSTRALIA v ENGLAND
First Test at Sydney:
AUSTRALIA 76 (J. Briggs 18, A. Lawson 16, G. Warren 14, N. Clay 13, K. Le Breton 10).
ENGLAND 32 (B. Kitchen 10).
Second Test at Sydney:
AUSTRALIA 67 (A. Lawson 16, G. Warren 15, J. Biggs 13, K. Le Breton 11).
ENGLAND 41 (J. Parker 11).
Third Test at Brisbane:
AUSTRALIA 72 (A. Lawson 17, G. Warren 16, J. Biggs 14).
ENGLAND 35 (J. Parker 12).
Fourth Test at Sydney
AUSTRALIA 68 (A. Lawson 18, K. Le Breton 15, G. Warren 11).
ENGLAND 40 (O. Hart 11, J. Parker 11).
Fifth Test at Sydney:
AUSTRALIA 68 (A. Lawson 17, G. Warren 16, J. Biggs 15, B. Longley 10).
ENGLAND 40 (O. Hart 11).
Sixth Test at Melbourne:
AUSTRALIA 50 (A. Lawson 18, B. Longley 12, M. Harding 12).
ENGLAND 58 (J. Parker 14, R. Clarke 14).
Seventh Test at Adelaide:
AUSTRALIA 70 (J. Young 17, B. Longley 16, A. Lawson 15).
ENGLAND 38 (J. Parker 14, R. Clarke 10).

1950
ENGLAND v AUSTRALIA
First Test at West Ham:
ENGLAND 47 (T. Price 10).
AUSTRALIA 60 (A. Lawson 12, V. Duggan 12, K. Le Breton 11, B. Longley 10).

Second Test at Belle Vue:
ENGLAND 58 (L. Lawson 14, E. Rigg 12, T. Price 10).
AUSTRALIA 50 (G. Warren 15, M. Harding 14).
Third Test at New Cross:
ENGLAND 63 (B. Roger 14, C. Roger 14, C. Brine 11, T. Price 10).
AUSTRALIA 45 (G. Warren 17).
Fourth Test at Wimbledon:
ENGLAND 62 (C. Brine 13, A. Hunt 12, T. Price 10).
AUSTRALIA 46 (G. Warren 15).
Fifth Test at Wembley:
ENGLAND 53 (C. Brine 16, T. Price 15).
AUSTRALIA 55 (G. Warren 15, K. Le Breton 12).

1950–51
AUSTRALIA v ENGLAND
First Test at Sydney:
AUSTRALIA 63 (A. Lawson 18, G. Warren 17, K. Le Breton 10).
ENGLAND 45 (J. Parker 14, E. Williams 10, E. Rigg 10).
Second Test at Sydney:
AUSTRALIA 65 (A. Lawson 15, J. Gates 15, B. Ryan 13).
ENGLAND 42 (J. Parker 16, E. Williams 10).
Third Test at Adelaide:
AUSTRALIA 60 (A. Lawson 16, B. Ryan 14, J. Biggs 11).
ENGLAND 48 (J. Parker 18, T. Miller 13, R. Clarke 10).
Fourth Test at Bathurst:
AUSTRALIA 67 (J. Gates 13, B. Ryan 12, A. Lawson 11, J. Arnfield 11, A. Hunter 10).
ENGLAND 40 (J. Parker 18).
Fifth Test at Adelaide:
AUSTRALIA 58½ (B. Leverenz 17, A. Lawson 16, B. Ryan 13½).
ENGLAND 49½ (J. Parker 13, E. Williams 12, R. Clarke 12).
Sixth Test at Brisbane:
AUSTRALIA 60 (K. Gurtner 12, A. Lawson 12, C. Spinks 10, B. Ryan 10).
ENGLAND 48 (J. Parker 16, T. Miller 16, E. Williams 11).
Seventh Test at Sydney:
AUSTRALIA 60 (A. Lawson 17, B. Ryan 11, L. Levy 11).
ENGLAND 48 (J. Parker 16, T. Miller 13, E. Williams 12).

1951
ENGLAND v AUSTRALIA
First Test at Harringay
ENGLAND 48 (F. Williams 11).
AUSTRALIA 60 (J. Young 16, A. Lawson 15).
Second Test at Bradford:
ENGLAND 59 (F. Williams 13, J. Parker 12, E. Rigg 12).
AUSTRALIA 48 (J. Young 16, J. Biggs 11).
Third Test at Wembley:
ENGLAND 49 (S. Waterman 13, F. Williams 12).
AUSTRALIA 58 (A. Lawson 17, A. Payne 16, J. Young 10).
Fourth Test at Birmingham:
ENGLAND 46 (E. Rigg 13, S. Waterman 10).
AUSTRALIA 62 (J. Young 18, J. Biggs 16).
Fifth Test at West Ham:
ENGLAND 49 (S. Waterman 17, E. Rigg 14).
AUSTRALIA 58 (G. Warren 12, R. Moore 11, B. Leverenz 10, A. Lawson 10).

1951–52
AUSTRALIA v ENGLAND
First Test at Sydney:
AUSTRALIA 69 (B. Ryan 16, L. Levy 14, A. Lawson 13, A. Payne 10).
ENGLAND 37 (J. Parker 14, B. Roger 11).
Second Test at Sydney:
AUSTRALIA 49 (B. Ryan 14, A. Lawson 13).
ENGLAND 59 (J. Parker 18).
Third Test at Sydney:
AUSTRALIA 76 (A. Payne 18, A. Lawson 16, B. Ryan 15).
ENGLAND 32 (J. Parker 9).
Fourth Test at Brisbane:
AUSTRALIA 66 (A. Lawson 17, K. Gurtner 15, L. Levy 12, B. Ryan 10).
ENGLAND 41 (C. Roger 11, M. Craven 10).
Fifth Test at Sydney:
AUSTRALIA 64 (K. Gurtner 18, C. Watson 15, A. Lawson 13).
ENGLAND 44 (C. Roger 9).

1952
ENGLAND v AUSTRALIA
First Test at Wimbledon:
ENGLAND 52 (C. Brine 13, B. Roger 12).
AUSTRALIA 56 (R. Moore 18, J. Young 16, M. Harding 10, J. Biggs 10).
Second Test at Wembley:
ENGLAND 52 (W. Green 12, B. Roger 11, F. Williams 10).
AUSTRALIA 56 (R. Moore 18, J. Young 16).
Third Test at Belle Vue:
ENGLAND 50 (K. Sharples 12, W. Green 11, A. Hunt 11).
AUSTRALIA 58 (J. Young 14, J. Biggs 12, A. Payne 12, R. Moore 11).
Fourth Test at New Cross:
ENGLAND 46 (B. Roger 11).
AUSTRALIA 62 (J. Young 18, R. Moore 18, G. Warren 10).
Fifth Test at Harringay:
ENGLAND 55 (D. Bradley 16, F. Williams 12).
AUSTRALIA 53 (R. Moore 15, J. Young 11, J. Biggs 10).

1952–53
AUSTRALIA v ENGLAND
First Test at Sydney:
AUSTRALIA 86 (G. Warren 18, L. Levy 16, A. Quinn 15, A. Lawson 14, B. Ryan 14).
ENGLAND 22 (J. Parker 6, R. Mason 6).
Second Test at Sydney:
AUSTRALIA 77 (G. Warren 16, A. Lawson 15, L. Levy 13, B. Ryan 13, K. Gurtner 11).
ENGLAND 31 (K. McKinlay 10).
Third Test at Brisbane:
AUSTRALIA 73 (A. Lawson 17, L. Levy 16, B. Ryan 12, K. Gurtner 11, K. Cox 10).
ENGLAND 35 (J. Parker 15).
NEW ZEALAND v ENGLAND
First Test at Dunedin:
NEW ZEALAND 36½ (R. Johnston 16, G. Mardon 12½).
ENGLAND 35½ (K. Sharples 17).
Second Test at Christchurch:
NEW ZEALAND 31 (G. Mardon 12, M. Neil 10).
ENGLAND 41 (C. Boss 15, K. Sharples 12).
Third Test at Hastings:
NEW ZEALAND 47 (R. Johnston 16, M. Dunn 12, P. Clarke 10).
ENGLAND 25 (B. Kitchen 14).
Fourth Test at Wellington:
NEW ZEALAND 35 (M. Dunn 13, R. Johnston 12).
ENGLAND 37 (B. Kitchen 12, C. Boss 12).
Fifth Test at Auckland:
NEW ZEALAND 47 (M. Neil 17, M. Dunn 13).
ENGLAND 24 (E. Williams 10).

1953
ENGLAND v AUSTRALIA
First Test at Norwich:
ENGLAND 46 (B. Bales 13).
AUSTRALIA 62 (R. Moore 18, J. Young 17, A. Lawson 13).
Second Test at Wembley:
ENGLAND 57 (E. Williams 15, T. Price 12, S. Waterman 12).
AUSTRALIA 51 (J. Biggs 13, J. Young 12, A. Lawson 11, R. Moore 10).
Third Test at Birmingham:
ENGLAND 61 (T. Price 14, S. Waterman 11, E. Rigg 11, A. Hunt 10).
AUSTRALIA 47 (J. Young 15, J. Biggs 13).
ENGLAND v NEW ZEALAND
First Test at Wimbledon:
ENGLAND 62 (S. Waterman 15, E. Rigg 15, F. Williams 14).
NEW ZEALAND 45 (R. Moore 18, G. Mardon 11).
Second Test at West Ham:
ENGLAND 32.
NEW ZEALAND 34 (T. Redmond 12)
(abandoned after 11 heats.)
Third Test at Bristol:
ENGLAND 77 (F. Williams 18, T. Price 16, S. Waterman 13, J. Lloyd 12).
NEW ZEALAND 31 (R. Moore 10).
Re-run at West Ham:
ENGLAND 56 (S. Waterman 15, E. Williams 14, F. Williams 13).
NEW ZEALAND 56 (R. Moore 14, M. Dunn 13, G. Mardon 10).

1954
ENGLAND v AUSTRALASIA
First Test at West Ham:
ENGLAND 60 (B. Crutcher 17, A. Forrest 15).
AUSTRALASIA 48 (J. Young 12, T. Redmond 10).
Second Test at Belle Vue:
ENGLAND 64 (A. Forrest 13, K. Sharples 12, E. Rigg 11, E. Williams 11, B. Crutcher 10).
AUSTRALASIA 44 (J. Young 15, G. Mardon 13).
Third Test at Bradford:
ENGLAND 56 (B. Crutcher 15, A. Forrest 10, E. Rigg 10).
AUSTRALASIA 52 (G. Mardon 13, R. Moore 11, B. Briggs 10).

1955
ENGLAND v AUSTRALASIA
First Test at Wimbledon:
ENGLAND 39 (A. Wright 10, F. Williams 10).
AUSTRALASIA 67 (R. Moore 18, J. Young 15, B. Briggs 12, P. Moore 11).
Second Test at Wembley:
ENGLAND 67 (F. Williams 17, B. Crutcher 16, E. Williams 11).
AUSTRALASIA 41 (J. Young 15).
Third Test at West Ham:
ENGLAND 42 (K. McKinlay 11, B. Crutcher 10).
AUSTRALASIA 66 (R. Moore 18, J. Young 18, B. Briggs 14).

Fourth Test at Bradford:
ENGLAND 61 (A. Forrest 18, B. Crutcher 14, K. Sharples 10).
AUSTRALASIA 46 (R. Moore 12).
Fifth Test at Birmingham:
ENGLAND 61 (K. Middleditch 13, A. Forrest 12, B. Crutcher 11, R. Mountford 10).
AUSTRALASIA 46 (B. Briggs 15, R. Johnston 12).
Sixth Test at Norwich:
ENGLAND 57 (B. Bales 13, A. Forrest 12, B. Crutcher 10).
AUSTRALASIA 51 (J. Young 17, B. Briggs 13, R. Johnston 10).

1956
ENGLAND v AUSTRALASIA
First Test at Bradford:
ENGLAND 55 (B. Crutcher 16, S. Waterman 11, K. McKinlay 10).
AUSTRALASIA 53 (B. Briggs 17, R. Moore 16, J. Biggs 10).
Second Test at Birmingham:
ENGLAND 65 (A. Hunt 18, K. McKinlay 14, B. Crutcher 13).
AUSTRALASIA 43 (R. Moore 14, B. Briggs 10).
Third Test at Poole:
ENGLAND 57 (P. Craven 15, B. Crutcher 13, K. McKinlay 12).
AUSTRALASIA 51 (R. Moore 11).
SWEDEN v ENGLAND
First Test at Kumla:
SWEDEN 65 (O. Fundin 17, O. Nygren 15, L. Pettersson 14).
ENGLAND 43 (K. McKinlay 10).
Second Test at Ostermalm:
SWEDEN 71 (O. Nygren 17, O. Fundin 16, R. Sörmander 15).
ENGLAND 37 (K. McKinlay 8, P. Craven 8).
Third Test at Stockholm:
SWEDEN 69 (O. Nygren 17, R. Sörmander 15, O. Fundin 14, PeO Soderman 12, U. Ericsson 10).
ENGLAND 39 (P. Craven 13).
ENGLAND v SWEDEN
First Test at Wembley:
ENGLAND 49 (B. Crutcher 14, A. Hunt 12, D. Bradley 10).
SWEDEN 59 (O. Fundin 18, R. Sörmander 11, O. Nygren 10).
Second Test at Wimbledon:
ENGLAND 52 (B. Crutcher 11, D. Bradley 11).
SWEDEN 53 (O. Nygren 12, O. Fundin 11, R. Sörmander 11, L. Pettersson 10).
Third Test at Norwich:
ENGLAND 66 (K. McKinlay 17, A. Hunt 11).
SWEDEN 42 (O. Fundin 15, O. Nygren 11).

1958
ENGLAND v SWEDEN
First Test at Southampton:
ENGLAND 59 (B. Crutcher 15, D. Bradley 12, P. Craven 12).
SWEDEN 49 (O. Fundin 16, O. Nygren 13).
Second Test at Norwich:
ENGLAND 50 (P. Craven 13, B. Bales 11).
SWEDEN 58 (R. Sörmander 18, O. Fundin 16, O. Nygren 15).
Third Test at Wimbledon:
ENGLAND 71 (P. Craven 18, B. Crutcher 15, R. How 15, K. McKinlay 11).
SWEDEN 37 (O. Fundin 15).
ENGLAND v AUSTRALASIA
First Test at Swindon:
ENGLAND 51 (P. Craven 16).
AUSTRALASIA 57 (B. Briggs 18, N. Street 12, P. Moore 12, J. Young 11).

Second Test at Oxford:
ENGLAND 44 (P. Craven 13, G. White 10, K. McKinlay 10).
AUSTRALASIA 64 (B. Briggs 17, N. Street 15, P. Moore 12, J. Young 11).
Third Test at Coventry:
ENGLAND 65 (K. McKinlay 15, B. Crutcher 14, P. Craven 14).
AUSTRALASIA 43 (B. Briggs 18, J. Young 13).
Fourth Test at Belle Vue:
ENGLAND 58 (P. Craven 18, K. McKinlay 14, R. How 12).
AUSTRALASIA 50 (R. Johnston 15, J. Young 10, R. Moore 10).
Fifth Test at Southampton:
ENGLAND 63 (B. Crutcher 15, P. Craven 12, K. McKinlay 12, D. Bradley 10).
AUSTRALASIA 45 (B. Briggs 17, J. Geran 12).
SWEDEN v ENGLAND
First Test at Gothenburg:
SWEDEN 61 (O. Nygren 17, O. Fundin 16, R. Sörmander 14).
ENGLAND 46 (P. Craven 13).

Second Test Hammarby:
SWEDEN 61 (O. Nygren 18, B. Nilsson 15, O. Fundin 12, R. Sörmander 12).
ENGLAND 46 (P. Craven 14, K. McKinlay 12).
Third Test at Malilla:
SWEDEN 48 (R. Sörmander 17, O. Fundin 11).
ENGLAND 60 (P. Craven 16, G. White 13).
POLAND v ENGLAND
First Test at Warsaw:
POLAND 27 (S. Tkocz 7, M. Polukard 7).
ENGLAND 81 (P. Craven 17, G. White 14, M. Broadbanks 12, K. McKinlay 12, D. Bradley 10, R. How 10).
Second Test at Rybnik:
POLAND 33 (J. Maj 13).
ENGLAND 75 (P. Craven 18, M. Broadbanks 15, G. White 14, K. McKinlay 13).
Third Test at Wroclaw:
POLAND 51 (M. Kaiser 15, K. Pociejkowicz 15).
ENGLAND 56 (P. Craven 17, K. McKinlay 14, R. How 13).

1958
ENGLAND v POLAND
First Test at Southampton:
ENGLAND 83 (D. Bradley 15, P. Craven 14, R. How 13, G. Jackson 11).
POLAND 25 (F. Kapala 9).
Second Test at Ipswich:
ENGLAND 77 (P. Craven 18, K. McKinlay 13, D. Bradley 13, R. How 10, G. White 10, N. Boocock 10).
POLAND 30 (F. Kapala 10).

Third Test at Leicester:
ENGLAND 84 (P. Craven 15, K. McKinlay 15, G. White 13, R. How 12, D. Bradley 10).
POLAND 24 (M. Kaiser 10).

1958–59
AUSTRALIA v ENGLAND
First Test at Brisbane:
AUSTRALIA 31 (K. Gurtner 12).
ENGLAND 29 (K. McKinlay 10).
Second Test at Sydney:
AUSTRALIA 44 (K. Gurtner 10, L. Levy 10, P. Moore 10).
ENGLAND 16 (K. McKinlay 9).
Third Test at Sydney:
AUSTRALIA 32 (P. Moore 10).
ENGLAND 28 (K. McKinlay 12).
Fourth Test at Melbourne:
AUSTRALIA 36 (P. Moore 10, J. Bainbridge 10).
ENGLAND 24 (K. McKinlay 12).
Fifth Test at Adelaide:
AUSTRALIA 21 (J. Young 10).
ENGLAND 39 (K. McKinlay 12, G. Hussey 10).

1959
ENGLAND v AUSTRALASIA
First Test at Southampton:
ENGLAND 52 (R. How 16, P. Craven 11, K. McKinlay 11).
AUSTRALASIA 56 (P. Moore 12, A. Lawson 12, B. Briggs 11).
Second Test at Norwich:
ENGLAND 62 (P. Craven 16, R. How 16, K. McKinlay 12).
AUSTRALASIA 46 (A. Lawson 13, R. Moore 13).
Third Test at Swindon:
ENGLAND 55 (P. Craven 13, M. Broadbanks 11, R. How 11).
AUSTRALASIA 53 (B. Briggs 16, R. Moore 14).

1959–60
AUSTRALIA v ENGLAND
First Test at Melbourne:
AUSTRALIA 21 (J. Bainbridge 11).
ENGLAND 38 (K. McKinlay 12).
Second Test at Sydney:
AUSTRALIA 26 (B. Bryden 8).
ENGLAND 34 (B. Andrews 11, M. Broadbanks 10).
Third Test at Sydney:
AUSTRALIA 16 (B. Bryden 7).
ENGLAND 44 (K. McKinlay 12, M. Broadbanks 10, G. Jackson 10).
Fourth Test at Brisbane:
AUSTRALIA 17 (B. Bryden 6).
ENGLAND 43 (K. McKinlay 12, M. Broadbanks 11).
Fifth Test at Brisbane:
AUSTRALIA 18 (B. Bryden 6).
ENGLAND 42 (K. McKinlay 12, M. Broadbanks 10).

1960
ENGLAND v AUSTRALASIA
First Test at Coventry:
ENGLAND 49 (P. Craven 14, K. McKinlay 11).
AUSTRALASIA 59 (R. Moore 17, R. Johnston 15, J. Young 13).
Second Test at Norwich:
ENGLAND 54 (P. Craven 18, R. How 18).
AUSTRALASIA 54 (R. Moore 13, R. Johnston 12).
Third Test at Ipswich:
ENGLAND 51 (P. Craven 15).
AUSTRALASIA 57 (B. Briggs 17, R. Moore 14, P. Moore 12).
Fourth Test at Leicester:
ENGLAND 52 (P. Craven 17, K. McKinlay 15, R. How 11).
AUSTRALASIA 56 (R. Moore 16, J. Young 10).
Fifth Test at New Cross:
ENGLAND 47 (K. McKinlay 12, I. Williams 11, S. Waterman 10).
AUSTRALASIA 61 (R. Moore 16, J. Young 15, P. Moore 15).
POLAND v ENGLAND
First Test at Wroclaw:
POLAND 68 (H. Zyto 13, M. Kaiser 13, M. Polukard 13, N. Switala 12).
ENGLAND 39 (P. Craven 21).
Second Test at Rybnik:
POLAND 56 (F. Kapala 16, M. Kaiser 13).
ENGLAND 51 (P. Craven 21).
Third Test at Leszno:
POLAND 52 (H. Zyto 16, B. Kacperak 12, M. Kaiser 11).
ENGLAND 56 (P. Craven 17, K. McKinlay 12, R. Genz 10).

1961
GREAT BRITAIN v SWEDEN
First Test at Norwich:
GREAT BRITAIN 58 (P. Craven 12, R. Moore 11, J. Chamberlain 11).
SWEDEN 50 (O. Fundin 18, B. Knutsson 11).
Second Test at Oxford:
GREAT BRITAIN 69 (R. Moore 15, R. How 14, B. Briggs 13, P. Craven 12).
SWEDEN 39 (B. Knutsson 16, O. Fundin 15).
Third Test at Belle Vue:
GREAT BRITAIN 68 (P. Craven 17, B. Briggs 15, J. Chamberlain 11, R. Moore 10).
SWEDEN 40 (B. Knutsson 15).
Fourth Test at Wimbledon:
GREAT BRITAIN 77 (R. Moore 17, P. Craven 16, B. Andrews 12, B. Briggs 11, R. How 10).
SWEDEN 31 (O. Fundin 14).
Fifth Test at Southampton:
GREAT BRITAIN 57 (P. Craven 14, B. Briggs 12).

SWEDEN 51 (O. Fundin 17, B. Knutsson 17).
SWEDEN v GREAT BRITAIN
First Test at Vaxjo:
SWEDEN 71 (B. Knutsson 17, R. Sörmander 17, O. Fundin 16, G. Nordin 10).
GREAT BRITAIN 37 (P. Craven 13)
Second Test at Gothenburg:
SWEDEN 65 (O. Fundin 18, G. Nordin 18, B. Knutsson 14).
GREAT BRITAIN 43 (P. Craven 11, R. Moore 10).
Third Test at Malmo:
SWEDEN 60 (O. Fundin 18, G. Nordin 15).
GREAT BRITAIN 48 (P. Craven 15, B. Briggs 13, R. Moore 12).
Fourth Test at Norkopping:
SWEDEN 70 (O. Fundin 18, B. Knutsson 17, S. Sjösten 13, R. Sörmander 13).
GREAT BRITAIN 38 (B. Briggs 12).
Fifth Test at Stockholm:
SWEDEN 71 (O. Fundin 18, G. Nordin 16, B. Knutsson 15).
GREAT BRITAIN 37 (P. Craven 11, R. Moore 10).

1964
GREAT BRITAIN v USSR
First Test at Wembley:
GREAT BRITAIN 73 (B. Briggs 16, R. How 16, N. Boocock 16, M. Broadbanks 10).
USSR 35 (I. Plechanov 16).
Second Test at Coventry:
GREAT BRITAIN 56 (K. McKinlay 14, R. How 12, N. Boocock 11).
USSR 52 (B. Samorodov 16, I. Plechanov 15).
Third Test at Belle Vue:
GREAT BRITAIN 71 (R. How 14, D. Fisher 13, B. Briggs 12, N. Boocock 12, K. McKinlay 11).
USSR 37 (I. Plechanov 14).

1965

GREAT BRITAIN v USSR

First Test at Wimbledon:
GREAT BRITAIN 71 (B. Briggs 17, N. Boocock 16, C. Monk 14, K. McKinlay 10).
USSR 36 (V. Sokolov 13, I. Plechanov 10).
Second Test at Coventry:
GREAT BRITAIN 66 (B. Briggs 18, N. Boocock 16).
USSR 42 (G. Kurilenko 12, I. Plechanov 10, V. Moiseev 10).
Third Test at Sheffield:
GREAT BRITAIN 73 (B. Briggs 17, N. Boocock 17, C. Monk 15).
USSR 35 (I. Plechanov 15).
Fourth Test at Belle Vue:
GREAT BRITAIN 69 (B. Briggs 17, N. Boocock 15, D. Fisher 11, K. McKinlay 10).
USSR 39 (I. Plechanov 15).
Fifth Test at Newport:
GREAT BRITAIN 63 (K. McKinlay 15, B. Briggs 14, C. Monk 11).
USSR 45 (G. Kurilenko 14, I. Plechanov 12).

1966

POLAND v GREAT BRITAIN

First Test at Bydgoszcz:
POLAND 77 (P. Waloszek 18, A. Pogorzelski 16, E. Migos 14, M. Polukard 11, M. Rose 10).
GREAT BRITAIN 31 (N. Boocock 7).
Second Test at Gdansk:
POLAND 62 (P. Waloszek 14, A. Woryna 14, A. Wyglenda 11).
GREAT BRITAIN 46 (B. Briggs 16, N. Boocock 12).
Third Test at Gorzow:
POLAND 74 (E. Migos 16, A. Pogorzelski 16, A. Wyglenda 13, J. Maj 11, S. Tkocz 10).
GREAT BRITAIN 34 (B. Briggs 15, T. Hedge 10).
Fourth Test at Wroclaw:
POLAND 77 (P. Waloszek 16, A. Woryna 13, K. Pociejkowicz 13, A. Pogorzelski 11, J. Trzeszkowski 10, A. Wyglenda 10).
GREAT BRITAIN 31 (B. Briggs 12).
Fifth Test at Czestochowa:
POLAND 38 (S. Rurarz 8, J. Maj 8, M. Rose 8).
GREAT BRITAIN 16 (B. Briggs 5, N. Boocock 5).
(Abandoned after nine heats.)

GREAT BRITAIN v POLAND

First Test at Hackney:
GREAT BRITAIN 61 (B. Briggs 18, C. Pratt 15, N. Boocock 13).
POLAND 47 (A. Woryna 10).
Second Test at Coventry:
GREAT BRITAIN 57 (B. Briggs 17, N. Boocock 14, J. Lightfoot 10).
POLAND 51 (A. Wyglenda 12, A. Woryna 11, K. Pociejkowicz 11).
Third Test at Sheffield:
GREAT BRITAIN 76 (T. Hedge 18, B. Briggs 17, N. Boocock 17, I. Mauger 11, E. Boocock 10).
POLAND 32 (P. Waloszek 8).

ENGLAND v USSR

First Test at Newcastle:
ENGLAND 49 (N. Boocock 13, B. Brett 12).
USSR 59 (V. Trofimov 16, I. Plechanov 15, B. Samorodov 11).
Second Test at Halifax:
ENGLAND 59 (E. Boocock 14, E. Boothroyd 11, N. Boocock 10, R. Mountford 10).
USSR 49 (I. Plechanov 14, V. Trofimov 11, Y. Chekranov 10).
Third Test at Wolverhampton:
ENGLAND 59 (E. Boocock 15, N. Boocock 12, T. Betts 11, T. Hedge 11).
USSR 49 (I. Plechanov 13, V. Trofimov 13, B. Samorodov 11).
Fourth Test at Exeter:
ENGLAND 60 (N. Boocock 16, R. Mountford 13, T. Hedge 11).
USSR 48 (B. Samorodov 16, I. Plechanov 14).
Fifth Test at West Ham:
ENGLAND 71 (N. Hunter 18, T. Betts 15, N. Boocock 13½, C. Pratt 12½).
USSR 37 (I. Plechanov 11).

1967

GREAT BRITAIN v SWEDEN

First Test at Wimbledon:
GREAT BRITAIN 46 (R. Luckhurst 13, T. Hedge 10).
SWEDEN 62 (G. Nordin 17, O. Nygren 16, O. Fundin 13).
Second Test at Coventry:
GREAT BRITAIN 46 (K. McKinlay 12, R. France 11).
SWEDEN 62 (G. Nordin 14, T. Harrysson 14, O. Fundin 11).

Third Test at Newport:
GREAT BRITAIN 62 (E. Boocock 15, C. Monk 12, B. Briggs 11).
SWEDEN 46 (T. Harrysson 15, O. Fundin 11, A. Michanek 11).
Fourth Test at Glasgow:
GREAT BRITAIN 66 (E. Boocock 15, N. Boocock 14, B. Briggs 12).
SWEDEN 41 (G. Nordin 12, O. Nygren 10, B. Persson 10).
Fifth Test at Belle Vue:
GREAT BRITAIN 44 (B. Briggs 14, E. Boocock 12).
SWEDEN 63 (B. Persson 14, A. Michanek 12).

ENGLAND v SWEDEN

Tour Match at Exeter:
ENGLAND 38 (E. Boocock 16).
SWEDEN 70 (O. Fundin 18, G. Nordin 14, T. Harrysson 12, G. Malmqvist 10).

GREAT BRITAIN v POLAND

First Test at West Ham:
GREAT BRITAIN 39 (C. Pratt 13)
POLAND 69 (A. Woryna 17, P. Waloszek 15, A. Wyglenda 14, A. Pogorzelski 11).
Second Test at Poole:
GREAT BRITAIN 59 (G. Mudge 10, I. Mauger 10, N. Boocock 10).
POLAND 49 (A. Wyglenda 12, P. Waloszek 12, A. Pogorzelski 10, A. Woryna 10).
Third Test at Wolverhampton:
GREAT BRITAIN 66 (N. Boocock 15, R. Trigg 13, E. Boocock 12, J. Airey 11, T. Betts 10).
POLAND 42 (E. Migos 15).
Fourth Test at Halifax:
GREAT BRITAIN 53 (E. Boocock 18, N. Boocock 10).
POLAND 55 (A. Pogorzelski 14, A. Woryna 14, Z. Pytko 13).
Fifth Test at Newcastle:
GREAT BRITAIN 77 (N. Boocock 17, I. Mauger 15, E. Boocock 14, C. Monk 12, D. Younghusband 12).
POLAND 30 (A. Pogorzelski 10).

1967–68

AUSTRALIA v ENGLAND

First Test at Sydney:
AUSTRALIA 53 (J. Airey 15, G. Guasco 14, G. Kentwell 12).
ENGLAND 55 (E. Boocock 14, R. Trigg 13, T. Betts 10).
Second Test at Brisbane:
AUSTRALIA 62 (G. Guasco 14, K. Gurtner 14, J. Airey 13).
ENGLAND 46 (K. McKinlay 15, E. Boocock 10).
Third Test at Sydney:
AUSTRALIA 43 (J. Airey 13, G. Kentwell 10).
ENGLAND 64 (E. Boocock 18, N. Boocock 15, K. McKinlay 13).
Fourth Test at Sydney:
AUSTRALIA 68 (G. Kentwell 18, J. Airey 17, G. Guasco 14).
ENGLAND 40 (K. McKinlay 12, E. Boocock 11).
Fifth Test at Adelaide:
AUSTRALIA 46 (C. Monk 12, G. Kentwell 11).
ENGLAND 62 (E. Boocock 18, N. Boocock 15, Ray Wilson 11).

NEW ZEALAND v ENGLAND

First Test at Auckland:
NEW ZEALAND 39 (B. Andrews 15, R. Timmo 12).
ENGLAND 69 (N. Boocock 15, E. Boocock 14, R. Trigg 11, T. Betts 11).
Second Test at Napier:
NEW ZEALAND 55 (R. Timmo 16, B. Andrews 14, B. Subritzky 11).
ENGLAND 53 (R. Trigg 12, T. Betts 10, C. Pratt 10).
Third Test at New Plymouth:
NEW ZEALAND 22(B. Andrews 8).
ENGLAND 86 (K. McKinlay 18, N. Boocock 17, E. Boocock 16, C. Pratt 14, R. Trigg 13).
Fourth Test at Auckland:
NEW ZEALAND 29 (R. Timmo 11).
ENGLAND 79 (E. Boocock 16, K. McKinlay 16, N. Boocock 16, C. Pratt 13).

Fifth Test at Christchurch:
NEW ZEALAND 47 (R. Moore 17, F. Shuter 10, B. Andrews 10).
ENGLAND 60 (K. McKinlay 18, N. Boocock 17, C. Pratt 15).

1968

GREAT BRITAIN v SWEDEN

***First Test at Wimbledon:**
GREAT BRITAIN 43 (B. Briggs 12).
SWEDEN 35 (B. Jansson 10).
***Second Test at Halifax:**
GREAT BRITAIN 51 (B. Briggs 11, E. Boocock 11).
SWEDEN 27 (O. Nygren 8).
Third Test at Wolverhampton:
GREAT BRITAIN 52 (J. Airey 14, M. Ashby 12).
SWEDEN 55 (A. Michanek 14, O. Nygren 12, S. Sjösten 11).
Fourth Test at Coatbridge:
GREAT BRITAIN 37 (M. Ashby 14).
SWEDEN 71 (B. Jansson 15, S. Sjösten 14, O. Fundin 14, B. Persson 14, T. Harrysson 10).
Fifth Test at Swindon:
GREAT BRITAIN 62 (M. Ashby 15, M. Broadbanks 14, N. Boocock 11).
SWEDEN 46 (B. Jansson 15, A. Michanek 14, S. Sjösten 10).
* World League.

GREAT BRITAIN v USSR

***First Test at West Ham:**
GREAT BRITAIN 52 (N. Hunter 12, M. Ashby 11).
USSR 26 (G. Kurilenko 7).
***Second Test at Exeter:**
GREAT BRITAIN 51 (M. Ashby 12, B. Andrew 11).
USSR 27 (B. Samorodov 10).
* World League.

ENGLAND v USSR

First Test at Coventry:
ENGLAND 58 (M. Ashby 13, E. Boocock 12, N. Hunter 11, T. Betts 10).
USSR 50 (I. Plechanov 16, G. Kurilenko 15).
Second Test at Newport:
ENGLAND 68 (M. Ashby 17, E. Boocock 15, N. Hunter 11, T. Betts 10).
USSR 40 (V. Smirnov 13, I. Plechanov 11).
Third Test at Belle Vue:
GREAT BRITAIN 77 (E. Boocock 18, N. Hunter 18, M. Ashby 13, R. Wilson 11).
USSR 31 (I. Plechanov 12).

GREAT BRITAIN v POLAND

***First Test at Hackney:**
GREAT BRITAIN 60 (T. Betts 12, C. Pratt 11, M. Ashby 11).
POLAND 18 (A. Woryna 7, P. Waloszek 7).
***Second Test at Coventry:**
GREAT BRITAIN 40 (N. Boocock 9).
POLAND 38 (P. Waloszek 14).
* World League.

ENGLAND v POLAND

First Test at Newcastle:
Rained off.
Second Test at Poole:
ENGLAND 55 (T. Betts 10, R. Luckhurst 10, N. Hunter 10).
POLAND 53 (A. Woryna 16, P. Waloszek 14, H. Glucklich 12).
Third Test at Sheffield:
ENGLAND 61 (M. Ashby 14, N. Boocock 11, T. Betts 10, Ray Wilson 10).
SHEFFIELD 47 (A. Woryna 14, P. Waloszek 12).

*** World League Final Table**

	P	W	D	L	Pts
Great Britain	6	6	0	0	12
Poland	4	1	1	2	3
USSR	4	0	1	3	1
Sweden	2	0	0	2	0

(includes Test Match in Rybnik:
POLAND 49 (S. Tkocz 10).
USSR 29 (V. Klementiev 13).

1968–69

AUSTRALIA v ENGLAND

First Test at Melbourne:
AUSTRALIA 43 (J. Airey 13, G. Mudge 12).
ENGLAND 65 (N. Boocock 16, E. Boocock 14, K. McKinlay 13).
Second Test at Adelaide:
AUSTRALIA 61 (C. Monk 18, J. Airey 16).
ENGLAND 47 (K. McKinlay 13, E. Boocock 11).
Third Test at Sydney:
AUSTRALIA 68 (J. Airey 16, J. Langfield 15, C. Monk 12, J. White 12).
ENGLAND 40 (K. McKinlay 17).
Fourth Test at Brisbane:
AUSTRALIA 51 (J. White 12, J. Airey 11, C. Monk 10).
ENGLAND 57 (N. Boocock 16, K. McKinlay 12, M. Broadbanks 10).
Fifth Test at Sydney:
AUSTRALIA 60 (J. Airey 17, J. White 14, C. Monk 12).
ENGLAND 48 (N. Boocock 13, K. McKinlay 12, E. Boocock 11, J. McMillan 11).

1968–69

NEW ZEALAND v ENGLAND

First Test at Auckland:
NEW ZEALAND 24 (I. Mauger 9).

ENGLAND 24 (N. Boocock 10,
J. McMillan 10).
Second Test at Napier:
NEW ZEALAND 25 (I. Mauger 11).
ENGLAND 23 (N. Boocock 10,
J. McMillan 9).
Third Test at Palmerston North:
NEW ZEALAND 11 (H. Cole 4).
ENGLAND 37 (N. Boocock 11, B. Kilby 10,
J. McMillan 10).

1969
GREAT BRITAIN v SWEDEN
First Test at Wimbledon:
Great Britain 68 (I. Mauger 18, R. Moore 14,
N. Boocock 11, B. Briggs 11,
R. Luckhurst 10).
SWEDEN 42 (B. Jansson 12).
Second Test at Newport:
GREAT BRITAIN 70 (B. Briggs 15,
I. Mauger 14, M. Ashby 12, N. Boocock 11,
E. Boocock 10).
SWEDEN 38 (T. Harrysson 13).
Third Test at Leicester:
GREAT BRITAIN 79 (I. Mauger 18,
B. Briggs 17, N. Boocock 13, Ray Wilson 13,
N. Hunter 10).
SWEDEN 29 (A. Michanek 12).
Fourth Test at Halifax:
GREAT BRITAIN 62 (E. Boocock 13,
Ray Wilson 11, J. McMillan 10).
SWEDEN 46 (T. Harrysson 9,
A. Michanek 9, S. Sjösten 9).
Fifth Test at Cradley Heath:
GREAT BRITAIN 63 (N. Boocock 17, Ray
Wilson 14, B. Briggs 12, I. Mauger 11).
SWEDEN 45 (A. Michanek 12,
S. Sjösten 10).
SWEDEN v GREAT BRITAIN
International in Malmö:
SWEDEN 54 (O. Fundin 15, S.Sjösten 12,
A. Michanek 12).
GREAT BRITAIN 54 (I. Mauger 17,
N. Boocock 14, J. McMillan 10).
ENGLAND v AUSTRALIA
First Test at Poole:
ENGLAND 66 (M. Ashby 15,
N. Boocock 12, E. Boocock 12).
AUSTRALIA 42 (G. Mudge 13, J. Airey 11,
C. Monk 10).
Second Test at Wolverhampton:
ENGLAND 8.
AUSTRALIA 4.
(abandoned after two heats.)
Third Test at Sheffield:
ENGLAND 69 (N. Boocock 17,
N. Hunter 14, A. Haley 12).
AUSTRALIA 39 (J. Airey 16, C. Monk 12).
Re-run at Wolverhampton:
ENGLAND 73 (T. Betts 18, R. Wilson 18,
N. Boocock 14½).
AUSTRALIA 35 (G. Mudge 11, J. Airey 10).
ENGLAND v NEW ZEALAND
First Test at Swindon:
ENGLAND 43 (N. Boocock 14,
M. Ashby 12).
NEW ZEALAND 65 (B. Briggs 17,
I. Mauger 17, R. Moore 15).
Second Test at Newcastle:
ENGLAND 47 (N. Boocock 14,
A. Haley 12).
NEW ZEALAND 61 (I. Mauger 15,
D. Gifford 14, B. Briggs 12, B. Andrews 11).
Third Test at Hackney:
ENGLAND 60 (N. Boocock 13, Ray
Wilson 13, T. Betts 13).
NEW ZEALAND 48 (B. Briggs 16,
I. Mauger 14).

1969–70
AUSTRALIA v ENGLAND
First Test at Perth:
AUSTRALIA 61 (J. Airey 17, C. Taylor 16,
J. Boulger 10).
ENGLAND 47 (E. Boocock 10,
J. McMillan 10).
Second Test at Adelaide:
AUSTRALIA 45 (J. Airey 15).
ENGLAND 63 (Ray Wilson 16,
E. Boocock 13, J. McMillan 11,
T. Clarke 10).
Third Test at Sydney:
AUSTRALIA 50 (J. Airey 18).
ENGLAND 58 (J. McMillan 13,
T. Clarke 11, A. Haley 11).
Fourth Test at Brisbane:
AUSTRALIA 56 (J. Airey 14, J. White 13,
D. White 11, B. Kingston 10).
ENGLAND 52 (T. Clarke 13, Ray Wilson 11,
A. Haley 10).
Fifth Test at Sydney:
AUSTRALIA 49 (J. Airey 15).
ENGLAND 59 (E. Boocock 15, A. Haley 14,
T. Clarke 13).
NEW ZEALAND v ENGLAND
First Test at Auckland:
NEW ZEALAND 36 (B. Andrews 10).
ENGLAND 72 (T. Clarke 17,
J. McMillan 17, E. Boocock 11, Ray
Wilson 11, N. Boocock 10).
Second Test at Auckland:
NEW ZEALAND 43 (I. Mauger 17),
England 65 (N. Boocock 17, J. McMillan 13,
E. Boocock 12, Ray Wilson 11).
Third Test of Christchurch:
NEW ZEALAND 40 (R. Moore 16,
I. Mauger 12).
ENGLAND 67 (N. Boocock 14, A. Haley 14,
E. Boocock 12, J. McMillan 11, Ray
Wilson 10).

1970
GREAT BRITAIN v SWEDEN
First Test at Glasgow:
GREAT BRITAIN 66 (I. Mauger 17,
N. Boocock 11, E. Boocock 11).
SWEDEN 42 (A. Michanek 14,
B. Persson 10, S. Sjösten 10).
Second Test at Halifax:
GREAT BRITAIN 48 (B. Briggs 14).
SWEDEN 60 (A. Michanek 17,
B. Persson 15, S. Sjösten 11).
Third Test at Exeter:
GREAT BRITAIN 66 (B. Briggs 17,
E. Boocock 16, R. Moore 11, Ray Wilson 10).
SWEDEN 42 (A. Michanek 14).
Fourth Test at West Ham:
GREAT BRITAIN 62 (B. Briggs 18,
I. Mauger 17, R. Moore 15).
SWEDEN 46 (A. Michanek 15,
B. Jansson 13).
Fifth Test at Newport:
GREAT BRITAIN 70 (B. Briggs 17,
R. Moore 16, N. Boocock 12, Bill
Andrews 11, I. Mauger 10).
SWEDEN 38 (S. Sjösten 10).
Sixth Test at Coventry:
GREAT BRITAIN 71 (I. Mauger 18,
E. Boocock 16, R. France 13,
J. McMillan 10).
SWEDEN 37 (A. Michanek 13).
SWEDEN v GREAT BRITAIN
First Test at Gothenburg:
SWEDEN 45 (A. Michanek 14,
S. Sjösten 12).
GREAT BRITAIN 63 (I. Mauger 18,
J. McMillan 15, E. Boocock 12).
Second Test at Malilla:
SWEDEN 73 (S. Sjösten 18, O. Fundin 15,
A. Michanek 14, T. Johansson 12).
GREAT BRITAIN 34 (I. Mauger 14).
Third Test at Stockholm:
SWEDEN 47 (A. Michanek 18).
GREAT BRITAIN 61 (I. Mauger 14,
M. Ashby 12, Ray Wilson 12).
ENGLAND v AUSTRALIA
First Test at Hackney:
ENGLAND 30 (C. Pratt 7).
AUSTRALIA 24 (J. Airey 9).
(abandoned after nine heats.)
Second Test at Newcastle:
ENGLAND 29 (N. Boocock 9).
AUSTRALIA 31 (J. Airey 10).
(abandoned after ten heats.)
Third Test at Cradley Heath:
ENGLAND 10 (T. Betts 17, E. Boocock 13,
N. Boocock 13, Ray Wilson 10).
AUSTRALIA 38 (L. Sharpe 14).
(abandoned after eight heats.)
1970
ENGLAND v NEW ZEALAND
First Test at Wimbledon:
ENGLAND 54 (T. Hedge 12, T. Clarke 12,
M. Ashby 10).
NEW ZEALAND 53 (I. Mauger 18,
B. Briggs 17).
Second Test at Belle Vue:
ENGLAND 66 (N. Boocock 12,
M. Ashby 12, A. Haley 11, E. Boocock 11,
T. Hedge 11).
NEW ZEALAND 42 (I. Mauger 18,
B. Briggs 17).
Third Test at Swindon:
ENGLAND 70 (B. Kilby 15, T. Betts 14,
Ray Wilson 13, E. Boocock 10,
M. Ashby 10).
NEW ZEALAND 37 (B. Briggs 18,
I. Mauger 10).
Fourth Test at Sheffield:
ENGLAND 64 (E. Boocock 14,
N. Boocock 13, A. Haley 11, B. Kilby 10).
NEW ZEALAND 44 (I. Mauger 18,
B. Briggs 15).
1970–71
AUSTRALIA v ENGLAND
First Test at Perth:
AUSTRALIA 58 (J. Langfield 13,
L. Hodgson 12, C. Taylor 11).
ENGLAND 50 (N. Boocock 15, A. Haley 12,
C. Pusey 12).
Second Test at Perth:
AUSTRALIA 61 (L. Hodgson 16,
J. Langfield 14, C. Taylor 13).
ENGLAND 46 (A. Haley 14, C. Pusey 10).
Third Test at Adelaide:
AUSTRALIA 55 (L. Hodgson 14,
C. Monk 14).
ENGLAND 53 (R. Trigg 14, N. Boocock 12,
G. Hunter 12).
Fourth Test at Sydney:
AUSTRALIA 52 (J. Langfield 13).
ENGLAND 56 (N. Boocock 14, C. Pusey 13,
B. Kilby 10).
Fifth Test at Brisbane:
AUSTRALIA 54 (J. Langfield 12,
B. Kingston 11, J. Boulger 10).
ENGLAND 54 (R. Trigg 14, N. Boocock 13).
Sixth Test at Brisbane:
AUSTRALIA 54 (B. Kingston 14,
J. Boulger 11).
ENGLAND 54 (N. Boocock 16, R. Trigg 12,
G. Hunter 10).
Seventh Test at Sydney:
AUSTRALIA 56 (B. Kingston 18, L.
Hodgson 12, J. White 10), England 52 (C.
Pusey 16, N. Boocock 10).
NEW ZEALAND v ENGLAND
First Test at Auckland:
NEW ZEALAND 48½ (G. Peterson 12).
ENGLAND 59½ (R. Trigg 15,
C. Pusey 12½).
Second Test at Auckland:
NEW ZEALAND 40 (I. Mauger 15).
ENGLAND 68 (C. Pusey 15, N. Boocock 13,
R. Trigg 13, B. Kilby 12, J. McMillan 12).
Third Test at Christchurch:
NEW ZEALAND 65 (I. Mauger 18,
A. Brown 13, R. Timmo 10).
ENGLAND 43 (R. Trigg 14, N. Boocock 10).
1971
GREAT BRITAIN v POLAND
First Test at Swindon:
GREAT BRITAIN 80 (R. Moore 14,
J. Airey 13, Ray Wilson 12, J. McMillan 11,
B. Cribb 10).
POLAND 28 (A. Wyglenda 8).
Second Test at Reading:
GREAT BRITAIN 78 (Ray Wilson 18,
N. Boocock 15, J. Airey 13, B. Briggs 12,
R. Moore 12).
POLAND 30 (A. Wyglenda 11).
Third Test at Leicester:
GREAT BRITAIN 77 (I. Mauger 18,
B. Briggs 15, Ray Wilson 15, R. Moore 13,
E. Boocock 10).
POLAND 30 (P. Waloszek 7, A. Woryna 7,
J. Trzeszkowski 7).
Fourth Test at Sheffield:
GREAT BRITAIN 66 (B. Briggs 16,
J. Airey 14, I. Mauger 13, N. Boocock 11).
POLAND 42 (A. Wyglenda 12).
Fifth Test at Glasgow:
GREAT BRITAIN 47 (I. Mauger 16, Ray
Wilson 10).
POLAND 61 (J. Mucha 14,
J. Trzeszkowski 11, A. Wyglenda 10).
Sixth Test at Belle Vue:
GREAT BRITAIN 57 (I. Mauger 18,
R. Moore 12, J. McMillan 11, J. Airey 11).
POLAND 51 (A. Wyglenda 13,
A. Woryna 11).
ENGLAND v SWEDEN
First Test at Wolverhampton:
ENGLAND 22 (Ray Wilson 7).
SWEDEN 32 (B. Jansson 8).
(abandoned after nine heats.)
Second Test at Wimbledon:
ENGLAND 51 (Ray Wilson 14,
E. Boocock 14).
SWEDEN 57 (B. Jansson 15, B. Persson 15,
S. Sjösten 12).
Third Test at Halifax:
ENGLAND 63 (D. Younghusband 18,
E. Boocock 14, B. Kilby 11).
SWEDEN 45 (A. Michanek 11,
B. Jansson 10).
ENGLAND v USSR
First Test at Exeter:
ENGLAND 54 (B. Kilby 17).
USSR 53 (Vladimir Gordeev 13,
V. Paznikov 11, G. Kurilenko 10).
Second Test at Poole:
ENGLAND 54 (Ray Wilson 18, M. Ashby 13,
P. Smith 10).
USSR 54 (G. Kurilenko 12, V. Paznikov 12).
Third Test at Wimbledon:
ENGLAND 61 (T. Hedge 14, R. Trigg 12,
M. Simmons 11).
USSR 46 (G. Mironov 14, A. Pavlov 10).
Fourth Test at Halifax:
ENGLAND 51 (Ray Wilson 15,
E. Boocock 10).
USSR 57 (G. Mironov 15, V. Paznikov 11,
A. Pavlov 10).
Fifth Test at Coventry:
ENGLAND 59 (T. Lomas 16, Ray
Wilson 11, N. Boocock 10).
USSR 49 (A. Pavlov 15, G. Chlynovski 11).

1971
UNITED STATES OF AMERICA v GREAT BRITAIN
First Test at Costa Mesa:
USA 48 (L. Shaw 10).
GREAT BRITAIN 42 (I. Mauger 12, B. Briggs 11).
Second Test at Costa Mesa:
USA 43 (R. Woods 13, S. Nutter 11).
GREAT BRITAIN 47 (B. Briggs 14, I. Mauger 12).
Third Test at Costa Mesa:
USA 49 (L. Shaw 10).
GREAT BRITAIN 40 (I. Mauger 15, B. Briggs 14).

1971–72
AUSTRALIA v ENGLAND
First Test at Sydney:
AUSTRALIA 60 (J. Langfield 16, J. Airey 15, J. White 12).
ENGLAND 48 (J. McMillan 14, N. Boocock 11).
Second Test at Brisbane:
AUSTRALIA 61 (J. Boulger 15, J. White 13).
ENGLAND 47 (N. Boocock 13, T. Lomas 10).
Third Test at Brisbane:
AUSTRALIA 46 (J. Airey 10, T. Hart 10).
ENGLAND 61 (C. Pusey 18, N. Boocock 13).
Fourth Test at Adelaide:
AUSTRALIA 57 (J. Airey 18, J. Boulger 16, C. Monk 14).
ENGLAND 51 (J. McMillan 12).
Fifth Test at Melbourne:
AUSTRALIA 44 (P. Crump 12, J. Langfield 10).
ENGLAND 64 (G. Hunter 15, C. Pusey 13, T. Lomas 10, M. Simmons 10, J. McMillan 10).
Sixth Test at Perth:
AUSTRALIA 49 (J. Airey 16, C. Taylor 10, L. Sharpe 10).
ENGLAND 69 (C. Pusey 13, N. Boocock 12, M. Simmons 11).
Seventh Test at Perth:
AUSTRALIA 31 (J. Langfield 14).
ENGLAND 77 (B. Harkins 17, N. Boocock 16, M. Simmons 16, C. Pusey 10).

1972
INTER-NATIONS TOURNAMENT
At Belle Vue:
AUSTRALIA 40 (J. Boulger 10).
NEW ZEALAND 38 (I. Mauger 15, R. Moore 11).
At Coventry:
ENGLAND 43 (Ray Wilson 9).
SWEDEN 35 (C. Löfqvist 12).
At Reading:
SWEDEN 40 (C. Löfqvist 13).
NORWAY and DENMARK 38 (D. Lovaas 12, O. Olsen 11).
At Hackney:
AUSTRALIA 39 (J. Boulger 11, G. Middleton 10).
SWEDEN 39 (H. Holmqvist 10).
At King's Lynn:
AUSTRALIA 39 (P. Crump 10).
NORWAY and DENMARK 39 (O. Olsen 12).
At Swindon:
SWEDEN 50 (C. Löfqvist 12, A. Michanek 11).
NEW ZEALAND 28 (R. Moore 9).
At Poole:
NORWAY and DENMARK 41 (O. Olsen 14).
ENGLAND 37 (R. Wilson 10).
At Wimbledon:
ENGLAND 51 (Ray Wilson 12).
NEW ZEALAND 26 (R. Moore 9).
At Wolverhampton:
NORWAY and DENMARK 55 (O. Olsen 15, O. Berg 10, D. Lovaas 10).
NEW ZEALAND 22 (R. Moore 10).
At Halifax:
ENGLAND 48 (Ray Wilson 12, N. Boocock 10).
AUSTRALIA 30 (G. Middleton 12).

Final Table

	P	W	D	L	F	A	Pts
England	4	3	0	1	179	132	6
Norway/Denmark	4	2	1	1	173	138	5
Sweden	4	2	1	1	164	148	5
Australia	4	1	2	1	148	164	4
New Zealand	4	0	0	4	114	196	0

1972–73
AUSTRALIA v ENGLAND
First Test at Perth:
AUSTRALIA 60 (J. Airey 18, J. Boulger 14).
ENGLAND 48 (B. Kilby 13, N. Boocock 11).
Second Test at Adelaide:
AUSTRALIA 50 (J. Boulger 16, B. Valentine 14).
ENGLAND 58 (A. Haley 14, P. Collins 14, N. Boocock 10).
Third Test at Sydney:
AUSTRALIA 63 (J. Boulger 15, J. White 15, B. Valentine 13).
ENGLAND 45 (P. Collins 15, N. Boocock 12).
Fourth Test at Sydney:
AUSTRALIA 58 (J. Boulger 15, K. Torpie 11, B. Valentine 11, J. Langfield 11).
ENGLAND 50 (N. Boocock 12, P. Collins 11).
Fifth Test at Brisbane:
AUSTRALIA 71 (J. Boulger 17, K. Torpie 15, D. White 13, S. Reinke 12).
ENGLAND 36 (C. Pusey 14).
Sixth Test at Brisbane:
AUSTRALIA 58 (J. Boulger 15, S. Reinke 11).
ENGLAND 50 (N. Boocock 10, C. Pusey 10, A. Haley 10).
Seventh Test at Sydney:
AUSTRALIA 62 (J. Langfield 18, J. Boulger 17, J. Airey 14).
ENGLAND 46 (G. Hunter 11).
NEW ZEALAND v ENGLAND
First Test at Auckland:
NEW ZEALAND 52 (R. Moore 14, B. Andrews 12).
ENGLAND 56 (B. Kilby 12, A. Haley 12, C. Pusey 12, G. Hunter 11).
Second Test at Christchurch:
NEW ZEALAND 77 (I. Mauger 18, B. Briggs 17, R. Moore 15, G. Stapleton 11).
ENGLAND 31 (C. Pusey 11).
Third Test at Auckland:
NEW ZEALAND 53 (I. Mauger 15, G. Stapleton 12, R. Moore 11).
ENGLAND 54 (B. Kilby 15, A. Haley 14).
Fourth Test at Wellington:
NEW ZEALAND 67 (I. Mauger 18, B. Briggs 16, R. Moore 11).
ENGLAND 41 (C. Pusey 14, E. Broadbelt 12).

1973
Daily Mirror INTERNATIONAL TOURNAMENT
At Sheffield:
ENGLAND 40 (Reg Wilson 11, P. Collins 10).
SWEDEN 38 (B. Persson 10).
At Hackney:
SWEDEN 49 (B. Jansson 12, A. Michanek 12).
USSR 29 (Vladimir Gordeev 13).
At Wolverhampton:
NORWAY and DENMARK 40 (O. Olsen 11).
NEW ZEALAND 37 (B. Briggs 9).
At Belle Vue:
ENGLAND 48 (Ray Wilson 10, A. Wilkinson 10).
NORWAY and DENMARK 30 (O. Olsen 10).
At Halifax:
POLAND 42 (E. Jancarz 10, H. Zyto 10, Z. Plech 10).
USSR 36 (Vladimir Gordeev 7, A. Kuzmin 7).
At Swindon:
SWEDEN 42 (C. Löfqvist 11).
NEW ZEALAND 35 (I. Mauger 10).
At Oxford:
AUSTRALIA 54 (J. Boulger 11, G. Curtis 11, J. Airey 10).
POLAND 23 (J. Mucha 11).
At Cradley Heath:
SWEDEN 45 (A. Michanek 11).
NORWAY and DENMARK 33 (O. Olsen 13).
At Exeter:
NEW ZEALAND 53 (I. Mauger 12).
POLAND 25 (Z. Plech 9).
At Leicester:
AUSTRALIA 45 (J. Boulger 11, J. Titman 10).
USSR 33 (Vladimir Gordeev 9).
At Poole:
NORWAY and DENMARK 43 (D. Lovaas 11).
POLAND 35 (Z. Plech 12, E. Jancarz 10).
At Ipswich:
ENGLAND 56 (Ray Wilson 12, J. Louis 11).
USSR 22 (A. Pavlov 4, A. Kuzmin 4, G. Chlynovski 4).
At Wimbledon:
NEW ZEALAND 50 (I. Mauger 12, B. Briggs 10, R. Moore 10, G. Peterson 10).
AUSTRALIA 28 (B. Valentine 7).
At Hackney:
ENGLAND 45 (J. Louis 12, Ray Wilson 10).
POLAND 33 (Z. Plech 11).
At Newport:
AUSTRALIA 40 (J. Airey 8).
SWEDEN 38 (C. Löfqvist 10).
At Cradley Heath:
NORWAY and DENMARK 47 (D. Lovaas 12, O. Olsen 11, O. Berg 10).
USSR 31 (Vladimir Gordeev 12, G. Chlynovski 10).
At Halifax:
SWEDEN 53 (S. Sjösten 12, A. Michanek 11, B. Persson 11, C. Löfqvist 10).
POLAND 25 (P. Waloszek 10).
At King's Lynn:
ENGLAND 44 (E. Boocock 13).
AUSTRALIA 34 (J. Boulger 11).
At Reading:
NEW ZEALAND 43 (I. Mauger 12, R. Moore 11).
USSR 34 (Vladimir Gordeev 10).
Abandoned because of rain:
ENGLAND v NEW ZEALAND (at Leicester) and
AUSTRALIA v NORWAY and DENMARK (at Coventry).
Semi-finals
At Belle Vue:
ENGLAND 48 (Ray Wilson 11, P. Collins 10).
NEW ZEALAND 30 (I. Mauger 13).
At Coventry:
SWEDEN 51 (C. Löfqvist 12, A. Michanek 12, S. Sjösten 10).
AUSTRALIA 27 (J. Boulger 7).
Final
At Wembley:
ENGLAND 39 (T. Betts 10, M. Simmons 10).
SWEDEN 39 (A. Michanek 11, C. Löfqvist 10).
Peter Collins beat Anders Michanek in a match race decider.
ENGLAND v REST OF THE WORLD
International Challenge at Wembley:
ENGLAND 30 (Ray Wilson 11).
REST OF THE WORLD 48 (O. Olsen 11, A. Michanek 10).
POLAND v GREAT BRITAIN
First Test at Wroclaw:
POLAND 76 (J. Mucha 15, Z. Plech 14, Z. Marcinkowski 14, E. Jancarz 13, H. Glucklich 12).
GREAT BRITAIN 31 (J. Louis 11).
Second Test at Rybnik:
POLAND 53 (P. Waloszek 13, E. Jancarz 12, J. Mucha 10).
GREAT BRITAIN 55 (Ray Wilson 13, J. McMillan 12, J. Louis 11, Reg Wilson 10).
Third Test at Gorzow:
POLAND 75 (Z. Plech 18, E. Jancarz 14, J. Szczakiel 14, M. Cieslak 12, P. Waloszek 11).
GREAT BRITAIN 33 (I. Mauger 9).

1973–74
AUSTRALIA v ENGLAND
First Test at Perth:
AUSTRALIA 55 (B. O'Leary 15, B. Sanders 11).
ENGLAND 53 (P. Collins 15, N. Boocock 10, Reg Wilson 10).
Second Test at Perth:
AUSTRALIA 33 (B. Sanders 8).
ENGLAND 75 (J. McMillan 15, G. Hunter 15, Reg Wilson 14, N. Boocock 14, P. Collins 12).
Third Test at Adelaide:
AUSTRALIA 44 (L. Sansom 13, S. Reinke 12).
ENGLAND 64 (P. Collins 15, J. McMillan 14, G. Hunter 11, N. Boocock 10).
Fourth Test at Sydney:
AUSTRALIA 50 (S. Reinke 13, J. Boulger 11, B. Sanders 11).
ENGLAND 58 (Reg Wilson 14, P. Collins 12, G. Hunter 10).
Fifth Test at Brisbane:
AUSTRALIA 46 (S. Reinke 11).
ENGLAND 62 (Reg Wilson 17, P. Collins 12, N. Boocock 11, G. Hunter 11).
Sixth Test at Brisbane:
AUSTRALIA 60 (S. Reinke 15, J. Titman 13, J. White 10).
ENGLAND 47 (Reg Wilson 14).
Seventh Test at Sydney:
AUSTRALIA 53 (J. Langfield 14, B. Sanders 14, R. Day 11).
ENGLAND 55 (P. Collins 14, Reg Wilson 13, E. Broadbelt 10).

1974
ENGLAND v SWEDEN
First Test at King's Lynn
ENGLAND 71 (D. Jessup 15, T. Betts 15, B. Kilby 13, Ray Wilson 10, M. Simmons 10).
SWEDEN 37 (S. Sjösten 17).
Second Test at Poole:
ENGLAND 66 (T. Betts 13, D. Jessup 13,

P. Collins 10, Ray Wilson 10).
SWEDEN 42 (S. Sjösten 16, T. Jansson 11).
Third Test at Sheffield:
ENGLAND 83 (P. Collins 18, T. Betts 17, D. Wyer 14, Reg Wilson 13, C. Pusey 12).
SWEDEN 25 (S. Sjösten 10).
Fourth Test at Hackney:
ENGLAND 73 (D. Jessup 15, J. Louis 15, C. Pusey 14, P. Collins 14).
SWEDEN 35 (S. Sjösten 15).
Fifth Test at Coventry:
ENGLAND 71 (D. Jessup 15, J. Louis 15, D. Wyer 15, Ray Wilson 12).
SWEDEN 37 (S. Sjösten 13).
ENGLAND v POLAND
First Test at Hackney:
ENGLAND 88 (J. Louis 18, P. Collins 16, B. Thomas 15, D. Jessup 14, Ray Wilson 13, T. Betts 12).
POLAND 19 (E. Jancarz 6).
Second Test at King's Lynn:
ENGLAND 78 (Ray Wilson 16, T. Betts 15, J. Louis 14, M. Simmons 13, C. Pusey 11).
POLAND 30 (E. Jancarz 11).
Third Test at Exeter:
ENGLAND 73 (M. Simmons 16, P. Collins 14, T. Betts 14, D. Jessup 11).
POLAND 35, (R. Fabiszewski 13, Z. Plech 11, E. Jancarz 10).
Fourth Test at Hull:
ENGLAND 69 (M. Ashby 18, M. Simmons 13, D. Jessup 12, T. Betts 10).
POLAND 39 (Z. Plech 13).
Fifth Test at Ipswich:
ENGLAND 78 (J. Louis 18, D. Jessup 18, Ray Wilson 13, M. Simmons 12).
POLAND 30 (Z. Plech 9).
Sixth Test at Halifax:
ENGLAND 65 (Reg Wilson 16, D. Wyer 14, Ray Wilson 13, J. Louis 10).
POLAND 42 (E. Jancarz 16, J. Mucha 10).
Seventh Test at Leicester:
ENGLAND 76 (P. Collins 15, M. Simmons 14, Ray Wilson 13, T. Betts 13, J. Louis 12).
POLAND 32 (Z. Plech 14, E. Jancarz 11).
ENGLAND v USSR
First Test at Swindon:
ENGLAND 66 (M. Ashby 17, T. Davey 16, D. Jessup 16).
USSR 41 (Vladimir Gordeev 13, G. Chlynovski 11, A. Kuzmin 10).
Second Test at Wolverhampton:
ENGLAND 61 (K. Holden 15, P. Collins 10).
USSR 47 (G. Chlynovski 14, Valeri Gordeev 12, A. Kuzmin 10).
Third Test at Wimbledon:
ENGLAND 71 (B. Thomas 16, T. Hedge 15, M. Ashby 12, K. Holden 10).
USSR 37 (G. Chlynovski 10).
Fourth Test at Cradley Heath:
ENGLAND 65 (B. Thomas 14, T. Davey 13, E. Broadbelt 12, H. Cole 10).
USSR 43 (Valeri Gordeev 10, Vladimir Gordeev 10, G. Chlynovski 10).
Fifth Test at Oxford:
Abandoned because of waterlogged track.
Sixth Test at Belle Vue:
ENGLAND 75 (P. Collins 18, C. Pusey 15, R. Greer 12, Ray Wilson 11).
USSR 31 (G. Chlynovski 14).
Seventh Test at Newport:
ENGLAND 17,
USSR 19.
(abandoned after six heats).

1974–75
AUSTRALIA v ENGLAND
First Test at Brisbane:
AUSTRALIA 62 (J. Titman 16, P. Crump 12, B. Sanders 11, B. Loakes 10).
ENGLAND 45 (D. Wyer 17, Reg Wilson 11).
Second Test at Brisbane:
AUSTRALIA 50 (P. Crump 12, J. Titman 11).
ENGLAND 58 (D. Wyer 14, Reg Wilson 13, E. Broadbelt 12).
Third Test at Newcastle:
AUSTRALIA 63 (P. Crump 18, B. Sanders 15, P. Herne 10).
ENGLAND 45 (D. Wyer 10).
Fourth Test at Sydney:
AUSTRALIA 55 (P. Crump 18, B. Sanders 15).
ENGLAND 53 (D. Wyer 12, E. Broadbelt 11).
Fifth Test at Liverpool:
AUSTRALIA 57 (B. Sanders 14, P. Crump 14, B. Valentine 13).
ENGLAND 51 (J. McMillan 11).
Sixth Test at Adelaide:
AUSTRALIA 59 (P. Crump 17, B. Sanders 16).
ENGLAND 49 (J. McMillan 10).
Seventh Test at Perth:
AUSTRALIA 46 (J. Titman 15, P. Crump 12, J. Langfield 11).
ENGLAND 61 (C. Morton 14, D. Wyer 12, E. Broadbelt 10, Reg Wilson 10).

1975
Daily Mirror INTERNATIONAL TOURNAMENT
At Sheffield:
ENGLAND 54 (P. Collins 12, D. Jessup 10).
SWEDEN 24 (T. Jansson 9).
At Exeter:
AUSTRALIA 42 (P. Crump 11, N. Street 10).
REST OF THE WORLD 36 (I. Mauger 13, J. McMillan 10).
At Leicester:
ENGLAND 50 (J. Louis 12).
AUSTRALIA 28 (P. Crump 13).
At Hackney:
SWEDEN 41 (A. Michanek 11).
REST OF THE WORLD 37 (I. Mauger 13).
At Poole:
AUSTRALIA 41 (P. Crump 9, P. Herne 9).
SWEDEN 37 (T. Jansson 11).
At Hull:
ENGLAND 41 (D. Wyer 11).
REST OF THE WORLD 37 (I. Mauger 15).

Final Table

	P	W	D	L	F	A	Pts
England	3	3	0	0	145	89	6
Australia	3	2	0	1	111	123	4
Sweden	3	1	0	2	102	132	2
Rest of the World	3	0	0	3	110	124	0

ENGLAND v SWEDEN
First Test at Poole:
ENGLAND 77 (P. Collins 15, J. Louis 14, D. Jessup 13, M. Ashby 12, Ray Wilson 10, M. Simmons 10).
SWEDEN 29 (T. Jansson 6, S. Sjösten 6)
Second Test at Leicester:
ENGLAND 66 (J. Louis 18, Ray Wilson 15, P. Collins 13, D. Jessup 10).
SWEDEN 42 (T. Jansson 10).
Third Test at Hackney:
ENGLAND 62 (J. Louis 18, D. Jessup 16, Ray Wilson 10, P. Collins 10).
SWEDEN 46 (C. Löfqvist 11).
Fourth Test at King's Lynn:
ENGLAND 70 (J. Louis 17, D. Jessup 14, Ray Wilson 11, M. Ashby 10, M. Simmons 10).
SWEDEN 38 (B. Persson 16, T. Jansson 10).
Fifth Test at Belle Vue:
ENGLAND 79 (J. Louis 17, P. Collins 16, Ray Wilson 14, D. Jessup 12, C. Morton 11).
SWEDEN 29 (T. Jansson 13).
ENGLAND v REST OF THE WORLD
International Challenge at Ipswich:
ENGLAND 63 (J. Louis 14, P. Collins 13, M. Simmons 11).
REST OF THE WORLD 45 (S. Autrey 11, I. Mauger 11, B. Sanders 11).
POLAND v ENGLAND
First (A) Test at Bydoszcz:
POLAND 71 (H. Glucklich 18, Z. Plech 18, E. Jancarz 12).
ENGLAND 37 (M. Simmons 10).
First (B) Test at Katowice:
POLAND 46 (A. Jurczynski 10).
ENGLAND 62 (P. Collins 17, J. Davis, C. Pusey 11).
Second (A) Test at Gorzow:
POLAND 50 (Z. Plech 12, J. Rembas 11).
ENGLAND 58 (D. Jessup 15, M. Simmons 13, D. Wyer 13).
Second (B) Test at Poznan:
POLAND 52 (J. Jarmula 15, Z. Kostka 11, J. Szczakiel 11).
ENGLAND 56 (P. Collins 18, J. Davis 12).
Note – On successive days, Poland and England teams met concurrently in matches regarded as full internationals.
SWEDEN v ENGLAND
First Test at Kumla:
SWEDEN 53 (T. Jansson 15, B. Persson 14, S. Karlsson 10).
ENGLAND 55 (P. Collins 16, M. Ashby 13).
Second Test at Eskilstuna:
SWEDEN 51 (T. Jansson 16, B. Jansson 10, T. Johansson 10).
ENGLAND 57 (P. Collins 14, M. Ashby 14).
Third Test at Stockholm:
SWEDEN 44 (B. Persson 12, T. Johansson 11, B. Jansson 11).
ENGLAND 64 (M. Ashby 18, P. Collins 15, D. Jessup 12).
Fourth Test at Vetlanda:
SWEDEN 40 (T. Jansson 16, B. Persson 14).
ENGLAND 68 (M. Ashby 14, D. Morton 12, M. Simmons 11, P. Collins 11).
Fifth Test at Mariestad:
SWEDEN 50 (A. Michanek 18, S. Sjösten 14, T. Jansson 11).
ENGLAND 58 (G. Kennett 11, J. Davis 11, M. Simmons 10, D. Jessup 10, D. Morton 10).

1975–76
AUSTRALIA v ENGLAND
First Test at Perth:
AUSTRALIA 41 (P. Crump 17).
ENGLAND 67 (P. Collins 14, J. Davis 12, C. Morton 12).
Second Test at Perth:
AUSTRALIA 34 (P. Crump 17).
ENGLAND 74 (P. Collins 17, C. Pusey 15, D. Wyer 13, J. Davis 12).
Third Test at Newcastle:
AUSTRALIA 32 (P. Crump 7, J. Titman 7).
ENGLAND 76 (P. Collins 18, J. Davis 15, C. Morton 13, D. Wyer 12).
Fourth Test at Sydney:
AUSTRALIA 38 (P. Crump 15).
ENGLAND 70 (D. Wyer 18, P. Collins 14, J. Davis 11).
Fifth Test at Liverpool:
AUSTRALIA 47 (P. Crump 17, B. Sanders 11).
ENGLAND 61 (P. Collins 17, D. Wyer 13).
Sixth Test at Sydney:
AUSTRALIA 62 (P. Herne 16, P. Crump 15, B. Sanders 11).
ENGLAND 45 (J. Davis 15, D. Wyer 10).
Seventh Test at Brisbane:
AUSTRALIA 50 (P. Crump 17).
ENGLAND 57 (P. Collins 15, D. Wyer 13, J. Davis 10).

1976
ENGLAND (WORLD CUP TEAM) v ENGLISH LIONS
At Leicester:
LIONS 42 (P. Collins 12).
WORLD CUP TEAM 36 (M. Simmons 9, D. Jessup 9).
REST OF THE WORLD v ENGLAND
International Challenge at Vojens, Denmark:
REST OF THE WORLD 43 (O. Olsen 12).
ENGLAND 41 (P. Collins 14).

1977
ENGLAND v REST OF THE WORLD
First Test at White City:
ENGLAND 63 (J. Louis 13, M. Lee 11, P. Collins 10, D. Jessup 10).
REST OF THE WORLD 45 (B. Sanders 13, O. Olsen 12).
Second Test at Ipswich:
ENGLAND 51 (D. Jessup 14, P. Collins 12).
REST OF THE WORLD 57 (P. Crump 13, O. Olsen 11, B. Sanders 11).
Third Test at Coventry:
ENGLAND 48 (M. Lee 12, D. Jessup 10).
REST OF THE WORLD 59 (O. Olsen 14, I. Mauger 12, B. Sanders 11).
Fourth Test at Reading:
ENGLAND 46 (M. Simmons 11, P. Collins 10).
REST OF THE WORLD 62 (O. Olsen 15, B. Sanders 13, J. Boulger 12, P. Crump 11).
Fifth Test at Hull:
ENGLAND 55 (M. Simmons 10, M. Lee 10).
REST OF THE WORLD 53 (I. Mauger 16, O. Olsen 15).

1977–78
AUSTRALIA v ENGLAND
First Test at Newcastle:
AUSTRALIA 38 (J. Titman 12, P. Herne 11).
ENGLAND 70 (P. Collins 18, J. Davis 17, D. Wyer 11, G. Kennett 10).
Second Test at Brisbane:
AUSTRALIA 51 (J. Titman 14, J. Boulger 13).
ENGLAND 57 (P. Collins 14, A. Wilkinson 12, J. Davis 12).
Third Test at Brisbane:
AUSTRALIA 61 (B. Sanders 17, J. Titman 15, J. Boulger 10, M. McKeon 10).
ENGLAND 47, (P. Collins 16, J. Davis 11, G. Kennett 10).
Fourth Test at Sydney:
AUSTRALIA 53 (B. Sanders 15, J. Titman 11).
ENGLAND 55 (P. Collins 14, J. Davis 10).
Fifth Test at Adelaide:
AUSTRALIA 56 (J. Boulger 14, B. Sanders 14, J. Titman 13).
ENGLAND 52 (D. Wyer 11, P. Collins 11, A. Wilkinson 10).
Sixth Test at Sydney:
AUSTRALIA 47 (B. Sanders 13, J. Titman 13).
ENGLAND 61 (P. Collins 17, G. Kennett 15, J. Davis 11).
Seventh Test at Perth:
AUSTRALIA 38 (M. McKeon 12, B. Sanders 10).
ENGLAND 70 (P. Collins 18, G. Kennett 14, J. Davis 14, D. Wyer 12).

INDEX TO RIDERS